RED TAPE

RED TAPE

*Adventure Capitalism
in the New Russia*

Bill Thomas and
Charles Sutherland

A DUTTON BOOK

DUTTON
Published by the Penguin Group
Penguin Books USA Inc., 375 Hudson Street,
New York, New York 10014, U.S.A.
Penguin Books Ltd, 27 Wrights Lane,
London W8 5TZ, England
Penguin Books Australia Ltd, Ringwood,
Victoria, Australia
Penguin Books Canada Ltd, 10 Alcorn Avenue,
Toronto, Ontario, Canada M4V 3B2
Penguin Books (N.Z.) Ltd, 182-190 Wairau Road,
Auckland 10, New Zealand

Penguin Books Ltd, Registered Offices:
Harmondsworth, Middlesex, England

First published by Dutton, an imprint of New American Library,
a division of Penguin Books USA Inc.
Distributed in Canada by McClelland & Stewart Inc.

First Printing, October, 1992
10 9 8 7 6 5 4 3 2 1

 REGISTERED TRADEMARK—MARCA REGISTRADA

LIBRARY OF CONGRESS CATALOGING-IN-PUBLICATION DATA:
Thomas, Bill, 1943–
    Red tape : adventure capitalism in the new Russia / Bill Thomas
and Charles Sutherland.
        p.   cm.
    ISBN 0-525-93502-9
    1. Soviet Union—Economic conditions—1985–1991.   2. Post-
communism—Soviet Union.   3. Soviet Union—Commerce.
I. Sutherland, Charles.   II. Title.
HC336.26.T5   1992
330.947′0854—dc20   92-52865
                                                          CIP

Printed in the United States of America
Set in Janson
Designed by Eve L. Kirch

To Belle and Brendan
To Nurit

Contents

Acknowledgments

We would like to express our gratitude to the following people for their assistance and encouragement:

First, to those whose connections, brains, and sheer bravado opened the doors behind closed doors: Givi Gomelauri, Tanya Klechko, Alexander Romanov, Volodya Sterlikov, and Galina Sullivan. To Sandy Stencel, for all her brilliant help, to Bob Kaper, for a year's worth of challenging insights, and to Dan Moldea, for his expert advice on everything.

While the views and opinions in *Red Tape* are solely our own, they were tested and retested without mercy on many others who generously gave of their time to listen and pretend we knew what we were talking about. Some we're surely forgetting; some we're sure would rather not be mentioned here. In any case, the following people all get major IOUs: Linda Bedeian, James Billington, Maxim Boycko, Etery Chitishvili, John Thor Dalberg, Richard Dean, Yuri Dubinin, Will Englund, Jim Fannon, Humbartsum Galstian, Alfred Giannantonio, Roy and Jewel Grutman, Ron Gunville, Bret Israel, Bill Keller, Ruslan Khasbulatov, Eugene Kirukhin, Todd Kliman, Rafael Kogan, Tanya Kolodzei, Boris

Komarov, Kathy Lally, Congressman Tom Lantos, Anna Lawton, Ted Lehman, Carol Long, Edward Luttwak, Dick and Diana McLellan, Jeremy Nicholl, Nikita Novokreshenov, Yuri Piskulov, Vladimir Pozner, Lena Romanov, Igor Rounov, Vladimir Shamberg, Luda Shaverdova, Mark Stencel, Dasha Sterlikova, Lev Sukhanov, Victor Volonski, and Winston.

Special thanks also go to Luba Sterlikova, whose logistical skills, tireless translating, and political savvy made doing much of the research and reporting in this book possible.

And finally, thanks—let's make that *bolshoye spasiba*—to Henry Dunow, agent extraordinaire, whose gentle yet firm hand guided this difficult project from start to finish, and to Laurie Bernstein of Dutton, whose unwavering support and deft editorial touch in the face of international turmoil brought it to life.

Authors' Note

THE NAME GAME

What do you call people who aren't even sure what to call themselves? For years the Communist Party tried to give Russians, Uzbeks, Georgians, and other ethnic groups a single Soviet identity. The identity didn't last, but the Soviet name may, especially since it's chiseled into buildings, stamped on passports, and otherwise plastered all over every other piece of property from Vladimir to Vladivostok.

Actually, "Soviet" is a good word to describe a diverse population that seems, for better or worse, to share a lot in common, including a mentality shaped by seventy-four years of communism. So in *Red Tape*, except when we are talking about individual nationalities, we will continue to call people Soviets.

In the case of the Soviet Union as a political entity, we had a somewhat different problem. Although the country no longer exists, many key parts of it—among them an airline, a state phone service, and a system of currency—are functioning (or not functioning) more or less as they always have.

Political changes require that we call the former USSR The Commonwealth of Independent States, even though the concept could be more of a transitional device than a lasting political arrangement. But don't be confused if, from time to time, we also refer to it as the Soviet Union, a term as psychologically valid as any to come along so far, and still the easiest way to identify a region that will probably defy other labels for some time to come.

RED TAPE

Keeping the Joneses Down with Us

Anyone who thinks real capitalism, with all of its supply-and-demand efficiency, has arrived in Russia hasn't been to the Don region lately. That's the rugged homeland of the Cossacks, a kind of civic-minded motorcycle gang on horseback, and, as history shows, when Cossacks don't like something, they're quick to make their feelings known. Which is what they did in early 1992 when some black marketeers in one village raised the price of fruit and vegetables. A group of Cossacks thought the increase was too high, and rather than waiting for a drop in demand to help lower costs to the consumer, they decided to saddle up and activate dealer incentives of their own. The Cossacks captured the offending black market bosses, hauled them into the local square, and gave them a public flogging until they agreed to declare an immediate discount.

It may have been just another version of command economics, but who can argue with the results? Goods appeared on the shelves, prices came down, and happy shoppers filled the stores.

There's a lesson here for all incoming entrepreneurs. The success of any business in the former Soviet Union can be ki-boshed without warning by unexpected native customs. If location

1

is everything, a place where almost nothing works in normal ways—including the laws, the markets, and the general populace—hardly sounds like a gold mine waiting to happen. But let's not forget, neither did Las Vegas before the casino business came to town. Venture capitalism is always a gamble. The trick to reducing the risk factor is knowing the territory before you get there. And in this case, prior knowledge isn't just a good idea, it's a matter of economic survival.

Red Tape is a book about doing business in countries that only a few years ago classified free enterprise as a crime, and still aren't sure whether the profit motive should be encouraged or constrained. Based on nearly a decade of business experience and hundreds of interviews with everyone from corporate executives to black marketeers, this book's subject is the Soviet money culture before, during, and after the arrival of capitalism. When we started writing, the government had just declared bankruptcy; halfway through, there was an attempted coup. By the time we finished, the Soviet Union was dissolved and up for sale under a new name and several possible revised configurations.

This is a book that introduces the buyers to the sellers, a sort of get-acquainted guide for dealmakers, consultants, and middlemen. Be advised at the outset that *Red Tape* is not an academic tome or an elevated view of the political economy. Instead, it's a ground-level look at the scramble for gross earnings that's become every native's and newcomer's nonstop obsession. It's about great expectations and great disappointments—and the miscalculations along the way that make it hard to tell them apart. In the following pages you'll meet never-say-die achievers and case-study flops; you'll see how some companies succeeded by being in the right place at the right time and how others were done in by a system that will take years to change.

As the title suggests, *Red Tape* isn't only about how Soviet business works, but how it *doesn't* work—and why. In that sense, it's also meant to entertain. Any historic upheaval that mixes capitalists, monarchists, do-gooders, and ex-KGB agents has a built-in potential for fun that speaks for itself.

Everything about the old Soviet Union was bolshoi (Russian for "big"), and the impact of communism's final collapse is like the Great Depression, Watergate, and the savings-and-loan crisis all rolled into one. A quick look at the financial scoreboard only begins to tell the story. Since 1990, output on Soviet collective farms has fallen by 20 percent, oil production has declined by 10 percent, the deficit has increased by a quarter, and the price of vodka has tripled.

But the problem facing the Soviet people goes much deeper than the bottom line. Can they create a new social and political culture capable of supporting a free-market economy? And can they do it before the new countries they live in go broke?

Halfhearted past attempts by replacement governments to reform the economic system without disturbing any of its cozy insider benefits is one example of why a true commonwealth of independent states could take generations to achieve. Another is the Soviet tendency to see buyers as victims and sellers as thieves—not exactly the mindset you'd expect to encounter on capitalism's newest frontier.

The ex-Soviet Union has gone through many changes over the past few years as it shed the legacy of socialism handed down by Marx, Lenin, and Stalin. However, it will have to go through many more before it becomes the Land of Opportunity envisioned by PepsiCo, Chase Manhattan, and the Heritage Foundation. Post-Soviet society and the post-Soviet consumer are products of historic circumstances vastly different from our own, which helps to explain why it would be unwise—and unprofitable—to apply Western economic ideals to post-Soviet reality.

To people steeped in decades of socialist double-talk, just keeping the terminology of capitalism straight can be a full-time job. For years, employment meant exploitation, profit was profiteering, and investment was speculation. No wonder a free-market economy is a complete mystery. In the minds of most Soviets a market is a food store where quality is nonexistent, selection severely limited, and service a specialized form of torment.

Take a basic American notion like "the customer is always right." Under communism, the customer was always *wrong,* and worse than that, an object of constant manipulation. Lenin and the founding fathers of the Soviet state designed a system in which supply could never keep up with demand, a situation that sentenced the average Soviet to spend an estimated 17 percent of his waking hours standing in line. Price reforms may have reduced some of the waiting time, but even after the communist era, buying anything in Russia or any of the other former republics means putting yourself at the mercy of a marketplace that's changed little since the first days of Bolshevism.

A week before the failed coup, we were two-hundred miles east of Moscow in the tiny Russian village of Tuikavo. There was only one store in town, and in it we came across a woman who qualified as Soviet sales clerk of the month. Untouched by anything resembling glasnost or perestroika, she not only made customers wait in a line that kept them standing for hours in the mud, when they finally got to the counter, she screeched at them like Ethel Merman in a bad mood. Her problem was a recent shipment of beer, which everyone wanted, and a rotten barrel of fish, which nobody did. Caught in the middle of a distribution snafu, the clerk had decided to sell beer only to customers who also bought fish, a policy that greatly displeased the locals. Yet the clerk's word was law, and rather than put up with mounting complaints, she simply closed the store in a huff and went on an all-day lunch break.

In any American town facing a similar dilemma, there would have been picket lines and calls to TV stations. If all else failed, some customers might even be mad enough to take over the store and help themselves to the beer. In a way, Soviet citizens *have* taken over the store. But bad habits die hard, and despite an end to communism, there are still lines, shortages, and clerks like the one in Tuikavo, running their shops just as they always have.

What's waiting for Western capitalists when they arrive in the new Russia, or what's left of the old one, are millions of potential customers eager for a consumer economy but almost totally ignorant of how one works. Even Russian President Boris

Yeltsin, who declared that "the entrepreneur will be the foundation of the new Soviet society," seems a little fuzzy on what it is an entrepreneur actually does. When he came to the United States shortly after his election in the summer of 1991, Yeltsin told an audience of financial analysts in New York that anyone who buys meat in Moscow and sells it as shish-kabob at a big markup less than a hundred miles away is guilty of criminal exploitation. He has since modified his views. But unlike most of his fellow countrymen, Yeltsin has the benefit of advice and counsel from the nation's top thinkers.

The rest of the Soviet population is learning about capitalism by sudden, if not total, immersion. The process so far has been a mixture of tentative steps forward and predictable slides back. After an independent farmer, supplying meat to a Moscow joint-venture restaurant, had his picture in the paper recently, his neighbors retaliated by burning down his barn. It was their way of saying: "Who does he think *he* is? That guy's no better than we are." Americans like to keep up with the Joneses. Communism taught Soviets to keep the Joneses down with them.

"For a long time, we've been like crabs in a basket," said Russian novelist Vladimir Voinovich, describing his country's psychology of oppression. "When one crab tries to climb out, the other ones pull him back."

As the old Soviet economy, based on collectivism and central planning, is replaced by a new one based on imported know-how and domestic self-interest, paranoid beliefs about the evils of financial success will be no match for the promise of a fast buck.

It often surprises visiting foreign businessmen that so many of the Soviets they meet are full-fledged capitalists, and have been for some time. In a country without junk bonds, mergers, or leveraged buyouts, the economic role models for most entrepreneurs, amazingly enough, are Americans. Our own fiscal problems might be making *us* question how smart we are, but Soviets are convinced that when it comes to making money, Americans are still the best teachers. The only things they need, they say, are the tools and the training to be more like us.

"I didn't know whether to feel sorry for them or to join them," said a U.S. computer executive hard hit by the recession. Later, after mulling over "the pros and cons of the situation," he decided to take on a partner in St. Petersburg, reasoning that a fresh start would do them both good.

Now that the communist apparatus is being subdivided into a thousand parts, chances for new starts abound. Of course, so does the risk of big losses. Then again, that's what "adventure" capitalism is all about.

"Everything here is difficult," a Russian saying goes. "But nothing is impossible." It took McDonald's of Canada fourteen years to negotiate the deal that brought Big Macs to Moscow. Talks between Chevron and government officials in Kazakhstan about tapping oil reserves there dragged on for three years. The breakup of the republics has removed one layer of bureaucratic confusion; just the same, in any deal, the first test of an outsider's endurance always takes place at the bargaining table.

While the odds are high that many who show up as saviors will leave as suckers, there's something about getting in on the ground floor, particularly a ground floor that spans eleven time zones, that keeps businessmen coming to Russia in ever-increasing numbers with ever-increasing schemes to make millions.

Seventy years ago, the director of the Soviet Central Labor Institute could have been predicting the capital-intensive times of today when he hailed "a new flowering of America" in Russia. What he was talking about, though, was *fordizm*, a Russian word for the theories of American carmaker Henry Ford, one of the world's foremost proponents of capitalism and among the first foreigners to do business in the Soviet Union. The early Bolsheviks didn't just buy thousands of Ford trucks, they bought the philosophy behind them. The need to build a new economy out of the one they had just destroyed forced communist leaders to forget about Party ideology and embrace Ford's "scientific principles" for getting the most out of workers. Not even Lenin himself could fail to admire the father of the assembly line.

Long before the United States recognized the Soviet state,

Ford engineers were there supervising the construction of automobile and tractor plants, the most famous of which in Nizhiny Novgorod turned out Russia's first proletarian passenger car. Sensing the potential for wealth, other American companies, such as Westinghouse and General Electric, all signed trade deals with the Soviet government, although none ever reached the status of the Ford Motor Company and its founder.

For years, the Ford name became synonymous with efficient, reliable workmanship, the last words anyone would use to define the current quality of Soviet labor. Inevitably, as the political pendulum swung in the opposite direction, Ford's lessons were lost on new generations of Soviet leaders. The Moscow factory that Ford engineers helped build was redesigned for the production of Zils, once the official limousine of the Politburo. And the rest is history.

It was Marx who noted that "personages of great importance . . . occur, as it were, twice . . . the first time as tragedy, the second as farce." Whether Henry Ford is having a second coming in the present influx of businessmen only time will tell. Certainly the pioneering industrialist would understand what drives so many to make the trip, and why they're now welcome with open arms.

For Americans, the former Soviet Union is California before they built the railroad—a place to put down your claim and strike it rich. For Soviets, America is the workers' paradise that communism had always promised, but never delivered. It only seems fitting that the two mythologies have found each other. Traveling salesmen, as Willy Loman, protagonist of Arthur Miller's *Death of a Salesman*, once said, are dreamers. But so are their customers. For every miracle pitch, there's somebody out there shopping for a miracle product.

In this book we have tried to focus on Soviet methods of doing business that survived the post-coup power shift more or less intact.

Red Tape was written literally on the run. At one point, a few days before the coup, even the KGB was chasing us. The problem, we later learned, was visiting a town that was off limits to foreigners. The fact that we had no idea where we were at the time would probably not have been a good excuse. As it turned out, however, other matters soon took precedence over bringing us in for questioning.

If many old Soviet customs, such as calling people comrade, have disappeared, others, such as distrusting foreigners, haven't. Nominal communists have become nominal capitalists, and the economy is stuck in the middle of the resulting identity crisis.

How does a businessman handle the risks that come with an unsettled situation? Under normal circumstances, an insurance policy or legal advice might take care of things. But in a place where the former until recently was unavailable and the latter is still unreliable, we think the best form of protection is to know the culture, which is the only sound basis for predicting all of the problems that can entangle you and your money.

Just ask anyone who's ever bought a business meal in Moscow, the only town in the world where restaurants regularly close for lunch.

The city is full of eating establishments that cater to corporate clientele, but getting reservations, ordering food, and paying the bill is the ultimate test of cultural and economic adjustment. And passing means knowing what to do well in advance. As in all things Soviet, a lack of knowledge going in can keep you a perpetual outsider.

Prices at Moscow's many new upscale bistros tend to be steep, yet flexible, and before you get to see a menu, it's important to establish how you're going to pay: by cash, plastic, or gold bullion. Places that say they accept "currency" mean they don't take rubles, even though some hard-currency establishments have "ruble rooms" for anyone willing to wait in line and put up with mean waiters. Despite limited convertibility, the variety of payment schedules can be endless. Many restaurants have "ruble lunches" and "hard-currency" dinners. Others sell food for rubles and booze for hard currency. Still others decide who pays rubles and who pays hard currency on the basis of what language they speak. Russian means rubles; anything else could cost you a week's worth of per diems.

Right up front, waiters will often want to see your credit cards, passport, and a sizable deposit on the tip. Eating at one of Moscow's class restaurants is like crossing an international border. If your papers aren't in order, you're not welcome. This is because good food for Soviets is a major expenditure, and deciding how it will be bought and paid for is like negotiating a six-course business deal. To a Russian, dining out in style is a chance to see how the rest of the world eats. To a Westerner, it's often the first introduction to a multilevel monetary system that, like any game of chance, should be approached with extreme—repeat, *extreme*—caution.

Doing lunch in Moscow can also reveal important aspects of the Soviet character that every businessman should study carefully. Since they've become accustomed to living on welfare, most Soviets treat foreigners as a hard-currency version of "big brother," an attitude that best shows itself in the presence of food, particularly expensive dishes. And when Russians make the reservations that's the kind you'll be eating and paying for.

Appetizers, soups, entrees, wines, desserts, and liqueurs—you've never seen anything disappear so fast or cost so much. In a gold rush that's the nature of the economy. It also happens to be the nature of the present economic relationship between Soviets and Westerners. Westerners want to exploit Soviets and their resources; Soviets want to exploit Westerners and theirs. It could be the perfect symbiosis or a perfect mess, but nobody can say it isn't a learning experience.

And the first lesson is never to believe everything you hear. Soviets have a well-deserved reputation for confusing things, though nothing lately is more confusing than the image of Soviet life as it's portrayed in the American press. During a one-week period in December 1991, the following two accounts of living conditions in the U.S.S.R. appeared in *The Washington Post:*

Friday, December 6: "These are desperate days in the Soviet Union... The newspapers are filled with reports of new shortages, worsening shortages or predicted shortages in everything from matches and wedding rings to hot water, newsprint and, most threatening of all, food. . . ."

Sunday, December 8: "I arrived at Moscow airport . . . with some trepidation . . . With rumors of famine, would I get enough to eat? During the ensuing four weeks of zigzagging across the region, however, I found that my fears were wholly unjustified. . . . Food was accessible and good. I savored fish in restaurants across the Baltic, devoured sweet grapes and good feta-style cheese in Georgia and dined on caviar and fresh vegetables in Moscow."

Long lines? Short supplies? Let's assume the second writer had hard currency to spend when he needed to, but so do most visiting businessmen. Far from being the Soviet Union of old, where everything was out of the question, everything today is negotiable, and by Western standards the prices for most things couldn't be much lower.

Maybe it's destiny that Americans and Soviets should finally meet at the end of what could be history's longest checkout line. For two nations separated for years by ideological and economic differences, political double-talk has been replaced by the equally mysterious inquiries of the marketplace: What's for sale? How much is it? Who's going to pay? When dealing with Soviets, these are always good questions. The answers, as *Red Tape* will show, can be full of surprises.

Asked how he would describe working with Russians, airline executive Jim Fannan, who once headed Pan Am's Soviet operations, put it this way: "Every day is an adventure in abnormal psychology."

That's a feeling we try to capture in *Red Tape*. Although this is a book about business, it's also about politics, culture, and strange behavior. How strange? Only in Russia would a salesman throw away expensive fruits and vegetables rather than insult his own manhood by lowering the price to attract buyers.

* * *

A market isn't just a place of commerce, it's a stage on which people act out their most basic hopes and fears. That's something else we try to explore in *Red Tape*. There are chapters on how a consumer revolt led to the defeat of the coup and the collapse of communism; on personalities like George Cohon, the relentless Canadian entrepreneur who brought McDonald's to Moscow; and on areas like Georgia and Armenia, where some of the most fruitful business opportunities exist if you're tough enough to brave a little guerilla warfare, toxic pollution, and a daily schedule of six-hour banquets.

Other chapters look at the law, a maze of contradictory rules and regulations that can tie up investments for years; at money, which can't be counted as profit until all the right bribes are paid; and at the black market, the only reliable source of goods and services, provided you don't mind dealing in stolen goods or being served by what locals refer to as "the trade mafia."

Red Tape was written to point out the pitfalls as well as the promises of new Soviet business ventures, and with that in mind we examine how the area's abundant natural resources can serve as an excellent substitute for convertible currency, how privatization can make smart buyers instant successes, and how knowing the applicable commercial customs can put anybody way ahead of the pack. There's also an up-close examination of the movie industry, a segment of the economy so full of con artistry it's the perfect microcosm for Soviet-style capitalism.

Our intention throughout *Red Tape* is to inform—or should we say, to warn—as well as entertain. And with that in mind, our first bit of practical advice is that no business traveler should even consider embarking on a trip to the now-defunct Soviet Union without bringing with him at least three essential things: several cartons of cigarettes (to use as money), a few packs of candy (to use as food), and a sense of humor (to use in case of emergencies).

Chapter One

Carryout Coup

"We lost the fight," said hard-line Soviet Colonel Victor Alksnis, giving a recap of the 1991 coup attempt on the "MacNeil/Lehrer Newshour." But exactly where or when the tide of events had turned against the communists, Alksnis wasn't really sure. It could have been when Boris Yeltsin defied the plotters while standing on top of a tank. It could have been a day later, when, one by one, leaders of the coup began to drop out with sudden colds.

"Let the historians decide," Alksnis sighed. "I don't want to think about it."

Yet to anyone on the "White House" barricades, it wasn't hard to identify at least one decisive moment. It came when the first provisions arrived from the Pizza Hut three blocks up the street. Russian officials knew that keeping thousands of hungry demonstrators chanting for democracy meant feeding them, and to do that meant placing the most important carryout order of the twentieth century.

On day two of the coup, as more and more tanks defected to the Yeltsin forces, the plaza in front of the white marble Russian parliament building took on the appearance of a heavily fortified drive-in restaurant. There were troop trucks, armored personnel carriers, and dozens of makeshift delivery vehicles to aid in the steady flow of pepperoni and cheese—to go. At the height of the struggle, fast food had become the ration of choice and a driving force behind the "Second Russian Revolution."

Not everyone, though, was satisfied with the direction the revolution was taking, and debate raged over the gut issues. "We had more to eat when Brezhnev was around," shouted those who supported the junta. "So what! That was a police state," resisters yelled back, swearing they'd go hungry rather than let the coup plotters succeed.

In fact, food may have been the reformers' only real ammunition. In a city that's supposed to be starving, free lunches were suddenly everywhere. A nice woman from the nomenklatura, the communist version of the upper class, was at the barricades giving away treats from an Irish hard-currency supermarket. Someone else was passing around bananas, a grocery item few Russians have ever seen, let alone eaten.

One American businessman in the crowd said he'd never forget the sight of resisters serving hot meals to the soldiers, or watching a young tank driver from Central Asia bite into a slice of pizza. "The look on his face told you the whole course of history was shifting."

Moscow is a city made almost entirely of concrete slabs—excellent raw material with which to build barricades. And the bigger the barricades grew, the more obvious it became: This was a political uprising powered largely by a consumer revolt, although *consumers* might be the wrong word to describe people who have never been inside a K-Mart, Trac Auto or 7-Eleven. In the communist world of haves and have-nots, the only real consumers were the same elite Party leaders who had engineered the coup in the first place.

In Pushkin Square, less than a mile from history in the making, it would have been difficult to tell that most Muscovites had anything more important on their minds than figuring out how many hamburgers and Cokes they could buy for 17 rubles. While the junta was threatening to rain destruction on the protesters and the protesters were vowing to fight to the death, the line outside the Moscow McDonald's was just as long as it always is. That in itself should have sent a powerful message to the coup conspirators, one of whom, former KGB head Vladimir Kryuchkov, went out of his way to denounce the new Western goodies Russians were so eager to buy.

"Exploiting our own mismanagement," Kryuchkov told the Supreme Soviet, "foreign capitalists are flooding the Soviet Union with contaminated foodstuffs full of high radioactivity and harmful chemical admixtures." To Soviet shoppers, convinced that their own food is life-threatening, Kryuchkov's warnings seemed slightly misplaced. Actually, if the plotters had only bothered to read some of the new signs all over town, they might still have their old jobs. Moscow, a city with M&Ms billboards but no M&Ms, was demanding M&Ms—and a lot more.

What the junta offered instead was a temporary suspension of all vodka rationing. But Soviets, who have had more than their share of baggy-pants politicians, were no longer willing to take orders—or handouts—from eight guys who could pass for finalists in a Three Stooges look-alike contest.

When it was clear that the Emergency Committee had lost its momentum, the "White House" crowd, which had grown by the final day of the coup to more than a million, picked up the rhythm. Soon the entire neighborhood was rocking to the beat. President Mikhail Gorbachev's temporary confinement at his twenty-eight-room beach house was over. And by the time a ghetto blaster in an open apartment window started booming Elvis Presley's "Hound Dog" into the streets below, Gorby's go-slow economic reforms were finished, too. Perestroika, as one eyewitness put it, had become "destroika" for the Party apparatus that opposed it.

The square in front of the Russian parliament building looked like a multinational melting pot—not the type Bolshevism tried to create by force, but one that seemed to materialize all by itself when the Army and the KGB threatened to turn the country back into a George Orwell novel. Unlike previous military crackdowns, this one, however, was greeted by a steady stream of jokes and sarcasm. Why hadn't the coup organizers put resisters out of commission by cutting off electricity and telephone service to the parliament building? "Yanayev was probably too drunk to find the switch," said a young man from Kiev. That little mistake, whatever the reason, tipped the balance of power by letting Yeltsin and company have access to photocopiers, fax machines, long-distance lines, and CNN.

It was open season on the old guard, and speaker after speaker urged Soviets to put aside their fear of the unknown and make a new start. Within days, scores of monuments to past communist heroes would bite the dust, including one to secret police founder Feliks Dzerzhinskii that stood for years in front of KGB headquarters. The attack was led by brokers from Moscow's brand-new commodities exchange, who first tried to pull it down with ropes. When that failed, the city council was asked to help out by sending over a few heavy-duty cranes. Three hours later, Dzerzhinskii's statue was lying in the street like a cast-iron King Kong.

"The junta wants to give us crumbs from the table," a priest told the demonstrators, whose shouts of dissatisfaction filled the air. This was a critical mass in every sense. For years deprived of consumer goods by a government going bust in the arms race, they wanted whatever the West had—and even if they couldn't come up with the downpayment, they wanted it now.

"God will help us," the priest replied, to the obvious reassurance of many. Considering the extent of the nation's financial plight, here was somebody finally talking business in a way Soviets understood.

"We're not going to turn our economic plans upside down . . . just to please the Americans," Gorbachev adviser Yevgeny Primakov said just before his boss took the worst summer vacation of his life. "There is no sense telling us to go down a certain path. We have our own path and we're going to stick to it. This is our fate, our country."

Lost in the happy overthrow of communism, Primakov's remarks go to the heart of Soviet crisis management.

Human history moves in cycles. Russian history moves in *circles*. The revolving-door effect has always created problems for foreigners, now being asked once again to save Russia and a reconstituted Soviet Union from decades of communist-inflicted woes.

Economic progress, Westerners like to believe, is evolutionary, the result of gradual improvements in the way people live, work, and enjoy themselves. Governments can stimulate and guide the process, some would say, but they can't impose it. History and political training have made most Soviets think the exact opposite.

In the past, whenever Russian rulers wanted progress, they merely ordered it. Not that orders were given that often. New ideas usually mean change, and Russia's traditional symbiotic power twins, the czar and the Orthodox Church, generally favored the status quo. Czar Nicholas I at one time even banned the word *progress* from the Russian language. Still, there have been occasions when leaders, for different reasons, tried to act like progressives. While he was busy starving Soviet citizens in the 1930s, Josef Stalin opened a chain of private hard-currency stores. After he returned from a 1959 visit to the United States, Nikita Khrushchev, fascinated by one-way streets, insisted that Moscow have them, too. And nearly every Soviet head of state has made an addition to the Exhibition of Economic Achievements, a monument to the Communist Party's domestic policy of bait and switch, where one-of-a-kind copies of Western consumer products, from hair dryers to sporty convertibles, were put on display for people to look at and wish they could have.

The intention was always to intimidate and coerce, the belief on the part of Soviet officials being that this was the best way to control the population and, most importantly, earn the respect of foreigners. As an old Russian proverb puts it: Beat your own people, and others will fear you.

If Soviets had an economic fate, as Primakov suggested, it's now part of a psychological dependence that communism spread throughout the entire empire. Despite an official end to the Com-

munist Party, the master-and-slave mentality it adapted from
Russian history and made an integral part of the Marxist system
won't simply vanish with the first two-for-one sale. That so many
Soviets still want someone like Stalin to lead them shows how
deep the national need is for a father figure to supervise the
Motherland. A *Los Angeles Times* poll conducted in 1991, four
months before the abortive coup, indicated that 57 percent of the
Russian people supported multiparty pluralism, while two out of
every five Russians favored a strong leader, rather than a democratic government, to solve the nation's many problems.

Some members of the emerging business class make regular
pleas for a dictatorship to transform the economy. Russians see
their leaders as both protectors and providers, and like them to
have the same strong-man qualities Yeltsin displayed during the
coup. But Yeltsin has confessed he can do virtually nothing to
rescue his country from its current financial mess without help
from abroad, another part of Russia's fate that has been repeating
itself for centuries.

Over one thousand years ago, Russians, admitting they were
incapable of whipping themselves into shape, asked the Scandinavians to do the job. According to Russian historical records,
several tenth-century Slavic tribes invited three Scandinavian
brothers, Ryurik, Sineus, and Truvor, to come to "the land of the
Rus" to see if they could get the place to work. "Our whole land
is great and rich, but there is no order in it," read the urgent plea
for help. "Come to rule and reign over us." The Scandinavians
took up the offer, and were compensated for their troubles with
money produced by the tax system they established.

From then on, Russian history has seen a never-ending pro-
cession of foreign rulers. Most of the Romanov dynasty, which
reigned over Russia for three centuries, had foreign blood. But
even that didn't help them much in overcoming the backwardness
of their subjects.

The greatest of the Romanovs was Peter the Great, who
occupied the throne from 1682 to 1725. As a young man, Peter
went to Europe to learn firsthand everything he could about

Western life. He visited universities, shipyards, factories, and the-aters, always taking notes on whatever he saw. When he got home, he set out to westernize Russia, much as Gorbachev tried to do 290 years later.

Peter devised a new Russian calendar, putting it in sync with the rest of the world. He improved education, transformed archi-tecture, and Europeanized fashion. To change Russian behavior, Peter reasoned, it was first necessary to change the way Russians looked. In keeping with his plan to emulate foreigners, he not only instituted a dress code for the nobility, requiring them to adopt Western styles and manners, he personally dry-shaved the beards off all of his aides and advisers to make them appear less barbaric to foreign visitors.

But, like Gorbachev, Peter had to contend with powerful opposition, particularly from the church. And to deal with his foes, he organized a secret police force, which, among other things, monitored the population's compliance with his new policy of "openness" to the West. The aim was to foster Peter's own form of perestroika and help to promote foreign trade. But the unin-tended effect was to stifle commerce.

Laws in Russia have never been applied as they are in the West, and in Peter's time no one knew for sure what was legal and what wasn't. As a general rule, anything that served the interest of the czar was permitted; everything else was illegal. After the Bolshevik Revolution, the same basic principle was followed by a succession of communist leaders who, until Gorbachev came along, had relatively little interest in doing business with West-erners. Even during the investment boomlet of the Gorbachev years, tax laws, banking charges, and the high cost of bribing officials usually reduced any business deal in the Soviet Union to an expensive exercise in overseas philanthropy.

For centuries, as despots and dictators came and went, Rus-sians retained their faith in the protective powers of their rulers. As those powers have failed miserably in recent years, the same faith has been transferred to the free market, the latest in a long line of cure-alls that Russians instinctively turn to when times are tough. Generations of utopian promises, predicting a workers' paradise in which no one would be required to work, haven't produced a nation of do-it-yourself buffs. The Soviet people have been conditioned to believe in miracles, to expect that some great force will solve their problems. Most, still reeling after the collapse of the communist state and the introduction of free prices, have no idea what hit them, or the foggiest notion of what to do next. But that doesn't mean they won't be getting plenty of outside advice.

It may be a coincidence that capitalism and religion returned to the Soviet Union at the same time, but it's no accident that the most active missionaries are consultants from the American Enterprise Institute, the Heritage Foundation, and the other conservative think tanks. Through Russia's new window on the West, it's possible to see an army of free-market futurists heading for the "primeval empire." One group, Junior Achievement of America, the world's oldest and largest business education program, is teaching the basics of capitalist thinking in 1,000 Soviet high schools. "Everybody there is talking about capitalism, but no one knows what it means," said James B. Hayes, chairman of Junior Achievement and the publisher of *Fortune* magazine. Courses are taught by Soviet instructors trained in the United States, using American economics textbooks translated into Russian.

"What good does it do to gloat," said William Eggers, a young privatization specialist with the Heritage Foundation. "It isn't a case where we defeated Russians and that's that. We beat them and now we're trying to join them."

American fast-food corporations aren't the only ones setting up shop in the former Soviet Union. For years, various organizations have been working behind enemy lines, selling their own brand of dialectical materialism. Everywhere you travel, all people talk about is going to church and making money, so combining the two activities seemed only natural. The owners of a publishing cooperative in Moscow said that in the space of three weeks they were approached by the Moonies and the Mormons with offers of financial help, technical assistance, and moral support.

The Seventh Day Adventists, who beat out Pat Robertson's

700 Club to win a three-year contract to show inspirational programs on Russian television, enhanced their bargaining position by putting something more than food for the soul on the table. "The Soviets wanted moral instruction in science and the Bible," said Los Angeles Pastor George Vandeman, the host of the broadcast and a strong proponent of agribusiness. "In Russia, tomatoes are one to two inches in diameter," Vandeman said. "Four years ago, we established a seminary in Zaokski, where we are training students in hydroponic gardening as well as theology—and producing some good-looking four-inch tomatoes and potatoes over six inches long."

Long before Graham Allison, director of the JFK School of Government, ever thought of calling his Soviet bailout scheme the Grand Bargain, the Heritage Foundation had connected with Yeltsin's high command, supplying free information on everything a developing country needs to know about a market economy, including a six-part Walt Disney cartoon that explained how Wall Street works.

"We were the first wave of capitalism," Eggers said proudly. "We see everything we've done up to now as an effort to make it easier for businesses to get started. American business, Russian business. What's the difference? We believe in free enterprise."

The stock-market cartoon could be a useful learning device for the Russians, but in a country whose only Nielsen ratings are KGB spy files, it's impossible to know how many people watched it the dozen times it ran on Russian television.

Just as competition is starting to appear in the marketplace, it's also showing up on the tube. Turn on post-communist TV and you never know what you might see. Watch one station and there's a star-search talent show from Odessa. Switch the dial and you get an actor reading excerpts from *The Gulag Archipelago* in front of a deserted Siberian prison camp. Weeknights it's everybody's favorite prime-time game show, "Field of Miracles," a "Wheel of Fortune" clone on which excited contestants spell words and win prizes. Except, in this case, the prizes are more like things most Americans have lost in their basements: a V-neck sweater, a transistor radio, or a pair of rubber boots. If players really get lucky, they can win a new Lada two-door, ready for immediate delivery, as opposed to the six-year wait it takes to buy one through normal channels.

How does all this apparent consumer readiness translate into commercial opportunity? According to the *Harvard Business Review*, "Western [companies] will not get very far unless they first understand that there really is no such thing as 'market share' to be captured in the Soviet Union just now; that the aggregated talent of Soviet citizens, however impressive, is not 'supply'; and their aggregated need, however dire, not 'demand.' "

Still, it's hard to underestimate the potential or the importance of beating the rush. A craving for all of the foreign goods money can buy is as much a part of life in the new Soviet society as avoiding contact with foreigners was in the old one. The difference is that Soviets today don't have any money—an inconvenience soon to be corrected by a multi-billion-dollar shopping credit from the industrialized nations that make the same products they want. It is, in a way, a fitting end to one chapter in economic history and the start of another.

On the side of a building near the southern loop of Moscow's Ring Road there is a faded advertisement for the Communist Party that shows a determined-looking man and woman with their fists clenched and their sleeves rolled up, and a message that reads: "We Are Building Communism." With all of the other work it has to do, it will probably be a while before the city council gets around to scraping it off.

The Soviet Communist Party promoted itself, but rarely what it produced. Advertising premiums were never considered useful in accomplishing its goals. If they had been, the coup plotters would have handed out free coupons for Baskin-Robbins. But they didn't get it. In the end, the communists were banished, if not entirely defeated, for being tightwads. What the proponents of democracy wanted—besides freedom—were CD players, Reeboks, camcorders, cellular phones, RVs, all-terrain vehicles, microwaves, and everything else that comes with living in what Russians like to call a "civilized" society, including consumer credit to pay the bills.

Karl Marx, communism's chief philosopher, concerned himself only with the necessities of life. The concept of material amenities eluded him, and Frederick Engels, his frequent coauthor, thought it best to keep it that way.

The prosperous owner of several factories, Engels knew that if Marx developed a taste for luxuries, he would be the one to pay. Marx, one of history's great freeloaders, spent his entire adult life asking other people for money, a habit he passed on to the Soviets. And this time it's the West that gets the bill.

Unlike their counterparts in Eastern Europe, most Russians and other Soviets have no memories of a free economy. For three-quarters of a century they lived in a nation that was both a police state *and* a welfare state. And as they plunge into a market system, there will be many people unhappy about the higher prices, unequal incomes, and greater demand for hard work that go with it.

Marx wrote volumes on the conversion of capitalism to communism. That the reverse process might some day need explaining apparently never occurred to him, an oversight that now has nearly every Soviet playing it by ear.

But an economy in transition—even a fake economy in transition—can offer many rich possibilities for investors. Through perestroika and glasnost, crackdowns and detente, business traffic moved in and out of the Soviet Union by its own internal guidance system. There are currently some 3,000 registered Soviet joint ventures. That less than half of them are actually working has done nothing to discourage new investors from trying their luck. Few, however, are prepared for the economic free-for-all that awaits them, or for the questions they will be asking themselves once they join in. Is the money really money? Are contracts really contracts? Has anything really changed? Communism may have been "a beautiful idea" on paper, as Boris Yeltsin has said, but cleaning up the debris it left behind will be a challenge extending well into the next millennium.

Since the days of the first Romanovs, Russian rulers have been conning the West, forecasting everything from wars to famine if other countries don't give them what they want. The ransom this time is drive-in-window privileges at the World Bank, a price most governments seem willing to pay for friendly foreign relations. But businessmen, putting their own money on the line, should remember the lessons of history or they might have to repeat them.

Capitalism defeated the communists. That much is clear. What isn't so clear is what the winning side has won—or how much it will have to pay the losers to find out.

Chapter Two

The Seventy-four-Year Misunderstanding

In the late 1940s, Joseph Stalin had a plan. What Moscow needed in order to be a first-class workers' utopia was skyscrapers. Inspired by pictures of New York City, but determined to create a Big Potato all his own, Stalin rolled up his sleeves and dictated every detail of the project himself. The look he had in mind is neo-Count Dracula. The result is a ring of seven identical gray buildings that tower over the city like high-rise mausoleums.

Actually, one is a university, one houses the Foreign Ministry, and others are apartments and hotels. From a distance they still retain some of their original Cold-War charm. But up close, like almost everything else in Moscow these days, they have the look of condemned property, falling apart from neglect and unfit for human habitation.

The same can't be said, however, of the luxurious Hotel Oktyabrskaya. Always out of place in the old Soviet Union, the Oktyabrskaya was never what it seemed to be. In fact, it wasn't even *where* it seemed to be. Rising above an abandoned construction site four blocks from Red Square, the Oktyabrskaya was always a Marxist mirage—not only was it hard to find, but for all practical purposes, it didn't exist.

It wasn't shown on street maps of Moscow or listed in the city's limited-edition phone book; no traffic cop would tell you how to get there, and taxicab drivers had never heard of it. As Russians often say in such cases, the hotel's whereabouts were an enigma. Here was a fifteen-story building that looked like a maximum-security Holiday Inn—minus the friendly sign on the roof—and to thousands of people who passed by every day, it might as well have been invisible.

But if the ultraexclusive Oktyabrskaya was a mystery to average Muscovites, who still aren't allowed past the front gates, they could never imagine what was going on inside. Surrounded by a ten-foot-high iron fence and guarded by the KGB, the hotel was built in pre-perestroika days for the secret enjoyment of the Central Committee, the Communist Party's now-defunct ruling body. It had two bars, a fitness club, and a glassed-in sun deck with Cuban banana trees. At the height of its socialist heyday, there was even a full-time nurse on duty to assist the health-conscious commissars who were once the only clientele. Aside from the normal plumbing problems, life at the Oktyabrskaya was so civilized and polite even the KGB agents said, "Have a nice day."

True, all the rooms were bugged; at this level of personal attention, that was to be expected. The listening device was a ten-pound table-model radio aimed at the bed and permanently attached to the wall by a quarter-inch phone wire. Who was tuned in on the other end was a matter of opinion, especially during the confused final years of the Party. Nevertheless, most regular guests were smart enough to jam the reception by turning up the volume on their television sets. This was one place where everybody who was anybody was also an amateur sound engineer.

After the communists departed, the bugging equipment they left behind proved to be a money-saving benefit for Western business. When several hotels signed deals with an in-room movie service, rather than having to install their own wiring, the foreign company simply used the KGB systems already in place.

The Oktyabrskaya, named after the month in 1917 when a coup d'etat put the Bolsheviks in power, was the last word in communist hospitality, and convincing evidence that Soviets were capable of running a non-lethal hotel. Until 1990, though, the only outsiders to know were visiting Third World revolutionaries and CIA moles. That's when the Central Committee proprietors took a good look at the books and decided to rent rooms to foreign businessmen in exchange for hard currency. Naturally, the policy shift upset a few reactionary types, and given the basic issues involved, it's easy to see why. For a political party that set out to destroy the value of money—a goal it achieved with remarkable success—the new occupancy plan not only represented one more lost privilege, but an open acknowledgment that checkout time was fast approaching for the Soviet economy.

Never before in the history of the Soviet Union had the leaders and the masses shared so much in common. The hard-currency craze that first went public in 1991 when Soviet citizens were legally allowed to own small quantities of the precious stuff soon became a nationwide financial panic whose effects on the already weakened ruble were predictably harsh. Halfway through the year, a pack of Marlboros had greater buying power.

In spite of Kremlin mood swings in the opposite direction, free enterprise had been creeping into the Soviet Union for decades. Today, with the black market and other related trade activities accounting for roughly 35 to 40 percent of the country's commerce, there isn't just one economy, but many, often working (or not working) side by side with no disruption to business as usual. But when a holy of holies like the Hotel Oktyabrskaya started ringing up sales in Deutsche marks, dollars, and pounds, not to mention playing host to investment panels, marketing seminars, and feel-good motivational workshops—all attended by top communist officials—it was clear that the Party line and the bottom line had become the same thing.

But then, to the Party's privileged few, they always were.

Many in the West have had the mistaken belief that the Soviet Communist Party wanted to destroy capitalism. In reality, Party leaders were trying to perfect it by removing the risks and giving themselves all the benefits.

"The corrupt communist knows that he is a petty thief and recognizes that other people also want to steal," wrote popular Russian author Tatayana Tolstaya. "He loves comfort . . . He wouldn't start a nuclear war with the West because that would destroy all those warehouses with . . . good things inside."

Rather than being the bloodthirsty bulletheads everyone imagined they were, most high-echelon Party members were more like country-club conservatives—people whose devotion to the material life would be surprisingly similar to that of corporate fat cats anywhere. This particular country club, though, had been going broke for years, and in the waning months of the regime, when the ideological equivalent of an eight-lane interstate came roaring through their golf course, the few remaining members could only look on in stunned disbelief.

What brought on such sorry times for these dispossessed duffers was the removal of the Party's most effective support mechanism. Other economies are driven by market forces; the Soviet version was driven by force. The fear of what might happen if they failed to produce was all that was needed to make people work. Those who slaved away while their bosses enjoyed themselves believed in communism, often because they didn't know enough to doubt it. And even if they had, what good would that have done? Well-being is a relative condition, and to question the behavior of higher-ups meant threatening the delicate network of private deals that made the entire system work, by degrees, for everyone, top to bottom.

Before it went into receivership, the Communist Party was to the Soviet Union what the U.S. banking industry was in America before the S&L crisis struck. For seventy-four years, the Party had money, power, and the authority to do whatever it wanted with both. It was the country's prime landlord and employment agency. It controlled every asset, manufactured good, and natural resource. Since it also ran the police, the military, and the government, it could behave like a mutant Rotary Club with firepower, and there wasn't much anybody could do about it. When Party faithful get together to reminisce about the good old days, those are the days they like to remember. And if anybody has cause for nostalgia, it's them.

It wasn't until Boris Yeltsin's exposé of life in the communist ruling class that ordinary Soviets could read a firsthand account of the good times that were really going on. *Against the Grain,* Yeltsin's 1990 autobiography, which used his own privileged circumstances as an example of official corruption, became an instant bestseller. After being elevated to the mighty Politburo, Yeltsin discovered that "on the summit of Olympus, the caste system was scrupulously observed.

"If you have climbed all the way to the top of the establishment pyramid . . . then it's full communism," he wrote. "It turns out that there was no need of the world revolution, maximum labor productivity, and universal harmony in order to have reached that ultimate, blissful state as prophesied by Karl Marx. It is perfectly possible to attain it in one particular country—for one particular group of people."

Yeltsin, who wept when Stalin died, and who resigned from the Party only thirteen months before the 1991 coup attempt, asked himself what he was doing in the company of such crooks. But the temptations were obvious. Assigned a government villa once occupied by the Gorbachevs, the Yeltsin family was cared for by a household staff that included three cooks, three waitresses, a maid, a team of gardeners, and a projectionist for their home movie theater. There were walk-in refrigerators in the basement and so many bathrooms upstairs that Yeltsin "lost count."

For people whose lives contained few if any creature comforts, the message hit home, and for delivering it, Yeltsin became for many Soviets a combination of Ralph Nader and Jesse Jackson. Maybe the stories about drinking too much were true. If so, they only reinforced his credentials as one of the boys, as opposed to one of the high-living hypocrites he wrote about in his book.

Perestroika was a plan for giving the authorities a better life, not the masses. What was this Yeltsin guy up to, anyway? Kremlin old-timers thought he was crazy. As Party boss of Sverdlovsk (since renamed Ekaterinburg), Yeltsin had no problem following orders to level the house where the czar's family was shot. Now he was telling people that Gorbachev and the entire Central Committee were a bunch of thieves. In Stalin's day, he would have been taken out and shot. But not even a TV blackout and three suspicious car wrecks could stop him. The only thing that slowed Yeltsin down was a heart attack, and when he got over that, he picked up right where he left off. The man was a legitimate contender and he was gathering crowds.

In Moscow, officials were in a panic. They banned public demonstrations, raised taxes, and armed rebel nationalists all over the country. If they couldn't stop Boris Yeltsin, at least they could take people's minds off him so the Party could get back to its first order of business—taking care of itself.

The communist system was founded on the concept of unequal treatment. Lenin believed the Party hierarchy was automatically entitled to extra perks. To lure the large numbers of new members he needed to do his dirty work in the 1930s, Stalin declared that sharing the wealth was for "a primitive sect of ascetics." Equality was something communists talked about, but never practiced.

The Communist Party of the Soviet Union was an apparatus designed for the seizure and control of power and property. Its closest parallel in the West wasn't a political organization or even a special-interest group but a Mafia family. If the CPSU had existed in the United States, it would have been prosecuted for racketeering. Communist officials claimed ownership of everything they could steal, and a nomenklatura of Party leaders and their families took full advantage of their status, giving themselves access to apartments, schools, and stores that were strictly off limits to ordinary Soviets.

Admission to the charmed circle of the two-million-member nomenklatura, a kind of totalitarian leisure set, was by invitation only. Just as they had to adhere to the Party line in politics, communist blue bloods were expected to follow the rules of an intricate social pecking order. New inductees climbed the ladder of success by serving those above them and cutting off those below. Because their parents' standing conferred certain class advantages on children, the offspring of power were expected to marry one another. Outsiders were not considered suitable mating material, and whenever one attempted to crack the ranks, defensive action could be swift.

In the 1970s, Soviet Premier Leonid Brezhnev disowned his loose-living daughter Galina and made himself the guardian of her only child. The girl, whose name was Victoria, soon became the focus of her grandfather's bearlike protective instincts. Brezhnev was determined not to let her turn out like her mother, who had deserted the nomenklatura for a circus strong man. So when Victoria entered college and started dating a poor music student named Gennady, Brezhnev saw red.

First, he had Gennady followed. Then he had his phone tapped. Finally, one night two KGB agents came to his room and told Gennady he was moving from Moscow to Leningrad.

"To Brezhnev, I was some kind of lowlife," said Gennady, who conceded he was lucky the KGB hadn't sent him to Siberia.

He and Victoria continued their relationship long-distance, and after two years in Leningrad, the KGB agents who had been trailing him the whole time said he could go back to Moscow. A few years later, Victoria and Gennady got married, but Brezhnev never apologized.

"Once at a party he offered me an American cigarette," said Gennady. "I guess that was his way of saying 'I'm sorry.' "

It was Gennady, though, who may have gotten the last laugh. When he and Victoria split up a few years ago, he moved into Brezhnev's dacha, a plush country house outside Moscow. How long he can stay in light of the changing political picture still isn't clear, but at least he can say he's lived on the communist answer to Easy Street. By mid-1991, that was a very busy thoroughfare.

Privatization was moving slowly everywhere else in the Soviet Union, yet in the old Council of Ministers, long an enclave of special privilege, the dacha (pronounced like "gotcha") business was booming. After repeatedly warning people about the dangers of converting state property to private ownership, officials apparently decided to experiment on themselves first.

Soviets, most of whom live in cramped cell-block apartments, love their country homes, but former Prime Minister Nikolai Ryzhkov had an absolute passion for them. Before resigning his job for health reasons, Ryzhkov proposed that "in order to cut down on costs for the state," thousands of luxury dachas should be sold to the government leaders who regularly used them free of charge. The suggestion was quickly approved by other council members and before long everyone was grabbing up houses at prices so low a special commission later estimated that insider trading had saved the buyers billions of rubles. Before the dacha scandal broke, Ryzhkov, who came up with the idea, had already bought two.

"If anybody still thinks it's democrats . . . who will lead us toward capitalism, he is dramatically mistaken," a concerned reader wrote in the magazine *Ogonyok*. "In fact, it was those who mourned publicly the most over [the loss of] the socialist achievement who were first in line."

Izvestia, once a Party house organ, charged that "yesterday's leaders, having scented the captivating smell of property, have seized land allotments, dachas, refrigerators and the whole deal with a death grip."

As the economy worsened and communists were calling it quits by the millions, life in the hard-pressed nomenklatura had become like one big "Phil Donahue Show," which, oddly enough, was being regularly co-hosted at the time by nomenklatura dropout and Kremlin "newsman" Vladimir Pozner. Already familiar to American audiences through his many appearances on "Nightline," Pozner, who was born in New York and grew up in Moscow, where his family moved in the 1940s, was a classic reformed communist: polished, contrite, and determined to take full advantage of capitalism by confessing his sins on TV.

Publicly, many in the nomenklatura tried to distance themselves from the imminent collapse of everything they once believed in. Letters of resignation from the Party were appearing in publications around the world. "I was a Party member for almost 33 years," read one in the *Washington Post,* written by a visiting Soviet journalist. "The decision to quit was painful but morally refreshing."

Privately, though, some in the dwindling ranks of the elite began to behave like passengers who wore their tuxedos and evening gowns the night the *Titanic* went down. If you've gotta go, it might as well be in the style to which you're accustomed.

During the week of the failed putsch, Atrodneya, a nomenklatura retreat in the suburbs of Moscow, was packed as usual with late-summer guests. Separated from a run-down apartment development by a wooded area and high cement wall, Atrodneya offered tennis, swimming, and that rarest of Soviet rarities: warm and friendly service. But as events of the coup unfolded, few vacationers could tear themselves away from their television sets and scenes of their entire world turning upside down.

"It was a nightmare," said one woman, who spent Coup Week at Atrodneya with her two children. But it wasn't a total loss, at least not from the standpoint of communists who'd been planning ahead.

"It's only a matter of time before the Soviet Union has a market economy," Mikhail Gorbachev happily told a 1990 meeting of the U.S.–U.S.S.R. Trade and Economic Council in Moscow. "The people who were here first," he promised, "are the ones who will reap the biggest rewards."

Using that logic, the people with the most to gain from capitalism were the communists—but they also had the most to lose, which may explain why many of them worked so hard at becoming capitalists while they still had an exclusive franchise on all incoming business deals. Having seen how their counterparts in Eastern Europe were treated after the Soviet pullout in 1989, smart apparatchiks started acquiring equity in a reformed economy at home long before anyone else.

In 1917, Party leaders predicted that old social classes would be destroyed and that new ones would rise up in their place. What no one foresaw at the time is that the replacements would arrive wearing the latest double-breasted Italian suits and handing out gold-lettered business cards. Orthodox communism may have been dying, but Communism Inc., as a new breed of Bolshevik *biznesmeni* saw it, was only going through Chapter 11, selling off assets and reorganizing itself under a plan designed to take maximum advantage of its own collapse. As early as 1988, business cooperatives were being created that worked like wholly-owned subsidiaries of the Party. In some cases, state property was converted into joint stock companies that, in turn, set up banks as fronts to disguise who the real owners were.

One of the lead roles in the conversion to a profit-oriented Party system was played by Komsomol, short for the Communist Youth League. Komsomol used to be a hard-line training organization that any Soviet with leadership ambitions had to join. Fail to prove your ability to give and take orders in Komsomol, and you could kiss your future prospects good-bye. At least that's the way it *was*.

By the early 1990s, Komsomol, with branches in schools and colleges throughout the country, had become a leading force in the new Soviet business culture. With direct access to government projects and millions of rubles in diverted Party funds, Komsomol was way ahead of the pack in the rush to go private. An estimated 20 percent of the private businesses in Moscow began as Komsomol projects, including Menatep, an investment group that had its origins in a Komsomol science center, and Cedobank, the first Soviet bank to issue experimental credit cards. Communist kids were out hustling their parents in ways no one could have imagined. They weren't so much bucking the system as playing a new angle. It was as if the Young Republicans had taken over an entire segment of the U.S. economy and were doing a better job at running it than the Old Republicans could.

Soviet peace foundations and cultural exchange groups that had once been front organizations for the Party were becoming small, and, in some cases, big businesses. As get-rich-quick schemes replaced political propaganda, the best and the brightest of what would have been communism's next generation of leaders were opening trade associations, ad agencies, and consulting firms.

Every bureaucrat with information to sell became a potential profit center. Losing their choke hold on the national economy only inspired officials to look for other ways to make—and take—money. Naturally, fees varied. Approval for an operating license could cost a seat on a joint-venture board. Help in dealing with the monetary system was even more expensive. One state bank administrator wanted a foreign company to give him a percentage of its earnings simply for explaining the official value of the ruble, which actually does take some work.

The new role models for these communist go-getters weren't the heroes of the revolution their parents looked up to, but crossover capitalists such as internationally famous eye surgeon and former member of the Central Committee Svyatoslav Fyodorov, who, despite bureaucratic red tape, started a lucrative private clinic and once bravely refused to pay an 80 percent tax on his hard-currency earnings.

In 1990, Fyodorov employed 169 doctors, who performed more than 270,000 eye operations a year, 4,000 of them on foreigners. To increase his convertible cash flow, he invested $64 million in a hospital ship to cruise the Persian Gulf, fishing for nearsighted oil sheiks. Yet Fyodorov's business plans went beyond the frontiers of medicine. With the Party apparatus constantly hounding him for payoffs, he steadfastly put together deals that made him the owner of a luxury hotel, a cellular telephone company, and a new Moscow gambling casino. He was such a whiz with numbers that Yeltsin once considered making him his chief economic adviser.

"People who get property . . . will have power," Fyodorov told *Fortune* magazine. Those who don't "will remain eternal hired hands." But who would get first crack at all of the new opportunities for wealth? The answer was obvious.

It's hard to meet a Soviet these days who doesn't want to go into business. It's even harder to meet a former communist official who hasn't already done it, often without changing jobs. Despite a high-level housecleaning, Party people still fill the bureaucracy, and still run it the same way they always have. Communists have kept top management positions, retaining control of factories and offices and winning many of the best contracts with Western companies. They've held onto power in part through connections, old Party ties that continue to funnel favors to communist-era cronies, and in part through necessity; in many fields the only ones who know how things work are the communists, who used to run the show officially and now do it by default.

If a Western bailout is called the Grand Bargain, maybe the Party's farewell should be called the Grand Charade. Rather than quietly disappearing, many key communists have quietly diversified instead. More than a year after the coup, sorting through all the layered combinations of investors in order to separate legitimate business ventures from those started with Party funds skimmed from the state is clearly a task so full of surprises it may never be tried.

"The situation is tremendously complicated," agreed economist and Speaker of the Russian Parliament Ruslan Khasbulatov, describing what could be the century's biggest inventory liquidation scam. But not many expected that getting to the bottom of the Party's financial affairs would be easy, or, in the end, even possible.

In what was formerly East Germany, one anticommunist group has set up a "witch-hunt hotline" that citizens are invited to call to expose Party members who have landed important, high-paying jobs after their fall from power. But the chance of a similar system working in the new republics is unlikely. Old Party regulars are too much a part of the structure to be removed without having the entire thing collapse.

The communists, of course, had no intention of walking off into the sunset without being paid in advance. And letting thousands of them get rich in the conversion to a market economy may be the price Soviets and the rest of the world have to pay to get rid of them. Then again, given the way they've rigged everything to keep themselves in business, who says they're leaving?

By the time of the aborted coup, the upper ranks of the Party were divided into opposing liberal and conservative factions: one trying to reserve a guaranteed piece of the action before the free market came, and the other trying to preserve the dream of financial security the Communist Party once held for them.

When putsch came to shove, the fight was finished in seventy-two hours. The battle, though, hadn't been over ideology. The real contest pitted communist against communist, and any Party regular who hadn't defected to the winning side by the time power changed hands was out of luck.

"Our people are not used to being worried about the future," said Alexi Volkov, the diehard communist boss of Moscow's Kievskaya section, as he watched his offices sealed by the police. "This has all been greatly unexpected, greatly unexpected."

The defeat of the conservatives changed the Soviet Union almost overnight from a gloomy, gray country full of entrenched opportunists to a gloomy, gray country full of hustlers.

Nowhere is the upsurge in post-Marxist business activity more noticeable than at the Hotel Oktyabrskaya. After an extensive management makeover, it's not the same place it used to be, except that it still requires payment from foreigners in hard currency. Gone is the giant white marble bust of Lenin on the first-floor staircase, the socialist book store in the lobby, and the bugged phones in every room. But there are still so many chauffeured black Volgas in the parking lot it looks like a state funeral. As for signs of capitalism, name a good or service, from condoms to campaign consulting, and somebody's there trying to buy it, sell it, or trade it for natural resources.

In the old days, when foreigners were routinely put up in the Hotel Ukraine, one of the city's seven Stalin-era skyscrapers, anyone who suggested that hotels should be designed for the comfort and convenience of the business traveler would have been branded an enemy of the people. Their real function was to help the KGB spy on visitors by keeping all of them in one convenient location.

For years, Soviets were trained to believe that businessmen were the embodiment of the capitalist conspiracy. "Speculators,"

Lenin wrote back in the 1920s, "should be shot at the scene of their crime." The idea that someday they'd be getting hand-delivered copies of *The Wall Street Journal* in what was once the Waldorf Astoria of communism would have been unthinkable. Now, with so much else going on, little things like that hardly get noticed.

"Good evening," said a youthful Oktyabrskaya desk clerk as he checked in an American oil company executive. "Will you be *paid* by cash or credit card?"

The young man's question, grammatical error included, made perfect sense. The hope of getting paid—or to be more specific, getting rich—brings more than 30,000 foreign businessmen to the Soviet Union every year. The cream of the crop usually stays at the Oktyabrskaya, where the room rates reflect the spirit of a free economy: $300 a night for a single, $400 for a double, and $750 for the former general secretary's suite. Capitalism may be a new concept in this part of the world, but the former Soviets have price gouging down cold.

In the registration line behind the American was an Italian movie producer, the head of a German drug company, and a group of South Korean CEOs. Former President Richard Nixon stayed at the Oktyabrskaya when he was in Moscow for sensitive talks with hard-liners and reformers a few months before the hostile takeover attempt.

Even at age 76, nothing could slow Nixon down on his mission to foster the peaceful spread of capitalism. One day, while taking a break from his busy schedule, he showed up at a private farmers' market, where he praised local vendors for their entrepreneurial spirit, which was on full display.

Not to be confused with a government store, where the produce section can usually pass for a compost heap and the meat looks like yesterday's road kill, a Soviet private market shows you all of the things free enterprise is capable of. The one Nixon visited in the Noviye Cheryomushki section of Moscow was a good example. There were turnips the size of softballs, potatoes as big as Arnold Schwarzenegger's biceps, and melons so firm and sweet that bees were getting loaded on the juice. As for the meat counter, it was nothing short of a four-star animal morgue, with whole sheep and pigs, cows' heads, ox tails, and skinned rabbits with the fur left on their paws, just the way they sell them in the finest American gourmet groceries.

The only problem was the customers. The prices were so high, most of them could only afford to browse and sniff. A chicken, at a hundred rubles, represented a week's pay, and a kilo of beef three weeks'. A half-dozen lemons from Azerbaijan cost the equivalent in American purchasing power of a weekend ski trip in Vermont. This wasn't food, it was blue-chip gastro-porn. And if nobody had the money to buy it, at least it was nice to look at.

Some of the farmers recognized Nixon from a previous trip he made to the same market years ago. However, one old man got him confused with Mikhail Gorbachev and began blaming him for everything that was wrong with the country's economy: inflation, low wages, and high taxes.

"That's not Gorbachev," his friends told him. "It's *Nixon.*"

"I don't care who he is," the old man replied. "To me, they're all the same."

Years of hardship have taught Soviets to take a dim view of politicians and their economic plans. Now that many former communist bosses are business executives, reaping the benefits of their past Party connections, that view has gotten even dimmer. Not everyone in the Soviet Union was opposed to the coup. Many actually welcomed it as a return to law and order and an end to the chaos of reform. After seven decades of socialism, six years of perestroika, and little to show for the defeat of totalitarianism but an improved climate for investment, the next phase in Russian history could have a distinctly unpleasant downside.

Unless Yeltsin and other leaders can put their countries on the road to a full market economy without driving it into a ditch, reformers could be swept out of office, as their counterparts were in Poland, by the same populist forces that put them there.

"Nationalistic trends, Nazi trends are growing stronger and stronger," warned Anatoly Sobchak, the reform mayor of St. Petersburg, shortly before Yeltsin first announced a timetable for the introduction of free prices. "If democratic governments in the republics, the local authorities, and the leadership in Moscow cannot stop inflation and falling living standards, then disenchantment and disaffection with democracy will set in." And if that happens, what follows could take the form of anything from large-scale riots to civil war.

With the communists collecting residuals and outside capitalists busy profiting and privatizing, if the free market fails to improve life for large numbers of ex-Soviet citizens—and do it in a hurry—millions could turn their anger on the government officials, economists, and the foreign entrepreneurs they hold responsible, and the outcome will definitely *not* be good for business.

Chapter Three

Russian Roulette

One day Mark Cowan was looking at a map of the world when suddenly he got the uneasy feeling that something was wrong. The CEO of the Jefferson Group, a Washington-based consulting firm, Cowan understood the identity problems of large organizations—how a company can sometimes be so big it seems to disappear behind the public perception of its own size. But could the same thing happen to a whole country, not to mention one that covers almost one-sixth of all the land on earth?

"The year was 1989, and everybody was talking about the market opening up in Eastern Europe," said Cowan. "It just didn't make any sense. You could put Poland, Hungary, and Czechoslovakia inside the Soviet Union and all of them together wouldn't amount to more than a little dot. To me, it seemed like this gigantic country was being totally neglected."

Well, not totally. Dozens of American companies were actively involved in setting up businesses there, and hundreds, maybe thousands more, were considering the possibility. Yet even among the established firms, the one thing they all needed was

help: meeting the right officials, keeping up with changing regulations, and, let's not forget, making money.

Help was exactly what Cowan's Washington consulting firm
sold, and even though his knowledge of the Soviet Union was
limited, his interest in corporate expansion wasn't. A Soviet
branch could be a lucrative addition to the successful fifty-person
lobbying operation he already had—and if he acted fast, who
knows how much business he could lock in?

The problem was that you don't just decide to open an office
in Russia, make a few phone calls, and it happens. Actually, nothing happens there—especially anything that works—unless it's
planned well in advance and monitored every step of the way.
And knowing *that*, as Cowan discovered, is only the beginning.

How do you sell access and influence in the place you know
virtually nothing about? First, you get busy learning as much as
you can.

Undaunted by the negatives and inspired by the prospect of
high earnings, Cowan spent the next six months studying Soviet
history, politics, and culture. He talked to diplomats, economists,
and intelligence experts. Everyone agreed that bringing capitalism
to the Soviet Union was a good idea.

But free enterprise was already there in the form of the black
market, a bustling nationwide system that put the official economy
to shame. The real challenge for incoming entrepreneurs would
be finding ways to take advantage of it. If Cowan wasn't too sure
where to begin, he wasn't alone. Fortunately, this is one area in
which lack of expertise never hurt anyone's chances of becoming
an instant authority. Part of being an informed Russia expert these
days means realizing how little most people know about what's
going on there. And profiting from the knowledge means being
able to sell it to those who know even less.

"No one has any idea what's happening in the Soviet Union,"
said a veteran executive with one international consulting company. "Not the Russians and definitely not us. So we decided if we
set up a local office, we can at least pretend to know something,
and maybe by being there we'll eventually find things out sooner

than most people. There's no question that our clients are paying for our education. But it's probably still cheaper than if they tried to do it themselves."

Companies in America have been spoiled by a domestic consumer market that's been on automatic pilot for decades. The fundamental error U.S. firms make when they do business overseas, particularly in developing countries, is that most are so into their sales pitch, they forget who their customers are.

"American businessmen see foreign markets through the eyes of sellers," Cowan said. "Most never take the time to learn anything about the countries or their customs. Right from the outset, I tried to see the Soviet Union from the Soviet point of view, through the eyes of the buyers."

Getting things into proper focus wasn't that easy, and Cowan almost immediately fell victim to the same short-sighted attitude he criticized. Once, he suggested to a group of Yeltsin's top aides that they sell the idea of capitalism to Soviets the same way consumer products are sold in the United States. You hire a big sports celebrity, such as Bo Jackson or Michael Jordan, stick a soft drink can in his hand, and let charisma do the rest. Why couldn't the Russians use chess masters and soccer stars to do the same thing for, say, privatization?

Yeltsin's men eyed one another and shook their heads. That just wouldn't work where they came from. "If a soccer player starts mouthing off about privatization, people would be very indignant," said one aide, pointing out that Russians tend to distrust any official spokesman. "They'd say, 'What the hell does he know?'"

Getting the Soviet Union to embrace the free-market system would require more than celebrity endorsements. What was needed was practical help in the basics of buying and selling. More important than a free-market ad campaign was proof that a free market could work, and that would require not just finding customers, but providing jobs, building a distribution system, modernizing industries, and refinancing an entire economy.

The former Soviet Union is different from any market most

American companies are familiar with, and those approaching it with the attitude that what works in the United States or Western Europe will work there could be in for an expensive lesson in commercial relativity.

One of the problems faced by Peter the Great was that hustlers from all over Europe saw Russia as a chance to make a fortune. Many set themselves up as consultants, both to the Russians and to unsuspecting Europeans, and as a result caused incredible problems with their bad advice. Peter, usually a gracious host, sent them home with some money in their pockets so as not to harm Russia's new image. But modern Russians couldn't care less about good publicity. They invite all comers and allow them to play the consulting game as long as they bring Western clients and pay their hotel bills in hard currency. If nothing else, it stimulates the tourist industry.

Cowan wasn't interested in helping Soviet tourism, but he did see a chance to make big money introducing American businessmen to a country that few knew anything about. And what made the whole thing such an undeniable piece of adventure capitalism was that he was just learning about it himself. The first thing he learned was that start-up problems in the Soviet Union weren't like start-up problems anywhere else in the world.

A former Reagan administration official, Cowan's government relations company had an enviable list of clients, with Arco, Bell Atlantic, and Lockheed among them. Doing business with the Soviets, though, would require more than just corporate connections and an inside-the-Beltway area code. To make Moscow an ongoing profit center meant finding Russians who not only knew the system but knew how to make it work. That's when Cowan heard about a former Kremlin foreign service officer who was living near Washington.

"Somebody told me to look up this Russian immigrant, Andrew Panov, who was selling blue jeans at a shopping mall in the suburbs. It didn't take more than a few conversations to see how well informed he was. I brought him into the company, and that's when our Soviet side got started."

Or rather, that's how half of it got started.

Panov was a real find. All the same, he was in America, and for a Russian branch office to work effectively, Cowan needed somebody in the Soviet Union on a day-to-day basis. As he saw it, there were three possible alternatives:

He could send a Russian from the United States—someone like Panov, for example. But that wouldn't work for two reasons. "First of all," said Cowan, "anyone who lived here wouldn't be up to date on what was going on over there. And second, Russians in the Soviet Union and Russians from abroad, as a rule, don't get along." Returning immigrants think Russians who stayed behind are lazy and stupid, and they usually end up bossing them around in a way that almost guarantees problems. So that approach was rejected.

He could send a lawyer, a typical solution for a lot of firms. In the Soviet Union, legal opinions are really political opinions, and the right lawyer can be a valuable operative. One of the most successful attorneys at making deals with the Russians is former Senator Gary Hart, who helped put together a multimillion-dollar fiber optics venture and even wrote a book to advertise his exploits and his law firm's availability for future missions. Regrettably, there weren't many American lawyers with the type of experience Cowan was looking for. "Can you picture some Washington or New York attorney sitting in his room in the Mezhdunarodnaya Hotel, waiting for the phone to ring, and not realizing it doesn't work?" So that approach got rejected, too.

Then there was a third possibility: finding a Soviet partner. Yet finding an honest one would be no simple task. There are probably thousands of Soviet consulting firms, and most of them give street-corner con artists a good name. Like any businessman in a similar situation, Cowan needed an organization that was dependable enough to deliver on its promises and crafty enough to help him and his clients negotiate the maze of Soviet rules and regulations. On top of that, whoever got the job would have to be good—very good—with money. What he was hunting for, in other words, was a well-practiced Soviet capitalist.

"We wanted somebody who could turn clients' rubles into dollars, and do it with a minimum amount of red tape," said Cowan. "There are lots of ways to convert rubles, but frankly we were after somebody who had the connections to get hard currency without all the hassle of bartering—and do it legitimately."

Officials from one of the companies he approached, Face to Face Moscow, said they could meet all of the requirements with no problems. Cowan, who had heard that before, decided to check them out. He had them set up meetings with government officials, which they did. Then he asked them to put him in touch with behind-the-scenes fixers, which they also did. A promising start. Next came the all-important money test.

This time it was the Russians who took the initiative. Face to Face, a marketing agency begun in West Germany in 1989 to help European businesses trade with the Soviet Union, wanted to buy 22,000 pairs of foreign-made tennis shoes, and its director general, Viktor Zaremba, asked the Jefferson Group to broker the deal. Sensing the opportunity to see if the firm could get the necessary financing—and make a nice percentage if they could—Cowan agreed.

Back in the United States, Cowan went to work searching for tennis shoes. When no American manufacturer was able to fill the order, he found a factory in Taiwan that could. In two days, samples arrived, and a week later the entire shipment was ready. Now the only thing missing was money. Cowan called Face to Face, instructed Zaremba to wire a quarter-million dollars to pay for the shoes, and the next thing he knew a bank in Moscow had sent the full amount to Cowan's Merrill Lynch account. The Russians passed the test with flying colors.

Besides having ties to a bank, Face to Face, which sounds more like a dating service than a consulting business, had several other built-in assets: forty operatives throughout the country, proven experience in foreign trade, and direct access to top policymakers in the Kremlin and Russian Republic. As an added benefit, the organization was originally founded as the marketing arm of the League of Scientific and Industrial Associations of the Soviet

Union, whose two thousand members—factories, research facilities, and industrial complexes—produced 65 percent of the country's gross national product and would be a useful source of candidates for joint ventures.

A good Soviet partner is anybody who can get things done, and Cowan was lucky to find one that apparently could. But, according to Mikhail Smirnov, a former trade director with the Russian embassy in Washington, foreign firms should always be on the lookout for cheap imitations.

"Most Soviet companies don't know how to do business," warned Smirnov. "So what they sell are connections, some of which may be helpful and many that aren't. A Soviet consultant might tell you he has someone you should know who turns out to be somebody he just met himself. An even bigger waste of time are companies that sign on with U.S. firms and then expect the Americans to give them a complete business education. There's only so much even the best Soviet partner can do, but a bad one can make doing almost anything impossible."

Then there's politics to consider. The ultimate success of any Soviet business venture depends on the cooperation of government officials, without whose paid assistance no commercial enterprise would ever get off the ground. In the economic Reign of Error that's accompanied reform, locating the right official patron is just as important as finding the right partner, and given the current rate of bureaucratic minicoups and property seizures, just as uncertain. Every relationship with a Soviet company, no matter how secure it seems, is subject to sudden, unexpected changes, which is why foreign firms should protect themselves by developing as many business contacts as possible, and as many political friends as they can afford.

The Jefferson Group began the process by signing a fifty-fifty partnership agreement with Face to Face in March 1991, making the Washington company the first American consulting firm to open a full-service branch in the Soviet Union. By August, the operation was set up in a Moscow office, and in addition to servicing corporate clients, was giving pro bono advice to the

Russian Republic's privatization council. Although the timing was pure coincidence, Cowan and his colleagues couldn't have been better positioned to capitalize on the failed coup.

While the competition was watching events on television, the Jefferson Group was way ahead of everybody. Some of the firm's Moscow employees were delivering free food to the resisters on the barricades, while others were waiting anxiously by the phone. The first thing they wanted to know when Cowan finally got through twelve hours into the takeover plot was "Are we still in business?" His immediate answer was a reassuring yes. How business would be done in the aftermath of the Soviet power shift was anybody's guess.

"What is certain," Cowan wrote in *The Washington Business Journal* a week after the abortive putsch, "is that the sustaining force behind the Russians' drive for democracy is their hunger for a better system. Not hunger for some vague ideal—hunger for a system that delivers. In 1917, the Bolsheviks' cry was 'bread and peace.' Now the Russian people are only beginning to understand that bread does not magically fill the shelves just because some bureaucrat orders it to appear . . . It was the fledgling market that sold the idea of reform. . . . And it is the market system that can put bread on Russian tables."

Cowan's article was an attempt to ease the minds of potential investors, but putting bread on Russian tables, to say nothing of sufficient cash in Russian pockets to pay for it, would require more than applied PR. Companies that want to do business with the Soviets may be motivated by the pioneer spirit, but those that profit need to have a specific, clearly defined project in mind before they ever get started. This is not the time or place for corporate prospecting. The foreign businesses that do well are those committed to establishing a long-term presence and willing to spend money up front to make money later.

Even so, the difference between success and failure usually comes down to which officials you have on your side—and how happy you can keep them with offers of free enterprise and old-fashioned kickbacks. No foreign company likes to talk about paying bribes; nevertheless, doing business in any form would be extremely difficult without them. Bribes are needed to set up meetings, to have licenses approved, and to arrange for train tickets and hotel rooms. One of the functions of any good Soviet firm is to keep its joint-venture partner "honest" by acting as a conduit for funneling payoffs to the proper authorities.

Despite the shutdown of the state propaganda machine, capitalists still have an image problem to overcome. Many Soviets think of Western businessmen as greedy profiteers, and in some cases they're right. One way to dispel the notion is for companies to give money to charities and other worthwhile causes, like cleaning up the environment. The downside is that too much emphasis on doing good works can easily turn a business into a welfare organization. "Line the pockets of your Russian partners," Cowan said, "and I guarantee you'll do better than if you build a Ronald McDonald House."

Incidentally, McDonald's philosophy is just the reverse. The fast-food corporation, which has been operating in Moscow since 1990, has made spreading goodwill a top priority, donating millions of rubles to various charitable organizations, constructing a medical facility for disabled children, and contributing food and supplies to orphanages and senior citizens homes.

McDonald's and other big companies, using a combination of hard work and image control, have succeeded in making their presence felt. Their impact on the system is another story. For all the talk about free markets, little has changed about the way Soviets do business. Entrepreneurs still have to bribe state-owned industries when they want to buy modern equipment. And state enterprises continue to receive government subsidies, while new companies are denied low-interest loans and forced to pay higher prices for supplies.

As for political reform in the ex-republics, that's also been slower than expected. In Azerbaijan, the first to hold a post-coup presidential election, only a single name appeared on the ballot, that of one-time Party head Ayaz Mutallibov, the incumbent boss of one of the most corrupt political machines in the country. In

Ukraine, Kazakhstan, and elsewhere, many of the same people who ran communist governments were firmly in charge of the transition to democracies, which often seemed no more democratic than the regimes they replaced. In Armenia the legislature privatized agriculture even before voters passed an independence referendum, but lawmakers elsewhere have retained strict control over their land and property, with many city councils operating more like high-volume real-estate companies than local governing bodies. The Moscow City Council, probably the most active business partner on the scene, is involved in hundreds of joint ventures, including hard-currency hotels, restaurants, and specialty shops that few Muscovites can afford to patronize.

Reform in Russia has become a free-market free-for-all as entrepreneurs, former bureaucrats, and ordinary citizens are all fighting for a place in the new economy. In contrast to the rapid and relatively smooth political change from communism to democracy, Russia's adoption of floating prices and private ownership has produced hyperinflation, long lines, and general public anxiety about what lies ahead. Rather than making life better, the conversion to capitalism, to many, has so far only made matters worse.

This is not the type of sales environment most U.S. companies are used to. American businesses have come to expect ready-made markets, where the biggest challenge is matching customers to products and products to customers. It isn't that easy when trading with Soviets. Markets, as most businesses know them, don't exist. Neither do the normal rules of supply and demand that govern Western commerce. Soviets need everything the West can supply. But that need, coupled with the inability to pay, hardly constitutes demand. Markets are made, not discovered, and the same goes for the people who support them. A Soviet consumer society will have to be bankrolled before it can be serviced, and doing that will take time, patience, and, naturally, capital.

The first thing Soviets will need before they can start spending like Westerners is a workable system of consumer credit. Without it, they'll be tied to a COD lifestyle that forces them to carry their money from store to store in plastic bags. At present, Soviet shoppers have to pay cash for everything they buy, assuming they have the cash and can find something to buy with it.

Charge cards, home mortgages, and car loans, an integral part of every Western economy, are unheard of in Soviet society, where the solution to increased purchasing power has always been to print more rubles. The average Russian would happily go into debt if it meant being able to own a microwave, a VCR, or a modern apartment. But without economic reform and extensive financial help from abroad that won't happen, and a real consumer market will never exist.

More than anything else, creating new economies will require the direct assistance of the same companies that expect some day to profit from them, and for many that will mean changing their entire approach toward making money. All of which makes introducing American businesses to Russia and the other commonwealth markets a delicate procedure.

"First of all, I never *tell* any companies to go there," said Cowan, who makes five or six trips to Moscow every year. "That's a decision they have to make for themselves. What I *do* tell them, if they want my advice, is to get help early and rethink their priorities—like their next quarterly earnings. For this kind of investment, a company really has to be willing to accept the idea of delayed gratification and tell Wall Street to shove it."

Some of Cowan's clientele have determined that the risk was worth it. Smith Corona wants to sell Cyrillic typewriters and needs marketing contacts; 3M is selling adhesives and needs advice on the regulatory situation.

Chevron, a client Cowan would like to land, has been tied up for years in oil drilling negotiations and needs all the help it can get. Chevron's experience should be a warning to other companies looking to make a quick and easy profit. Given carte blanche by the old central government to drill anywhere they liked, Chevron executives selected a place where oil was virtually seeping out of the ground. But the Soviets could do that themselves, and they let company officials know their skills could be put to better use at more difficult drilling sites. Negotiations to determine exactly where Chevron will sink its wells and how much it will cost for the privilege are still going on.

The right consultant can handle some problems, but to avoid the type that takes years to resolve, it's wise to make sure your company's expectations are realistic from the start. To minimize the risk factor, a number of U.S. corporations have formed investment groups. The biggest is the American Trade Consortium, made up of Chevron, Archer-Daniels-Midland, Eastman Kodak, RJR Nabisco, and Johnson & Johnson. ATC's game plan is ambitious, but it offers a good illustration of the contortions all companies have to go through to do business in a place where business was banned for seventy-four years.

Under the terms of the agreement worked out with commonwealth officials, hard-currency profits from the Chevron oil project would be shared with other companies in the consortium, which in turn would use the money to start joint ventures of their own. Each consortium company could negotiate its own separate deals, but each deal would depend on Chevron earning enough hard currency to meet everyone's needs.

Consulting companies may be learning the Soviet system by trial and error, but that doesn't mean they're not out shopping at the same time. Cowan is no slouch when it comes to picking up side deals for his firm. Besides investing on its own, the Jefferson Group piggybacks onto investments with clients, and is currently putting together a venture with Smith Corona to sell office supplies in Russia. Many consulting firms have made similar arrangements, crossing the line to become business owners themselves. Soyuz Transworld, another Washington company that specializes in matching American and Soviet partners, takes equity in all of its deals, according to founder Michael Govan. Soyuz represents Timex, McDonald's, and Union Pacific, and recently purchased a factory in St. Petersburg to manufacture paper cups and plates that it plans to sell to the McDonald's restaurant in Moscow.

The question for Western client companies to ask themselves is how impartial a consultant's business suggestions can be when he's both an adviser and a shareholder. Then again, some clients might be comforted by the fact that a consulting firm would think enough of a project to invest its own money in it. In either case, it's important to pick your consultant carefully. A fully equipped Moscow office with its own Russian-speaking Western staff is a must. So is a proven record of service. A good way for companies to guard themselves against falling prey to unscrupulous or uninformed advisers is to be just as cautious when selecting a consultant as consultants tell them to be when selecting a Soviet partner.

Not long after his appointment as U.S. ambassador to Moscow, Robert Strauss sounded the same warning. "In this city right now . . . you've got to keep in mind, every sleazebag in America and every sleazebag in Europe is over here trying to get rich quick. And the first ones on the ground are always the first ones to steal something that isn't nailed down."

Cowan, too, is a firm believer in covering his bets, and he urges any business considering a Soviet operation to do the same. That means retaining an American law firm with experience in Soviet legal affairs. But even then, it's difficult to keep up with all of the new rules and regulations.

"When government officials in Russia are asking for daily advice on what laws to create, how can Western lawyers pretend to know the current legal situation?" asked Galina Sullivan, former executive assistant to Occidental Petroleum chairman Armand Hammer. But at least they're a safer bet than Soviet attorneys, many of whom were originally trained as KGB informers and now work as industrial spies.

It also means developing ties with more than one Soviet partner. Not only will this lead to added business opportunities, but if one partnership turns sour, which can easily happen, there will be others to fall back on. Cowan has four, and he's always looking for more.

Relaxing in his Washington office a few blocks from the White House, Cowan said, "We have relationships with a company called the Russian Business Agency, the Russian Afghan War Veterans—that's not like the VFW, it's a business—

and two banks, the Business Russia Bank and Bank of the East."

Cowan would not discuss any specific services he's provided for his clients, or what success he's helped them achieve. Others in the firm conceded the companies they represent "haven't made any money, but we have saved them a lot."

Only a few years ago, conservatives, like Cowan, were calling the Soviet Union the Evil Empire. Now they're among the first in line to cash in on the expected bonanza. In his more poetic moments, Cowan is fond of calling the Soviet market "the last great mountain" and the Soviet people "a vast pool of talent." These are inspiring images, but climbing that mountain without falling off and swimming in that pool without being pulled under is risky business.

How risky? Take banks. In most countries, businesses and banks are natural allies. In the former Soviet Union, they're more like natural enemies. Russian banks do everything they can to prevent businesses from making money and, failing that, try to steal as much as they can from any funds put on deposit.

Imagine going to a country's main foreign exchange bank to withdraw dollars from your account, put there by you for safekeeping, only to be told that the bank doesn't have your money anymore. That's exactly what happened on November 5, 1991, when businessmen and embassy officials showed up at Moscow's once-almighty Vnesheconombank, trying to take out their hard currency.

And what did the bank do with the money? It didn't lend it to Arizona land developers, or spend it on TV set and toaster giveaways. No, what bank officials did was use it to service a foreign debt so big it makes places like Haiti, Bangladesh, and Mali seem like solid investments.

"It's quite an unusual situation for us," said Vladimir Sterlikov, head of Vnesheconombank's foreign relations department, responsible for putting the best possible spin on the dilemma. "The cash flow to the centralized fund is . . . limited nowadays, which means we have problems with liquidity."

What Sterlikov meant is that the republics had stopped paying their hard-currency tribute to the central treasury, and the bank, strapped for cash, appropriated its clientele's deposits to settle accounts with the government's foreign creditors.

Will Western companies have to pay the Soviet Union's debts before they can do business there? The idea isn't as farfetched as it sounds. Yes, it does take a special breed of businessmen to try their luck in these parts. Amazingly, they come, however, and even more amazingly take out money—or, if not money, profits in barter.

"It can be done," said Cowan. "But not by somebody who doesn't know what he's doing or isn't connected to someone who does. Russia is a resource-rich country, and these are talented, cultured, highly educated people. They just don't have any idea what capitalism is. They think they do, but they don't." Cowan's not sure how long the learning process will take—nobody is—but a story he told suggests it could go on for some time.

An American friend of his was walking down the street in Moscow with a big-shot politician who was very proud of having converted from communism to capitalism. Pointing to all of the vendors selling their products, the politician said, "See, everybody's a capitalist now." Then, turning to the American, he admitted there was still one thing about capitalism that had him confused. "I understand what free enterprise is," he said. "But how do you know what prices to charge?"

That's a good question, even if the answer could be a little hard to explain to a Russian. The idea of a buying public influencing the price of goods simply by deciding whether or not to buy them is an alien concept, especially to government officials, who tend to see the free market as a license to steal, a license they'd like to keep exclusively for themselves.

Chapter Four

Attention Shoppers

Part of Ronald Reagan's strategy for winning the Cold War was needling Mikhail Gorbachev with jokes about the sad shape of the Soviet consumer economy. The fact that Gorbachev apparently had no sense of humor on the subject only made Reagan more determined to keep up the offensive. Every time the two men got together, the former president had new material. But the ultimate showdown came during the 1987 summit meeting in Washington.

After a typically dry speech by Gorbachev to a group of American businessmen, Reagan stepped up to the mike and went on the attack with a gag he'd been practicing for months.

"Have you heard the one about the Russian guy who wanted to buy a new car?" he asked the Soviet leader. "Well, he goes in to fill out the paperwork, and a clerk tells him he has to pay 9,000 rubles in advance. And to make things worse, he can't pick the car up for *ten years.*

'Ten years!' says the man.

'Take it or leave it,' the clerk says.

'Okay,' says the man. 'I'll take it.' And the clerk tells him his car will be ready on November 10, 1997.

'Will that be in the morning or the afternoon?' the man asks.

'What difference does it make?' says the clerk. 'It's ten years from now.'

'Yeah, I know,' the man says. 'But the plumber's coming in the morning.' "

Score one for the Gipper. Everybody in the Soviet delegation was laughing, including Gorbachev. But he "had to be crying on the inside," said Tony Dolan, a former White House speechwriter.

As Reagan's joke points out, shopping in the Soviet Union was a complicated process. And the disappearance of communism has done little to change things. In a country without suburban malls, supermarkets, factory outlets, convenience stores, mini-marts, or mail-order catalogues, not to mention credit cards, checking accounts, and automatic teller machines, finding something to buy— and the money to buy it with—can be an endless, and usually fruitless, struggle.

The problem hits home even at the highest levels. Decades of uncontrolled military spending and government corruption, said former Foreign Minister Eduard Shevardnadze, "have left the Soviet people and the nation destitute."

This, however, is destitution with a special twist. In Moscow and St. Petersburg, people live a hand-to-mouth existence that compares to life in America during the Great Depression. They hoard toilet paper, sell empty vodka bottles, and consider a box of matches a precious trading commodity. In the Russian countryside, and in the villages and towns of the former republics, conditions are worse. Goods such as butter, sugar, and soap, which are scarce in the big cities, haven't been seen in some areas since Brezhnev's time.

But appearances—particularly appearances in the former Soviet Union—can be deceiving, which is one reason Russian economist Maxim Boycko didn't quite know what to expect when he started work on a 1990 survey comparing consumers in Moscow and New York. Even the basic concept of the study seemed a little misleading. The Soviet Union didn't have consumers, certainly not in the New York sense. It had recipients, people who took whatever they were given, or, more likely, whatever they happened to find.

Besides that, there was the matter of conducting the survey itself. Would Russians even be willing to answer the questions? Or would they just assume Boycko was a KGB agent looking for economic subversives? Until a few years ago, public opinion polls were against the law in the Soviet Union. Asking people what they wanted might lead them to want more, and that could create all sorts of problems for a government unwilling and unable to provide it. Besides, Soviets weren't supposed to have opinions.

But Muscovites, as it turned out, were eager to talk. "Soviets have been lied to for so long, they're anxious to tell the truth," said Boycko, a research specialist at the Institute of World Economy and International Relations in Moscow. "And when the subject is their basic well-being, it's hard to keep them quiet."

Sponsored by the National Bureau of Economic Research, an independent think tank in Cambridge, Massachusetts, the survey was the first scientific inquiry into the minds of Soviet shoppers, a total of 391 of whom were randomly selected and asked 34 questions. The scholarly purpose of all of this was to discover "the fundamental parameters of human behavior related to the success of free markets." But for the 29-year-old Boycko, son of respected Soviet economist Vladimir Shamberg and someone brought up to believe in numbers, it promised to yield insights into a topic he had only theorized about. Then again, as a Moscow shopper himself, maybe it would only confirm something he knew all along.

"Clinically speaking," said Boycko, "all Soviets operate under an incredible amount of market-related stress. Shortages and long lines have made people here ruthless competitors for what little there is to buy."

On the other hand, he added, those same circumstances have also made Soviets the most avid students of supply and demand anywhere in the world. The contrast between empty shelves in the stores and tables full of food in most people's homes, or between complaints about expensive meat and potatoes and the large numbers of overweight, apparently well-fed citizens, has always been one of the great mysteries of Soviet life.

In theory, the Soviet Union was an economic basket case, but in reality, Soviets, in crisis after crisis, have demonstrated an amazing talent for survival. If there's a line, they get in it. There's probably something worth having at the other end. If there's an item they want, they buy it. Chances are it won't be there in five minutes. Acting on instinct and determination, Soviets have developed an uncanny ability to locate almost anything they need, find enough money to make the purchase, then carry it home on their backs.

"They may be hard-pressed financially, but they're resourceful," Boycko said. And in that respect, he cautioned, they can be full of surprises.

"Visit any place where buying and selling occurs, and time and time again, you see evidence of rational behavior under extremely irrational circumstances. Wherever there's a crowd, there's an opportunity for private enterprise. When the communists ran things, the black market thrived on the frustrations of people tired of waiting for hours to buy junk. It still does."

Only now, so do armies of hustling self-starters who use legitimate businesses both as wholesale suppliers and as sources of customers. Boycko pointed to the three-year-old Moscow McDonald's as an example. On busy days, when people waiting to get in can number in the thousands, profit-minded patrons often buy three or four orders of over-the-counter burgers and fries, eat one, and auction off the rest to the highest bidders at the end of the line.

Actually, the long lines of Soviet shoppers have all sorts of hidden income potential. Some people sell their places in line; others get paid by the hour to queue up for somebody else. Anyone who thinks it will take armed intervention for these folks to adapt their market skills to a free economy has never studied the intricacies of Soviet linear dynamics.

In a country where the average worker's salary equals a modest $100 a year, it's the rare individual who has never dabbled in some form of freelance capitalism. Boycko likes to quote a familiar

Russian curse that even encourages it: "May you be condemned to live on your salary." Which almost nobody does.

But none of this gave any hint of the findings he and his American colleagues would uncover in their survey. Released in the form of a modest booklet titled *Popular Attitudes Towards Free Markets: The Soviet Union and the United States,* here was evidence that refuted nearly every preconception held in the West about Soviet consumer readiness.

The data not only reveals that capitalist Americans and communist-trained Soviets hold virtually the same opinions on such things as profit incentives, competitive pricing, and property values, it also shows that Soviets, whom most experts consider hopelessly behind the Eastern Europeans when it comes to marketplace skills and perceptions, are just as savvy as anyone you'd come across prowling the sales racks in Bloomingdale's.

For years, the Kremlin put off market reforms because, it said, the Soviet people weren't ready for them. First, they had to overcome their hostility toward business. Then they had to accept ideas like an eight-hour workday and the unequal distribution of income. After that, there would have to be years of reeducation, retraining, and all of the other things the communists once used as excuses to buy time to stash away loot.

"It's not very easy to develop a stratum of talented people with a good understanding of the market," wrote former Soviet Deputy Prime Minister Leonid Abalkin the same year Boycko and his group started their work. "For that, it is necessary to put aside fixed patterns of thinking, inherited from the past, to consider afresh our morals and our system of values in general." But, as Boycko and his fellow economists discovered, the only thing Soviets really need to be practicing capitalists is *capital.*

Take, for instance, the widely held belief that Soviets would much rather earn uniform wages than work harder for higher pay. Boycko and his pollsters asked Muscovites and New Yorkers: "Do you think people work better if their pay is directly related to the quantity and quality of their work?" The response: More Russians said yes than Americans. Of the Soviets questioned, 90 percent agreed that pay and productivity are directly related; 86 percent of the Americans did. For years, the communists promoted the myth that Soviets enjoyed being equal in poverty. Work was its own reward, according to Party propaganda. But clearly the workers had a different opinion.

Surveyors then asked the two groups how each would react to the offer of a 10-percent reduction in their work hours per week, if take-home pay was also reduced by the same amount. Again, both gave basically the same response. Among the Soviets, 51 percent said they would reject the offer, while 58 percent of the Americans said they would. For almost the same percentage in each group, money was more important than time off.

On questions designed to separate economic conservatives from risk takers, the response was more lopsided, but equally interesting. Both groups were asked this question: "Imagine you are offered a new job that increased your salary by 50 percent. The new job is no more difficult than your present one, but not everyone is good at this line of work. It could turn out that after a year or two in this new job you will be told that you are not doing well and will be let go. Your chances of keeping and your chances of losing it are about equal. Given this situation, would you take the risky, high-paying new job? In answering, assume that if they let you go, you could, after some time, find something more or less similar to your old job." A total of 79 percent of the Americans said they would take the risk, compared to 52 percent of the Soviets.

On the surface, the answers might seem to indicate that Americans are more adventuresome than Soviets in their attitude toward changing employment. But the gap between the two groups on this question may have more to do with smart shopping on the Russians' part than a fear of taking chances.

"It could be that Soviets and Americans responded differently to a 50-percent raise, not just to the element of risk," said Boycko. "To New Yorkers, a 50-percent increase in salary represents a lot of money. But to most Muscovites, as our discussions after the poll shows, 50 percent isn't that much."

Salary jumps of 200 to 500 percent would be more in line with what Moscow joint ventures and cooperatives are now offering. Then, too, the survey question left out any mention of hard currency, small amounts of which would make any salary package that much more attractive to Soviets.

The current Moscow job market operates like a Las Vegas casino, and the fact that so many Russians indicated a willingness to play, even for what most would consider such small stakes, is "a very encouraging sign," Boycko said.

But work for most Soviets has always been a game, if not a game of chance, at least hide and go seek. At the same time the Communist Party was corrupting the nation's management class, its attempt to create a dictatorship of the proletariat may have booby-trapped the labor force for the next generation.

Communism glorified labor to the point where it no longer had any relationship to skill, financial reward, or the constructive use of time. The communist concept of employment was like the American idea of life, liberty, and the pursuit of happiness. A job wasn't a career. It was a sacred guarantee. In practice, for many Soviet workers "labor" meant attendance at work. In the last few years, it's even stopped meaning that. A growing fear among people in all walks of life is that a free economy will require them to do something they've never done before; namely, work for a living. During three-quarters of a century, communism has produced many social ills, but a nation of workaholics isn't one of them.

"That was certainly true when the communists were in charge," said Boycko. "But I'm not sure it will mean much once it's every man for himself. In a free market, people do whatever they have to do to earn money. They don't have any choice."

When the economic pressure is on, in fact, Soviets have repeatedly proven their ability to rise to the occasion, as they did when the Commonwealth of Independent States lifted price controls on many goods in early 1992. Or as they did during the famous ruble recall a year earlier. In America, when the Federal Reserve wants to control inflation, it raises interest rates. The old Soviet Finance Ministry took a more direct approach.

It simply declared money obsolete and started collecting it.

The last surprise recall under the communists caught people sleeping on billions of suddenly out-of-date fifty- and one-hundred-ruble notes. Soviets don't trust state banks, and most of them keep their nest eggs hidden under mattresses. But a strict limit on the amount of old bills each person could exchange for new ones, a three-day deadline for turning them in, and long bank lines changed that.

In the midst of one of the worst January cold spells in memory, many Soviets faced the threat of losing their entire life savings. But soon word spread of a way around the government-created bottleneck. Instead of lining up at the banks, people flocked to telegraph offices to wire themselves money. In a move worthy of Wall Street half an hour before the four o'clock closing, they paid with old rubles and picked up new ones the next day. Obviously, prospering under capitalism isn't the same as playing beat the reaper with Soviet rubles, but the message to be gained here is that most Soviets can wheel and deal with goods and money in ways the average capitalist couldn't imagine.

While the socialist system guaranteed everyone jobs, health care, and housing, the quality was so low they were hardly worth having. People learn from an early age, as poet Irina Ratushinskaya put it, "to fend for yourself, expect nothing from the state, and hope the authorities will leave you alone." Under the communists, anyone who wanted more than the minimum went out and traded for it. That rule still applies, and the deals it produces in apartment exchanges and goods-for-service swaps can be as elaborately structured as a corporate merger—which brings up another myth the survey explodes.

One of the frequently cited barriers to doing business with Soviets is their historic prejudice toward "speculators," a catch-all term that no longer conjures up the Bolshevik image of fat bankers swimming in bags of gold. Instead, it's come to mean anyone who steals goods earmarked by the government for one group and sells them to another at a profit.

Speculation is closely associated in the minds of many Soviet citizens with the country's "backdoor" economy, so named because products meant to be sold in state stores so often ended up disappearing out the back door and into the hands of the privileged or the black market.

In 1990, a report by the Soviet Academy of Sciences estimated that on-the-job theft from factories and shops accounted for the annual loss of more than 50 percent of all goods produced in the Soviet Union. The report concluded that most of those goods—usually the highest-quality products the system could turn out—were eventually sold on the black market.

Yet under the communists, the economy would have come to a complete halt without the black market, and for one very good reason. Run by a loose-knit partnership of corrupt politicians, gangsters, and thousands of small-time salesmen, it did something the official economy never could—supply customers with things they wanted at prices they were willing to pay.

Black marketeers also became the middlemen in the Communist Party's policy of special favors. Black market products smuggled from the West bought loyalty, rewarded faithful service, and eventually created a Soviet consumer class whose demands for more and more foreign goods helped to topple the government.

Today, as the black market becomes the real market, whatever hostility there may have been against speculators is disappearing.

Boycko and his pollsters asked this question: "If the price of coffee on the world market suddenly increased by 30 percent, what do you think is likely to be to blame?"

The answers went like this:

	SOVIETS	AMERICANS
1. Interventions of some government.	17%	13%
2. Such things as a bad harvest in Brazil or unexpected changes in demand.	51%	36%
3. Speculators' efforts to raise prices.	32%	51%

More Americans than Soviets thought speculators were responsible for manipulating prices. Although speculators continue to be blamed by reform governments in Russia and the other former republics for creating shortages, causing inflation, and stirring up social unrest, the public seems to think otherwise.

The same was true when people were asked about competitive real estate prices. Always a sacred commodity under communism, the land, it was said, belonged to everyone. But here again, people who have never even heard of the Hamptons or Palm Beach seem to have a fairly impressive grasp of what a choice piece of vacation property is worth. Another poll question: "A new railway line makes travel between city and summer homes positioned along the rail line substantially easier. Accordingly, summer homes along the line become more desirable. Is it fair if rents are raised on these homes?" The responses were almost identical. Fifty-seven percent of the Soviets said yes, as did 61 percent of the Americans.

Throughout the survey, Soviets showed that they were concerned about fair pay and fair prices. But does this indicate an unwillingness to mix it up in a free marketplace? Actually, as the poll results indicate, it was the Americans who appeared to be more uncomfortable with competitive economics than Soviets.

True, New York isn't Peoria, and Moscow isn't Magnitogorsk. Outside big cities in the United States and Russia, economic attitudes tend to be more cautious and conservative. Yet the survey offers encouraging evidence that Soviets are not only well prepared for a market economy, but probably capable of taking advantage of it in ways few foreign investors ever suspected.

Boycko refers to a passage in de Tocqueville's *Democracy in America* to illustrate an interesting point about human nature he thinks the study makes. Writing in 1850, de Tocqueville found that the American "love of money" had less to do with national character than a stable economy organized around free enterprise and private initiative.

> What I say about the Americans applies to almost all men nowadays. Variety is disappearing from the human race; the same way of behaving, thinking, and feeling are found in every

corner of the world. This is not only because nations are more in touch with each other and able to copy each other more closely, but because the men of each country, more and more completely discarding the ideas and feelings peculiar to one caste . . . are . . . getting closer to what the essential man is, and that is everywhere the same. In that way they grow alike, even without imitating each other. One could compare them to travelers dispersed through a huge forest, all the tracks in which lead to the same point. If all at the same time notice where the central point is and direct their steps thither, they will unconsciously draw nearer together without either seeking, or seeing, or knowing each other, and in the end will be surprised to find that they have all assembled at the same place.

Americans and Soviets may be similar in the ways outlined by de Tocqueville; however, New Yorkers and Muscovites differ significantly, at least in one major respect. American visitors to the Russian capital often remark on the rudeness of Muscovites they meet on the streets.

"But they're certainly no worse than New Yorkers," Boycko said. The essential difference, as he's observed it, is a matter of throw weight and economics, not aggression. In New York, pedestrians move in straight lines and plow through anything in their path. People in Moscow, usually loaded down with the day's provisions, tend to swing their cargo from side to side as they rush forward. It's not that they're more inconsiderate than anyone else, Boycko concluded, they just take up more air space.

Chapter Five

Corporate Commando

"How old do you think I am?" asked Jhoon Rhee, bounding up from his living room couch and standing at perfect attention. "I'm sixty," he said, not waiting for an answer. "And how many sixty-year-olds do you know who can do this?" With that, Rhee dropped to the floor and began doing push-ups in such rapid succession it was impossible to keep count. Two minutes later, he was back on his feet. "Discipline," he said, without the slightest hint of heavy breathing. "I do one thousand of those every day."

On the mantle of Rhee's Northern Virginia home, there's a picture of Boris Yeltsin. On the dining room wall there's an oriental rug from Kazakhstan with a picture of Rhee woven into the middle. And on his coffee table there's a copy of the February 1991 issue of *International Affairs* magazine, the official publication of the former Soviet Foreign Ministry, inside of which is an article written by Rhee about a business philosophy he calls "Happyism."

The wealthy owner of a chain of East Coast karate schools, Rhee thinks he's found a way to rebuild the Soviet economy, and Happyism is the key. "Many Soviets are interested in doing business," he wrote. "They are motivated to work, but all of them, without exception, need a basic business education, starting with the fundamental principles of Adam Smith." Implement those principles, and the Soviet Union "will be the happiest nation in the world."

A capsule summary of Rhee's three-part prescription for putting Soviets in the mood to embrace laissez-faire economics goes like this: "Knowledge in the mind, honesty in the heart, and strength in the body."

Since that also happens to be the motto of his martial arts schools, it would be easy to dismiss Rhee as a crackpot self-promoter; easy, but not advisable. Soviets, in fact, have taken to his teachings in a big way. In less than two years after his first visit to Russia, sixty-five new Jhoon Rhee schools were in full operation there. But Rhee doesn't just teach students how to break boards with their bare hands and kick cinder blocks to bits.

"Happiness, as America's founding fathers understood, comes from hard work and dedication," he said. "And that's what Soviets need to learn. To Americans, things like individual initiative and personal responsibility are second nature. To Russians, they're almost totally unknown. Before the Soviet people can be retrained as capitalists, they have to be retrained to trust themselves, trust their talents, their ideas, and their ability to do things on their own."

Rhee, who emigrated to the United States from Korea thirty years ago, has taught Tae Kwon Do to the late movie actor Bruce Lee, former heavyweight champion Muhammad Ali, reporter Jack Anderson, and hundreds of corporate executives, foreign diplomats, and members of Congress. However, teaching karate in the Soviet Union—and teaching his Soviet partners how to manage their businesses—represented a special challenge.

"It's interesting," Rhee said. "In the United States, businessmen have the know-how, but lack the inspiration. In Russia, they have all the inspiration you can imagine, but don't have the know-how or the training. Even though the politics has changed, people's tendency is to do things the same way they did under the communists, and that assures that nothing will ever get done.

Every Russian I've met has a head full of business projects. Yet very few know what to do to get them started or keep them running."

If small businessmen were evangelists, Rhee would be a religious fanatic. He admitted he gets a little carried away at times, then explained that's only because he's so excited about the economic changes taking place in the former Soviet Union, once a country he despised but now is determined to help.

His theory is that business and philosophy go hand in hand. "It's a matter of balance," he said. "Integrating knowledge, character, and strength, I teach people the physical qualities of Tae Kwon Do. I also teach them that these same physical qualities must be translated into human qualities that can be applied in our daily lives."

As Rhee tells his students, the lessons of karate apply just as easily to the business world. Alertness, perseverance, timing, and self-control—all things that karate teaches—are also useful attributes in any business. Even an act like bowing to one's opponent, he said, translates into respect for one's colleagues and the competition.

Rhee first traveled to the Soviet Union in late 1989, when he was invited to stage a martial arts ballet in Moscow as part of a cultural exchange program. The sponsoring organization was nervous about government reaction to the demonstration—karate was technically illegal at the time. Nevertheless, Rhee was confident the show would be a big hit—particularly because it featured a ballet he choreographed to the Soviet national anthem called "Mikhail Gorbachev's Glasnost"—and it was.

Right from the start, Rhee was making plans to bring his karate schools to the Soviet people. A ban against teaching or participating in the sport was largely ignored; still, regulations would have to be changed before any formal classes could be given. Not only was private business against the law, in this case, so was the business product.

Rhee was determined to have the law against karate overturned, and embarked on a crusade to enlist the aid of as many

Soviet officials as he could. Having taught karate to more than two-dozen children of Soviet embassy personnel in Washington helped to open a few doors, as did Rhee's nonstop media campaign. After a story about his program appeared in *Izvestia,* Rhee got an invitation to deliver a lecture on martial arts at the Moscow State Sports Academy, and during his appearance he took full advantage of the opportunity. He emphasized the importance of thinking over fighting. He talked about how karate lessons improved concentration and performance in school. He talked about how his karate-oriented seminars for businessmen prepared them to deal with the demands of the corporate world. Quoting Patrick Henry, Benjamin Franklin, and Thomas Jefferson, he talked about how the discipline of karate and profits from karate franchises could spread happiness and prosperity all over the Soviet Union.

America, the Founding Fathers, democracy, free enterprise, money—Rhee was pushing all the right buttons. When he finished, he had everyone in the audience convinced that karate was the most important thing in the world. What made Rhee's job easy, aside from the fact that he sincerely believes in his message, was that everything he said was ideally suited to the psychological needs of the market he was appealing to. If any group of people was ready for a pep talk on human potential, it was the Soviets. Bombarded for years by official paranoia, here was a population dying to feel good about itself. Maybe it was Norman Vincent Peal's power of positive thinking coming a half century late, but compared to the Central Committee's decades of depressing pronouncements, it sounded pretty inspiring. Rhee's lecture was followed by a meeting with the deputy minister of sports, and within days the State Sports Committee passed a rule legalizing all Asian martial arts.

By the time his nine-day trip had ended, Rhee was conferring with entrepreneurs from Russia, Armenia, Georgia, Kazakhstan, and Ukraine about opening karate schools in their republics. Before they could run the schools, though, they would have to know more than just Tae Kwon Do. They would have to learn about advertising, accounting, employee relations, and all other skills needed to manage a successful business. But step one in teaching Soviets to be businessmen, Rhee realized, would be teaching them self-reliance, a character trait that had been systematically discouraged for seventy-four years.

Many Asian cultures thrive on order and responsibility; Soviets shy away from both. In Korea, people also work hard to find ways to express their individuality. Martial arts is a good example. Soviet society, however, affords no such outlets. Trained to support the collective and downplay the individual, most Soviets are far more comfortable deferring to the authority of some larger body than deciding anything by themselves.

That attitude pervades the Soviet workplace. Russians love to boss people around, but consensus, not expedience, is the most important element in the decision-making process. In some companies the concept of togetherness is carried to such extremes that entire staffs, including secretaries and receptionists, take part in every meeting, and when there's a vote, the result is always unanimous, a strategy designed to make everyone responsible for the outcome.

Within such organized disorganization, personal initiative has never been encouraged. Instead of being rewarded, as it is in the West, ambition was looked upon by the communists as a sign of selfishness and greed. This doesn't mean that wives stopped pushing their husbands to bring home extra money. To want more than others was fine as long as you kept your feelings hidden. Let them show and you were immediately singled out as a *chasnik,* or private trader—somebody who does business on his own and thinks he's better than everyone else.

Even after the demise of communism, the pressure on Soviets to appear satisfied with what little they have remains one of the few controlling forces left in their society. Yet, as people pursue a dwindling amount of supplies, it becomes more and more difficult for them to pretend satisfaction. Under the old regime, it was in no one's interest to work faster or better, and those who did were often punished, sometimes killed. Now, with new governments unable to provide even the basic essentials, anyone who wants more and works harder to get it is often seen as a criminal corrupted by capitalism.

In the West, a little criticism might be considered a small price for success, but it can place a heavy burden on Soviets, for whom family and friends make up an indispensable economic and psychological support system. In a society in which almost nothing works, relationships are more than a social convenience, they're a necessity for survival. Take away friends and relatives with the right connections to get things done, and life for most Soviets would be inconceivably grim. Capitalism, to many, means cutting those connections and making it on your own, a prospect that can fill the average Soviet with crippling doubt.

"People here still have a tremendous fear of being successful," noted an American businessman with many years of experience working with Russians. "First, because they think success will isolate them from their peers, and secondly, because they don't think they can handle the demands that go with it. It's a terrible weakness of the will. I've never seen anything like it in any other country. Part of the blame has to go to the communists, but part, maybe even a larger part, goes back to centuries of hardship and oppression the communists couldn't begin to match."

In this connection, one of the initial sensations foreigners often have when they arrive in Moscow is the feeling that something is missing from society and from the daily lives of ordinary people. Why, Rhee wondered, was everyone always so rude? Why was everything always lost, unobtainable, or broken? Then, one day, it all made sense. The Soviets had art and music, poetry and drama, but beneath that, they seemed to have no idea about order, no understanding of the way things worked, and no appreciation or knowledge of the skill it takes to keep them working.

It was hardly a unique observation. Many prominent Russian intellectuals felt the same way. "We never had a good civilization, but we always had a good culture," said Viktor Yerofeyev, one of the Soviet Union's most successful contemporary writers.

It's civilization that holds a society together, gives it cohesion and structure, and civilization is what had been taken away from

Soviets. The effects of its absence are visible everywhere, in the way people treat one another and in the way they treat their surroundings.

Sometimes, it seems as though everything man-made in the former Soviet Union is either falling apart or destroyed. Once-beautiful cities are in shambles, small towns look like junkyards rising up from the mud, and throughout the countryside ancient buildings and churches lie in ruin, not just from neglect, but from vandalism. In the Russian village of Vypolsovo, not far from Vladimir, an old monastery that looks like it took a direct hit from Nazis during World War II is actually being hacked to pieces by the local residents, who are tearing it down for the bricks. Similar acts are repeated on a daily basis throughout Russia, large parts of which now look like the end of a demolition derby.

The first reaction of most Westerners to such wanton destruction—after the initial shock of seeing it wears off—is to get out the rubber gloves and disinfectant and start cleaning the place up. Not that Soviets couldn't do it themselves. It's just that the job is so big, it's difficult for them, or anyone else for that matter, to know where to begin.

"I couldn't believe how backward things were," said Rhee. "It reminded me of my life in Korea thirty-five years ago. Every time I saw an American, I thought there goes a rich man. That's what I wanted to become, and that's how Soviets feel today."

No wonder audiences applauded Rhee's talks. They were hungry for new ideas from the West. In a country in which any imported creed was once prohibited, Rhee's philosophy of free enterprise, discipline, and respect for others was like a delayed revelation. Karate can help to make you the master of yourself, he had told Soviets, and when you master yourself you can change your world. It was nothing more than a standard American pep talk. But maybe a pep talk is exactly what Soviets need to hear.

Almost overnight, Rhee became the country's Pied Piper of self-improvement. People who had never heard of brown belts or black belts wanted to take karate lessons and start karate schools. Economists, army officers, government officials, policemen, and poets all signed up, but not one of them knew the first thing about business. So Rhee, by this time making regular trips back and forth between the United States and the Soviet Union, decided to teach would-be school managers everything they needed to know, from making sales calls to signing contracts.

"The idea of a private contract was the hardest thing for them to understand," he said. "Contracts are based on trust, and since they had never trusted anybody before, why should they trust a piece of paper? But trust and honesty have to begin in the heart. Without that, all the laws in the world are useless. That's what martial arts philosophy is about, and the beautiful thing is that it can be transferred directly to business."

Although Rhee's students are interested in earning money, Rhee himself is not. Profits from the karate schools go to the school owners. And profits from Rhee's business seminars, which are open to any interested Soviet entrepreneurs with ten thousand rubles to spend, go to a charitable foundation, which then dispenses the money to educational projects.

"I've been very successful, and I really feel that success unshared is unfulfilled," Rhee once told a reporter. "I have a nice home, all of my children are out of college now and healthy and happy, and I want to give the rest of my life for society. I'm going to make some history."

The first phase of the effort is to create as many Soviet small businessmen as he can—businessmen who are smart, disciplined, and honest. Rhee knows his program works, because it's the same one he's been using back in the United States, where, free of charge, he teaches inner-city schoolchildren how to get along with one another and bring home better grades by instructing them in Korean karate and the philosophy that goes with it. In his own way, Rhee can be very convincing when he explains how it works.

"The thing I teach the children, when we talk about life, is that the purpose of living is to be happy. But unless they are nice to people, people are not going to appreciate them, and they are never going to be happy. If that is clear in their minds, then they will be nice to each other."

That, Rhee said, is how he hopes to change the world. "My goal is to make truth, beauty, and love the basic rule by which we deal with each other. You can't even have a game between the Redskins and the Cowboys with two different sets of rules. Well, we have literally five billion rules in the game of life today . . . which is why human history has been nothing but bloodbaths. What we must do is to bring a single value system to bear on our universal problem."

For Rhee, the most effective value system is one that's based on work—hard work. Karate, as he sees it, is not about knowing how to defend yourself, but about learning to whip yourself into shape—something the Soviets need to do—and the process begins on Day One.

At Rhee's first twelve-day business seminar in Moscow in 1991, one of the organizers asked him for the schedule, and was told that classes would run from 6:00 A.M. to midnight.

"It's impossible for Soviet people to work for eighteen hours a day for twelve straight days," the man said.

"It's just as impossible for Americans, Koreans, or anybody to do it, if they're not properly motivated," said Rhee, who assured the organizer that students would be motivated.

When Rhee gave his first business seminar in America in Fort Worth, Texas, starting on July 4, 1986, more than sixty karate school owners and other businessmen from all over the country attended. The session lasted for four days and ran from sunup to midnight each day.

"It was like Marine boot camp, with lectures on business ethics and early American history thrown in," recalled one participant. "There were company executives, salesmen, lawyers, all kinds of people. We got up at six in the morning, ran a few miles, heard Rhee talk, did exercises, heard Rhee talk, ran again, heard Rhee talk some more, and went to bed. By the way, if you talked while Rhee was talking, you had to do a hundred push-ups."

All but five of eighty-seven Soviet students successfully completed Rhee's first course in Moscow, and sixty-five of the graduates went on to open karate schools. Of all the Western companies
that have come to the Soviet Union in recent years, Rhee's alone
has a policy to leave behind more than it takes out. Everyone talks
about the vast potential in Soviet human resources, but Rhee
actually has a development plan, even if the end product is a little
harder to quantify than timber and oil.

"It's an attitude," said Rhee. "I believe that the mind and body
work together as one. The action of your body creates a state of
mind in which you want to do something. If you develop a state
of mind where you pay undivided attention, how can you not
develop good work habits?"

The main obstacle is that Soviet minds have been at rest for
more than seven decades. The reform movement, unfortunately,
hasn't done much to change things. The new Soviet society is
virtually indistinguishable from the old one, except now, with the
Communist Party no longer telling people what to do, most people don't do anything.

Russians have a long history of adopting ideas from other
cultures. They took their religion from Byzantium, their bureaucracy from Sweden, their architecture from Italy, and their concept of government from Germany. It says a lot about the Soviets'
lack of drive and determination that so many of them continue to
trust their fate to some outside force, whether it's the government,
the free market, or a corporate benefactor from abroad.

During the Cold War, Russians measured themselves against
the Americans, and now they're patterning many of their reformed institutions, from the presidency to the KGB, on American
models. It's one thing, though, to copy the plans, and another thing
to put them into operation. Few Soviets need to be persuaded that
capitalism and democracy work for other people, but many Soviets do need to be convinced that these institutions can work for
them.

In a society in which no one used to accept responsibility for
anything, Rhee was telling people that their economic success and

future happiness depended entirely on themselves—not as a group, but as individuals. "Karate is a means to an end," Rhee said. "What counts is the discipline. If Russians want what the West has, no one's going to give it to them. The communists couldn't, and no one else can either. They're going to have to earn it." And that starts, he tells them, by getting up every morning, jumping out of bed, and doing a few hundred push-ups.

Chapter Six

Big Mac Attack

It all began on July 24, 1959, the date of the famous "kitchen debate" between Richard Nixon and Soviet Premiere Nikita Khrushchev. Nixon seems to have an instinct for being in the right place at the right time, at least in the Soviet Union. But in boosting his political career by getting into an argument with Khrushchev, the then vice president also helped to expose the first glimpses of Soviet consumer anxiety.

The celebrated face-off came at an exhibit of U.S. household products in Moscow, and while the Russian leader denounced capitalist materialism, Nixon boldly disagreed, claiming that Americans had more modern conveniences at their disposal than anyone else on earth. As proof, he pointed to an automatic dishwasher, a family-size box of Brillo, a frost-free refrigerator, and a twelve-ounce can of Pepsi—all props in a display of a typical American kitchen that passing Soviets stared at as if it had just arrived from another planet.

Standing nearby was Donald Kendall, chairman of Pepsi Cola, who introduced the first U.S. soft drink to the Soviet Union—a country for which hard liquor has been the beverage of choice

81

since the tenth century. In 1959, Pepsi was still unknown to most Soviets, and following the debate, Kendall thought Khrushchev might like to try a free sample.

"In those days," he recalled, "we had an advertising slogan that went: 'Be Sociable, Have a Pepsi.' Well, I toasted Khrushchev with a glass of Pepsi, and when he heard that slogan, he got a big smile on his face. 'No, no,' he said, lifting his glass to correct me. 'Be *Socialist*, Have a Pepsi.' He really had a great sense of timing."

So did Pepsi. From then on, the company has been a major presence in the Soviet Union and an acknowledged leader in the art of doing business there. Pepsi's landmark soft-drink-for-vodka deal, an elaborate barter transaction that let the Soviets sell Pepsi Cola in their country and Pepsi sell Stolichnaya vodka in the United States, has become a textbook example of how to profit by trading with the Russians.

During the intervening years, the company's sales campaign has extended far beyond soft drinks. In 1990, PepsiCo and its Soviet partners signed the biggest contract in the history of U.S.-Soviet trade. The agreement, which represents more than $3 billion in retail sales, not only allows for increased back-and-forth shipments of vodka and Pepsi, but adds a new element to the bargain—the construction of ten Soviet commercial shipping vessels to be built for rubles, then sold or leased on the international market for hard currency.

What makes Pepsi's latest achievement so remarkable is that the groundwork was laid over thirty years ago, when the Soviets were publicly vowing to bury the West. Yet, as Kendall suspected, what they really wanted to do was copy the West. In fact, the Soviet desire for Western goods and products, even in the midst of the Cold War, was a signal that, starting with the first Russian Pepsi generation, the Soviet Union would never be the same.

For decades, Donald Kendall has had many would-be imitators, but nobody could rightfully be called his successor, nobody, that is, until George Cohon, president of McDonald's Restaurants of Canada, came along.

In 1976, Cohon first got the idea to sell Big Macs in the Soviet

Union. Always on the lookout for expansion opportunities, he approached Soviet officials attending the Montreal Olympics with a proposal to have a McDonald's restaurant open for business in time for the 1980 Olympic Games in Moscow. There were Mc-Donald's in places like Turkey, the Philippines, and Chile. Why couldn't there be one in the Soviet Union, too? The Soviet invasion of Afghanistan and a subsequent Olympic boycott answered that question, but Cohon didn't give up.

For the next six years, he negotiated with the Soviet Foreign Ministry, the Trade Ministry, and the Finance Ministry. Talks to build a Moscow McDonald's outlasted the tenures of three Soviet leaders. Eventually, Cohon's persistence paid off. By 1986, he was discussing possible locations for a restaurant with the Moscow City Council. But council members, like local politicians anywhere, wanted to know what was in it for them. From the communist point of view, the one that dominated proceedings in those days, the quid pro quo was as basic as a free lunch at capitalist expense. If McDonald's wanted to operate in their fair city, they would have to give city officials a respectable share of the profits. And so negotiations continued.

The runaround finally ended a year later, when Mikhail Gorbachev decided that having a McDonald's in town might be the perfect way to prove to the Soviet people that perestroika was working, or, on the other hand, just the right distraction to keep their minds off the fact that it wasn't. It may not have been bread and circus, but McDonald's did have buns, and the Moscow Circus was usually out of town, performing in the West for hard currency.

Under the terms of the agreement Cohon worked out with the city council, McDonald's of Canada owns 49 percent of the enterprise; the remaining 51 percent belongs to Mosobshepit, the city's food-service administration, whose responsibility it is to run all of Moscow's 11,000 public cafeterias and restaurants.

On the surface that might seem like an ideal matchup, two food giants joining forces to bring the first Mickey D's to the Soviet Union, but Mosobshepit and McDonald's had about as much in common as a Quarter Pounder and a quarter pound of gristle. Mosobshepit knew absolutely nothing about running a quality eatery. Of course, it didn't have to, since what Soviets call "eating out" bears no resemblance whatsoever to the same experience in the West.

Enter a typical Soviet restaurant and you enter a place that not only makes you lose your appetite, but your self-respect. The service is bad, the premises are filthy, and the meals are inedible. By the end of the day, tables and chairs in most public restaurants are piled so high with leftovers and dirty dishes it's impossible to find a seat. And even when you can, it's necessary to slip the waiter a bribe before he lets you enjoy the unenviable privilege. Many of Moscow's growing number of cooperative restaurants offer food and service comparable to anything you'd find in other world capitals, but their public-sector counterparts are a gastronomic disaster area.

What made Mosobshepit the ideal partner wasn't its culinary appreciation of entrees and salad bars. As the city's biggest landlord, Mosobshepit controlled vast tracts of Moscow real estate, including some of the best commercial property in the city. With a partner like this, Cohon could take his pick of dozens of choice sites, not only for McDonald's first restaurant, which he decided to locate on Pushkin Square, one of the city's busiest intersections, but for more restaurants (the contract calls for twenty more) and other commercial developments.

In a conflict of interest that would be illegal in America, Mosobshepit functions as McDonald's business partner, real-estate agent, and government overseer. But in the Soviet Union, even in the reformed version, such crossover arrangements are the rule rather than the exception.

Outside of a few tightly regulated co-op businesses and trade associations, free enterprise remains an alien concept in Soviet society. A large percentage of new commercial activity in Russia and other republics is firmly in the hands of local governments, whose officials seem disinclined to surrender any of their deal-making authority to private entrepreneurs.

"It's half corruption and half market arrangement," said Mikhail Berger, an economics columnist with *Izvestia.* Local councils operate like huge urban conglomerates, with their hands in so many economic pies that the real business of running city government is neglected.

Often cited as an example of a politician turned business mogul is Moscow's reform Mayor Gavril Popov, once an economics professor at Moscow State University. "During the almost two years Popov's been in power, he could have done a lot," Konstantin Borovi, president of the city's largest commodities exchange, told *The Washington Post.* "He could have organized a properly functioning retail trade system with the collective farms in the Moscow area, but he has done nothing. The Moscow authorities have interfered with private businessmen at every turn."

Cohon knows about interference, but fourteen years of knocking on doors also had an upside. It introduced him to every important person in the Soviet Union. And when you're involved in any business deal that leaves your investment hostage in the host country, it pays to get acquainted with as many powerbrokers as possible. During the coup attempt, as other businessmen envisioned their money going down the drain, Cohon picked up the phone, made a few calls, and realized in no time that there was nothing to worry about.

On August 19, 1991, the first day of the coup, Cohon was vacationing with his family in the Crimea, just a few miles from where Gorbachev was being held under house arrest.

"We flew from Yalta to Tblissi, Georgia," he said. "I was able to get to an international phone line and I called a lot of people that I know. . . . One of the people I talked to was Vadim Bakatin. He's the new reform-minded head of the KGB [although he's since been replaced], someone I know very well. And his line was something that stuck in my head: 'This won't last. The people aren't for it. There's no leadership at the top. You can't do this in this day and age.' So I never once said, Gee, I'm sorry McDonald's is here. That thought never entered my mind."

More than a decade of negotiating had earned Cohon access

to the highest levels of Soviet officialdom. Russian bureaucrats use endless meetings to wear down their opponents. The approach is partly a control strategy and partly an attempt to hide their incompetence. But surviving the process, as Cohon's experience demonstrates, can pay off in residual benefits that money can't buy.

Hardened by centuries of oppression, Russians respect in foreigners the same quality of endurance they possess. Combine this with their passion for camaraderie and terms such as "enemies" and "allies" soon become interchangeable. For all of their fabled toughness, Russians have a way of mixing work with recreation that makes corporate conflicts seem to disappear. A government administrator or factory director you're completely at odds with in the afternoon could be toasting you that night as his best friend. It's largely a game, but play along, which isn't that difficult after a few rounds of vodka, and you could develop a useful personal relationship with someone you hardly know and probably can't stand. Doing business with Soviets is an exercise in learning to live with—and profit from—just such contradictions.

George Cohon came to know the Soviets as well as any outsider could, and one thing he knew with absolute certainty was that McDonald's couldn't survive one week if it had to rely on the local infrastructure to meet its needs. It was essential for the restaurant to have an uninterrupted flow of meat and potatoes. But without its own private network of suppliers and distributors, a modern food processing center, and staff trained to work according to the McDonald's philosophy of labor rather than Marx and Lenin's, the project would be doomed to failure.

The plan Cohon devised to protect the company's investment and build future earnings is a blueprint for success that any joint venture could use. No business can last long in Russia without guaranteeing itself access to the basic materials and services it must have to function. And how Cohon did that by mixing McDonald's know-how with available resources, teenage help, and a stockpile of rubles is an applied lesson in venture capitalism.

Normally foreign businessmen are expected to provide their

Soviet partners with get-acquainted trips abroad. In this case, Cohon believed, the junkets were a vital part of the training process. It was important for Soviets to see what a fully operational McDonald's food chain looked like.

"When they saw our meat suppliers, our training facilities, our productivity at the restaurant level, they got so excited," said Cohon, a 54-year-old lawyer from Chicago, who opened his first McDonald's store in London, Ontario, in 1968. "They knew that there are things we could show them that would help them run their restaurants better."

The rationale for joint ventures is simple: The foreign partner provides the financing and technical expertise; the Soviets bring access to cheap production and vital knowledge of how the system works. In this case, however, Cohon wasn't particularly interested in cheap production, and he already knew how the system worked.

Despite the built-in problems of an arrangement that required foreign companies to assume all of the risk, by the late eighties, joint ventures were springing up everywhere in the Soviet Union. It hardly seemed to matter that an old law (no longer in effect) relegated outside firms to minority-partner status; here was a chance to be a part of economic history, and few big Western companies could resist the temptation. Sheraton, Philip Morris, and IBM got into the act. Pan Am and Aeroflot, the official Soviet airline, became partners in a Moscow-to-New York route. The Moscow City Council signed agreements with Baskin-Robbins to open ice cream stores and with Pizza Hut, a subsidiary of PepsiCo, to open pizza restaurants. But nothing came close to matching what George Cohon had in mind—a top-to-bottom, vertically integrated supply line that ran directly from the rolling fields of Mother Russia to the computerized cash registers at McDonald's.

With agricultural experts from Europe and America, Cohon began looking for Soviet collective farms to supply McDonald's with meat, pickles, potatoes, flour, and cheese. It didn't take long to find out that few collective-farm products could measure up to the company's standards.

"We never wanted to become farmers," said McDonald's quality-control specialist Terry Williams. "But it was increasingly clear that we would have to get into the agricultural end of the business a bit deeper than we had anticipated."

A cheddar cheese plant located in the Volga region passed inspection, and a state-owned cattle farm near Moscow agreed to produce the type of beef McDonald's required. French fries, though, were starting to look like an endangered side order. The Russians had plenty of potatoes. It was just that Russian potatoes, tasty as they may be (whether consumed as a solid or as vodka), are no bigger than tennis balls—not nearly the right size to produce a McDonald's french fry.

So a new strain of spud, the Russet Burbank, was brought into service. With company agronomists watching and taking notes, the imported potato thrived in Soviet soil. The first harvest in 1989 beat anything area farmers had ever seen. McDonald's was producing twice as many potatoes per hectare (30,000 pounds) as its nearest competition. In one planting season, the company had revolutionized Soviet potato farming.

"We showed that the way we do it gets better results," said a McDonald's potato specialist from Holland, one of fifteen foreign scientists brought in to oversee the experiment. "The local farmers were very impressed."

Just as important as growing food, however, was McDonaldizing it—trimming, grinding, molding, slicing, and dicing it into the universally recognizable shapes and sizes that McDonald's patrons everywhere expect to see when they place their orders. At this crucial stage in the operation, nothing could be left to chance, which meant nothing could be left to the Soviets.

Russians would be phased into the management team, but they were wisely kept away from the design-and-construction end of the project. Soviets actually work on very few of the new buildings going up in Moscow. It was Germans who painstakingly refurbished the Metropol Hotel; Finns who restored the stately Savoy. The tradition dates back to the days when Ivan the Terrible imported Italians to build the Kremlin. Peter the Great did the same when he wanted to make St. Petersburg look like a cold-water copy of Venice.

Russians automatically assume if something is made by foreigners, it has to be better, and they're usually right. So the Soviets were impressed when Yugoslavs were brought in to build the restaurant, when Americans supervised work on the processing center, and when Germans, Finns, and Poles installed the imported machinery from Sweden, Canada, and the United States.

Russians *were* in on the planning. After all, it's their country and they do control 51 percent of the business. But as anyone who's ever made plans with Russians knows, 90 percent of the time is taken up figuring out how to get around obstacles that wouldn't be there in the first place if Russians weren't involved.

Cohon and his McDonald's of Canada assistants are full of praise for their Soviet partners, and they should be. Russians require constant stroking and reassurance, and McDonald's first-name corporate style and fail-safe management principles were perfectly suited to their needs.

"Planning a joint venture is . . . like planning an experiment in genetic engineering," wrote attorney Jeffrey M. Hertzfeld in the *Harvard Business Review.* "New enterprises, like transplanted strands of DNA, will become the organizing matter of new commercial life . . . new forces of production that sustain wealth."

The Soviets' first goal, though, isn't sustaining wealth, it's learning how to produce it, and the only practical way to do that is for them to be trained in precisely the way Cohon has done. Without having Western companies teach them about marketing, information gathering, technology management, financial analysis, quality control, strategic planning, and all of the other necessary ingredients in a well-organized enterprise, Soviets would be hopelessly lost. McDonald's is an example of the effect one firm can have. Its original $50 million investment hasn't just created 1,500 restaurant jobs, it's introduced thousands of farmers, scientists, engineers, and future executives to ideas about business and money that will eventually transform the Russian economy.

"This is a country that has always rewarded mass obedience, instead of individual initiative," said Jeffrey Zeiger, manager of Tren-Mos, a Trenton, New Jersey, joint-venture steak house in Moscow. "If something breaks, it stays broken. If something doesn't work, it never gets fixed. Nobody wants to make the effort or take the responsibility. Foreign businesses are showing Russians how to do things right the first time. But when you're used to working for two days then getting two days off, which is the way it's done here, just being on the job Monday through Friday is like science fiction. But I have to say they're learning."

When Cohon ran a one-day ad in a Moscow newspaper that read, "Wanted: workers for the new McDonald's restaurant on Pushkin Square," over 27,000 job applications arrived. Office clerks, artists, bureaucrats, and college students—everybody wanted to work for McDonald's. But not everyone could pass the rigorous screening process or the intense training that followed.

Customer service is not a Soviet tradition. Except in a few pricey hard-currency shops and restaurants that cater mainly to foreigners, customers are considered an annoyance. Store clerks and waiters in most countries don't qualify as high-status professionals. In the Soviet Union, however, they're in the enviable position of having first crack at all of the incoming food and merchandise, which is one reason why many of the best goods disappear before the public ever sees them.

McDonald's, with its obsessive emphasis on "food, folks, and fun," represented a complete departure from the normal Soviet style of serving the public. The company taught its Russian employees to smile at customers, to say "hello," "thank you," and "come again." Buying something in the Soviet Union is usually a cross between a scavenger hunt and tug-of-war. Cohon wanted to change that experience for two reasons: to create "a proper McDonald's environment" and to make sure that that environment wasn't destroyed by the ongoing hostility between customers and the help that turns most Soviet businesses into an over-the-counter battlefield. A generous system of incentives was installed to keep McDonald's staffers happy even under the most trying conditions. After five years of service, all employees are eligible for bonuses; after ten years on the job, they get their choice of a diamond ring or a new car. Even *Pravda*—the old *Pravda*—conceded that the communists couldn't beat that.

All of this preparation was aimed at meeting a single overall objective—selling hamburgers, a food product that could trace its ancient history back to a meat dish eaten by one of the many Soviet ethnic groups, the Tartars, but refined, restructured, and renamed by McDonald's.

On his first visit to the United States, in 1936, then-Soviet minister of food industries Anastas Mikoyan came across a hamburger stand in New York and marveled at the way it worked: how beef patties were cooked on one side and then the other; how the clerk placed the finished product on a bun, added a piece of pickle and a few squirts of ketchup and mustard, and in less than a minute or two the thing was ready to eat. In an essay published years later, Mikoyan described each step of the process with such a precise attention to detail you would think he'd made some great scientific discovery. But to a Soviet in the 1930s, after years of revolution, civil war, and starvation, maybe that's what a hamburger was.

That's *certainly* what it was to Ray Kroc, a traveling milkshake-machine salesman, who made a deal with two brothers named McDonald in 1954 to franchise their California drive-in restaurant. Kroc edited the menu, applied the latest concepts in mass marketing, and soon there were Golden Arches from coast to coast, continent to continent.

"What Aaron Montgomery Ward, Richard Sears, Alvah Roebuck, and F.W. Woolworth did for dry goods . . . Ray Kroc did for fast food," observed columnist George Will in praise of the McDonald's phenomenon. "[Kroc's] enterprise expresses the prosaic idea on which American prosperity rests: *things add up.* Enough billions of fractions of anything . . . add up to a lot of something. . . . Like many entrepreneurs, Kroc's genius is for acting on the obvious, or what seems obvious after he has acted on it."

The late founder's owl-shaped face, embossed on a commemorative plaque just to the left of a bank of cash registers, was symbolically watching the take as 30,000 customers came pouring through the doors when Cohon opened the Moscow store for business in January of 1990. As it turned out, that would be the worst daily crowd in the history of the restaurant, the biggest and busiest in the world. On an average day, the Moscow McDonald's feeds 50,000 people, most of whom stand in line for up to two hours before getting in.

During its first year, using a basic no-frills menu, Cohon sold six million soft drinks, five million orders of french fries, four million milkshakes—and 3,960,004 Big Macs.

Anything big in the Soviet Union is regarded as important. It doesn't matter what it is or what it does. In a society in which size is a substitute for quality, bolshoi, as the Russians say, means the best. When the Soviets invent their own microchip, a Russian joke goes, it will be the biggest microchip in the world. And when Soviets had a chance to buy Big Macs, they went wild. After twenty months, the original price had doubled to nearly ten rubles, almost a day's pay for the average Soviet worker. But the demand only increased and the line outside got longer.

In fact, the length of the McDonald's line is one of the Russian economy's leading economic indicators. Prices go up and the line shrinks for a day or two, until the need for "Beeg Meks" increases and the crowds come back in greater numbers than before.

George Cohon calls his success an example of "hamburger diplomacy," reverting to McDonaldese to explain what happens when deprived taste buds experience a Big Mac and a whole series of socioeconomic changes begins. But how does McDonald's make money when all of its profits so far have been in the form of rubles?

Other Western shops and restaurants in Moscow normally require payment in hard currency, or, like Tren-Mos, some combination of hard currency and rubles. McDonald's takes in only rubles, earning in the neighborhood of half a million a day, some of which it converts into dollars to pay for imported restaurant products, but most of which it keeps.

As to making use of his revenue, Cohon explained, part of the trick is being patient, and the other part is being shrewd. "Don't

MCDONALD'S MOSCOW MENU
A WAGE-PRICE ANALYSIS

ITEM	U.S. PRICE* (DOLLARS)	SOVIET PRICE† (RUBLES)	SOVIET PRICE‡ (WORK HOURS)
Big Mac	1.95	69	24 hr. 17 min.
Hamburger	.59	35	12 hr. 19 min.
Double hamburger	1.65	51	17 hr. 57 min.
Cheeseburger	.69	39	13 hr. 43 min.
French fries (medium)	.99	25	8 hr. 48 min.
Milkshake	.99	35	12 hr. 19 min.
Apple pie	.99	40	14 hr. 4 min.
Ice cream	.99	33	11 hr. 36 min.
Coke (medium)	.79	30	10 hr. 33 min.
Coffee, tea (small)	.59	7	2 hr. 27 min.

*Prices in effect at McDonald's Store No. 00689, Washington, D.C., May 6, 1992.
†Prices in effect at McDonald's Store No. 1, Moscow, Russia, May 1, 1992.
‡Based on an estimated average Soviet monthly wage of 500 rubles.

think in terms of being a pirate," he said. "Think in terms of being a pioneer. I had a meeting with Gorbachev . . . and we got into an in-depth discussion about the difference between pioneers and pirates. If you go to the former Soviet Union and your intention is to go in, make a quick buck, and get out, I don't think they need those kind of people. But if you go with the intention of McDonald's and other large companies, that you're going to be there for the long haul, then I think the time is now and it's right."

But even pioneers like to get their hands on some solid cash now and then, and Cohon's no exception. He disagrees with the notion that he was hanging onto tens of millions of pieces of unconvertible paper money. He's been busy converting them in real-estate deals and barter projects. Using his connections with Mosobshepit, he's building a twelve-story office building in the heart of Moscow's business district where suites will rent for hard currency. He's trading commodities. "There are ships pulling out right now with products that are being sold for hard currency that we bought for rubles," said Cohon. And he's planning to open more restaurants. The next one in Moscow will have a hard-currency menu with everything you'd expect to find in a full-service McDonald's.

"Cohon is occupying ground on a market that, sooner or later, will inevitably become highly interesting," noted Mikhail Berger of *Izvestia*.

And Cohen couldn't agree more.

He likes to quote critics who said it couldn't be done. First, everyone told him, "You will never come to an agreement with Soviet officials on a joint business." Then, they said, "You won't be able to build anything in Russia." After that, the advice was, "Don't look in this country for local raw materials suitable for preparing foods according to accepted standards." Finally, he heard, "Where will you find individuals like the smiling, hard-working, pleasant young people who helped to create the McDonald's reputation?"

Cohon's usual reply: "You obviously don't appreciate the Soviets enough. Remember who has won the most Olympic medals." He's too polite, of course, to mention all the illegal steroids they used to get them.

Now, Cohon likes to talk about the persistence it takes to do business with the Soviets, the meticulous planning that went into building McDonald's self-contained supply network. And the ingenious ways he's turning rubles into real money.

But most of all, he likes working the front door of McDonald's—"I will never deny myself the pleasure of welcoming the first customers at the entrance"—watching as the long line of Russians moves slowly in his direction, and knowing from experience that good things come to those who never give up.

Chapter Seven

Money Apartheid

Nobody was paying much attention at the time, but former Soviet Prime Minister Valentin Pavlov, one of the eight plotters who tried to overthrow Mikhail Gorbachev, may have exposed preparations for the historic conspiracy months before it ever went public. Evil Western capitalists, Pavlov told the world in February of 1991, were devising a scheme to undermine the ruble, destroy the Soviet economy, and depose Gorbachev. The idea seemed so preposterous that most people treated Pavlov and his charges as a joke. How could anyone do a better job of undermining the ruble and destroying their economy than the Soviets themselves? As for getting rid of Gorbachev, that seems to have been a Kremlin project dating back at least to 1988.

Still, there was something about Pavlov that made him hard to dismiss. Shaped like a 250-pound Mr. Potato Head with a Big Bopper flattop, to many he never looked smart enough to be coup material, let alone the chief architect of Soviet fiscal policy. But, as things turned out, he may have been the perfect guy for both jobs.

There are two distinct schools of thought on Pavlov that

converge on one crucial trait. "The man is a financial genius," an important Moscow banker said just weeks before the junta's attempt to seize power. Ironically, most of Pavlov's critics agreed, although to them he was a genius with a distinctly sinister side, as shown by the part he played in the three-day putsch. But in the communists' brink-of-disaster economy, Pavlov also had an undeniable talent for manipulating money, and in early 1991, he proved just how clever he could be.

The economic picture was not at all bright. The Soviet debt crisis was getting worse, the money supply was increasing geometrically, and the rubles-for-dollars ratio was going through the roof. This last factor was of particular concern to Pavlov and other Kremlin officials, in that it meant the black market was prospering and they were not.

Without a Dow-Jones Industrials average to gauge how well the economy is doing, the black-market price for rubles makes a handy substitute. For example, in March of 1990, when Lithuania declared its independence from Moscow, one dollar bought 23 black-market rubles. In December of 1991, when Ukraine voted for independence, a dollar could buy 120 rubles. Just as the stock market is a gauge of Americans' confidence in their economy, the black market shows what Soviets think of theirs.

In the first months of 1991, with the illegal ruble-to-dollar exchange rate hovering around 33-to-1, the government was facing a major challenge from the black market. There were so many worthless rubles in circulation, the only thing saving the economy from total collapse was the fact that a large part of it ran entirely on barter and foreign money. But if the black market continued to divert hard currency, Kremlin officials would soon be unable to pay for their own luxuries, to say nothing of imported necessities for general use, such as food, and machinery and spare parts for printing presses that were churning out rubles so fast they created a national paper shortage. The government was caught in a vicious circle: The more of a mess it made of its finances, the more the black-market economy profited. And the more the black-market economy profited, the worse the official economy got.

The Soviet Union was the only country in the world that practiced money apartheid against its own currency as a matter of national policy. The statement on the back of every ruble, ordering its acceptance throughout "the entire territory of the union for payments by all institutions, enterprises and persons" has always been more of a decoration than a requirement, which explains why many Russians call their bank notes wallpaper. The situation had gotten so bad that even Aeroflot, Intourist, and the Bolshoi Ballet—all government enterprises—were refusing to accept rubles.

Foreign companies felt the same way. In one anything-but-rubles deal with the Russians, Control Data Corporation agreed to accept partial payment for its computer products in Soviet-made greeting cards, for which the wily Russians demanded—and got— the full retail price for each card.

Even by communist standards, this was not the sign of a healthy economy, and any attempt at a cure had to begin with *(A)* cracking down on the black market and *(B)* taking a serious chunk out of the publicly held stockpile of rubles. Pavlov's basic plan was to stabilize the value of the ruble by destroying as many of the little green and yellow varmints as possible. Ideally, he would have liked to install paper shredders next to every cash register in the country and grind the miserable things to a pulp the minute they were spent. But he didn't have the technology, and if he did, it would take decades to install. What the current crisis called for was swift action, and Pavlov was ready with an air-and-land operation worthy of Goldfinger.

No government can just start taking people's money away without the appearance of legitimacy, and Pavlov came up with an excuse in the form of a conspiracy theory so weird that it would make sense only to Russians. It went like this: The Colombian drug cartel, the CIA, the Vatican bank, and several thousand assorted currency swindlers were out to destroy the Soviet economy and topple Mikhail Gorbachev by flooding the country with rubles. Overlooked in Pavlov's cover story was the fact that the Soviet government had been doing precisely the same thing by printing millions of brand-new rubles every day.

To give the plot the look of reality, Pavlov filled an Aeroflot plane with a few tons of decoy rubles and had it flown to Zurich, where the precious cargo was loaded into trucks for a prearranged discovery by KGB agents who would bring the nasty business to light. Armed with irrefutable "evidence" of an international conspiracy, Pavlov declared an immediate recall of all fifty- and hundred-ruble notes. Given the fact that these denominations are virtually the only ones used in the black market, the move was expected to bring business to a halt and give the money changers fits. The other intended target, the ruble-hoarding masses, would be put in an equally tight spot. The recall would force them to bring their dough out of hiding to exchange bigger bills for small ones—and when they did, Pavlov would hit them with his Sunday punch.

The big surprise awaiting anyone with rubles to return was that lines at the banks were too long and the hours too short to beat the three-day deadline. It didn't help matters that no banks had enough small bills to make change or that the temperature had dropped to 25 below zero. But that was all part of the plan.

By the time it was all over, 10 billion rubles were collected and many billions more rendered useless. The relief, though, was only temporary. Within weeks the economy was right back in the same fix. The black market was open for business, people were hoarding money again, and rubles were running off the presses at an even greater rate than before.

A year and a half later, with Pavlov in jail for his role in the coup attempt, other minds were trying to solve the former Soviet Union's financial problems, the most urgent of which in terms of its effect on business was the convertibility of the ruble. The Russian ruble has never been accepted as real money at home or abroad, and free trade in the currency markets will put it to the ultimate test. History shows that easy convertibility of weak currencies leads to a massive transfer of capital into stable foreign money. After World War II, it took European countries thirteen years to introduce fully convertible currencies, and most of their economies were in far better shape than the economy of any commonwealth country is now.

The Russians call hard currency, like American dollars, British pounds, and German marks, *valuda*, a term that means something of value, as opposed to the ruble, commonly regarded as having no value at all. Even the origin of the word *ruble* is in doubt. Some say it comes from the Russian noun *rubi*, meaning silver; others say it comes from the verb *rubit*, meaning "to cut." That makes sense, considering how many times it's been devalued over the years.

Until Peter the Great introduced monetary reforms that gave birth to the ruble in the late seventeenth century, Russians used a combination of native kopeks and foreign currencies that they altered by stamping them with big Ms for Muscovy. The practice of using other people's money has always been a popular Russian pastime. When the Bolsheviks came to power, leaders tried to abolish cash in all forms, replacing it with a system of vouchers called labor units. But the experiment was a complete flop, and by 1918, some 2,000 types of foreign money were circulating in the Soviet Union.

The first Bolshevik currency, the chic-sounding chervonet, was soon replaced in rapid succession by the silver ruble and the silver politnik, both of which were devalued faster than they could be printed. Then, in 1928, came the ruble as we know it today, which Stalin, in a move to safeguard Soviet gold, declared to be nonconvertible into other currencies—a decision that officially began the Soviet Union's economic isolation from the rest of the world.

For a political party that started out denouncing money as a bourgeois tool, the communists seemed to spend more time and energy tinkering with it than they did creating an actual economy. Devaluations, multiple exchange rates, recalls, and import-export restrictions have all been tried and retried. The ruble may not be worth much, but that doesn't mean it's not complicated.

Rather than being money fit for a great world power, as the Soviet government once liked to pretend, rubles are more like

IOUs from somebody who couldn't pass a Woolworth's credit check. The ruble is currency in its most elastic and creative form. It has so many different values, depending on who's spending it and what they're spending it for, it sometimes seems that the solution to the ruble's multiple personalities disorder isn't economic at all, but psychiatric.

On the basis of one exchange rate, the Soviet government could claim up to 90 percent of a foreign company's profits in taxes. On the basis of another, the same company could pay almost 100 percent less in taxes and walk away with a nice profit.

How much is the ruble really worth? No one seems to know for sure. And just when somebody thinks he does, there's always somebody else ready with a different figure. Does a company with 1 billion rubles in assets have holdings worth $500 million dollars (based on the old commercial exchange rate) or $25 million (based on the black-market rate)?

If the ruble was a mystery when the Soviet Union had one government, it could get downright metaphysical in a commonwealth with eleven or twelve. Under the 1991 union treaty, each republic was entitled to have its own individual ruble. In a revamped common market–style economy, it's assumed, this approach will decentralize financial planning and facilitate overall accounting procedures. However, some former republics are also developing their own separate currencies, and many have said they will determine for themselves what exchange rate to attach to the ruble. In 1990, Ukraine became the first republic to introduce its own money, a sort of "shadow currency" in the form of coupons used for the purchase of scarce consumer goods and food products. The thought is almost inconceivable, but within the next few years, once you factor in free-market pricing and hyperinflation, there could be even more useless money floating around than there is already.

Before the Soviet Union ceased to exist in December of 1991, the ruble had so many different values it often ended up being worth whatever amount people using it could agree on. In business deals involving rubles, the first thing to be decided was always the exchange rate. And that's where the real fun began. There were so many official and semiofficial rates it was almost impossible to keep all of them straight. If you think the IRS tries to make money confusing, take a look at the following list of a dozen values one ruble could have:

1. *The international ruble.* For years, the exchange rate for this ruble stayed around $1.75. Although totally contrived, the government achieved the appearance of legitimacy by posting the international rate on digital currency boards in Soviet airports and expensive hotels, pretending that it fluctuated daily.

2. *The commercial ruble.* This ruble, in theory, was good for all business transactions and usually worth 57 cents. The problem was that no one ever used it. In 1990, the commercial rate replaced the industrial rate, which tended to vary dramatically among Soviet ministries, depending on the size of a transaction and/or the political priority of the product involved.

3. *The tourist ruble.* Also referred to as the special ruble, this ruble was intended for foreign tourists in the Soviet Union. Its official value was a penny, although banks in Russia could set their own rates.

4. *The auction ruble.* The rate of this ruble was determined by bank officials prior to hard-currency auctions. Available only to business and joint ventures, its value changed from bank to bank and auction to auction.

5. *The foreign ruble.* This ruble, now just a bad memory, was used in transactions outside the country, particularly in areas of Eastern Europe, and its worth was determined by on-the-spot negotiations.

6. *The petroleum ruble.* Used in oil purchases, this ruble's rate changed according to world prices and the mood swings of Soviet sellers.

7. *The blocked ruble.* Sometimes called an enterprise ruble, this ruble was reserved for specific transactions with Soviet

industries. Blocked rubles were worth varying amounts, but could be spent only on goods produced by the industry in which they were earned.

8. *The accounting ruble.* Accounting rubles were used as off-setting amounts of cash in commodities transactions with Soviet industries. The hope was that the buyer or seller had them in a bank account somewhere.

9. *The golden ruble.* This was a sales term applied to tourist items priced in rubles but paid for in hard currency, usually at the international rate.

10. *The wooden ruble.* This was another sales term that referred to items priced in rubles but sold for hard currency at less than the international rate.

11. *The expired ruble.* As the name suggests, this is an out-of-date ruble with no official worth. But some expired rubles have a greater value as collector's items and souvenirs than the rubles that replaced them. In Moscow's Ismailova market, a 1905 ten-ruble note could cost as much as five-hundred modern rubles.

12. *The street ruble.* This is the ruble that's actually in people's pockets. Street ruble rates are more vulnerable than any others to rapid economic fluctuations, which average Soviet citizens still refer to as "fuck-u-ations."

In addition to official government ruble exchange rates, which have always been subject to point-of-purchase negotiation, the black market also has rates that slide up and down, depending on the needs of the moment. Let's suppose a load of sought-after merchandise or food happens to arrive in a Moscow neighborhood. The value of the ruble can skyrocket in seconds. Black-market arbitrageurs suddenly appear on the scene, and the result is an instant "spot market" for rubles.

That's what happened when a truck loaded with bananas pulled up to the curb recently on Prospect Mira, a busy street in downtown Moscow. Within minutes there were hundreds of people eager to make deals, including an old lady with several bags of foreign money, who opened an outdoor exchange bank on a nearby bench. Because the vendor wanted to be paid in hard currency, the potential buyers had to act fast before the bananas were gone. The old lady announced her rates and the buying began. Sometimes bidding on hard-to-find items can start an inflationary spiral that ends in a riot, but this time supply equaled demand, and within a few minutes the crowd and the bananas were gone.

Black-market rubles are traded by an army of self-trained professionals from all walks of life, but particularly by people who have regular contact with foreigners, the principal source of hard currency. Bartenders, taxi drivers, hotel clerks, waiters, students, shopkeepers, tour guides, and translators are all active in the black market—and most can make change in any international currency, as an attorney from Virginia found out after asking a cabbie in Moscow to sell him some rubles. When the American mentioned that he had a $100 bill, but only wanted to buy $50 worth of rubles, the disappointed cab driver replied, "OK, but I'll have to give you change in Swedish Kroner."

Especially adept in dealing with foreign exchange rates are prostitutes, who, because of their international clientele, have to keep close tabs on the currency market. It's so rare to find a prostitute in Moscow, St. Petersburg, or other large cities who's willing to work for anything but hard currency that hookers have become the subject of the same type of jokes among Russians that Americans tell about lawyers.

One goes like this: A foreigner goes to a brothel and picks out one of the girls and takes her to a back room. Five minutes later, after hearing the girl's screams, the madam comes rushing in to see what's wrong.

"Are you all right?" she asks. "What's he doing to you?"

Says the hooker, "He's trying to pay me in rubles."

As complicated as it is to figure out the value of the ruble, that's nothing compared to trying to get your hands on some when you need them. Going through all of the red tape required to withdraw rubles from a company or personal bank account can take months—and still not produce any money.

Unaffected by political reform, the Soviet banking system works something like the U.S. Securities and Exchange Commission, monitoring all business activity, but paying special attention to the financial dealings of foreign joint ventures. In order to open a Russian bank account, a foreign company must have a letter from its bank at home, confirming that it has no outstanding debts. Because virtually all successful Western businesses carry some form of debt, getting around this precondition requires some ingenuity.

When Columbia–Tri-Star, the movie company, wanted to open a bank account in Moscow for rubles it had earned distributing films in the Soviet Union, there was no way it could supply a letter saying it was debt free. "We have loans from all our banks," said Milt Fishman, Columbia's vice president and general counsel. What they should have done was set up a $500 petty cash account at another U.S. bank and gotten a letter saying they didn't owe any money.

Soviet banks also have the authority to decide whether a company is spending its money wisely or not. Bankers control business assets by approving (or disapproving) quarterly budgets that have to be sent in long before any withdrawal. And even then, getting them to okay a request often has less to do with the soundness of the budget than the size of the accompanying bribe. Banks can decide that a company's expenditures are too large or too small, or that company personnel are being overpaid. When that's the case, the bank will frequently return a budget with instructions to make the necessary corrections and resubmit it, which is sometimes another way of saying add more money to the original bribe. Most Soviet bankers have no formal training in banking or accounting, but they *have* learned the business lessons of communism.

The American partner in a small glassware company remembered what happened when he needed some rubles. After arriving in Moscow for business meetings, he and his Soviet partner went to withdraw 2,000 rubles from their company's bank account. The bank official refused, saying the request was not in the company's quarterly budget. "But we're *under budget* for the quarter," the American explained to the banker. The answer was still no. When he told the banker he needed the money to eat, he was given the address of a cheap restaurant, but no rubles. Finally, he had to borrow money from his partner, who was also short on cash and had to take up a collection from company employees.

Checking accounts would be the simple solution to the problem, but checking accounts have never existed in the Soviet Union. In 1990, a small number of Soviet banks let their customers use checks, as part of an experiment, but the project turned into a fiasco when no one would accept them as payment. Taking rubles was bad enough. Taking *checks* for rubles was more than most Soviets could deal with.

It's not surprising that Soviet banks are so strict. Letting depositors manage their own funds means that the banks would lose a large part of their monitoring and control authority. So until the law is changed, most financial transactions, business or otherwise, will continue to be conducted on a cash-and-carry basis, which means that if you want to buy something expensive, you'd better show up carrying the cash.

Credit cards would be easier to transport than bags of money, but Soviets aren't allowed to have those, either. And even if they were, aside from the hotels and expensive shops that cater to foreigners, there aren't many places where credit cards can be used. Nevertheless, having a credit card is the ticket to shopping privileges most Soviets only dream about, and to take advantage of this, many of the country's most prominent citizens regularly resort to fraud. A former Kremlin official, who has since gone into business for himself, explained how it works. "It's easy," he said, with the type of pride that only a former communist could exhibit in such circumstances. "I have many foreign friends, so once or twice a year I buy credit cards from them. I give them $1,000 for each card and they report them stolen." In the meantime, the former official has a field day charging clothes, imported food, and anything else he can find. Since perestroika began, he estimates, he's run up tens of thousands of dollars in unpaid bills.

When foreigners use plastic to pay their hotel bills, eat at expensive restaurants, or make purchases in fancy shops, the arbitrary value of the ruble can create another set of problems. Soviet hotels and other institutions welcome American credit cards because they afford greater flexibility in the use of conversion rates. And since they always get soaked with the highest rates, foreigners, tourists, and visiting businessmen can find themselves paying $300 for a room or $200 for a dinner that should have cost a few hundred rubles. It's too complicated for the card companies to correct the rip-off at its source; besides, the "error" allows them to make extra money, too, from interest on the card holder's higher balance.

Computer verification could put a stop to credit-card crime. Unfortunately, American Express and Visa have had to delay setting up their systems. The equipment involved is so sophisticated it's on the list of restricted U.S. technology, and adjustments to the hardware have put the project behind schedule.

If Russian banks could be trusted, many of the credit and cash-flow problems that hinder foreigners from doing business would be eliminated, or at least be significantly reduced. Then again, if that happened, they wouldn't be Russian banks. Banking procedures are primitive, illogical, and usually criminal. But that's nothing new. The best way to survive in any hostile environment is to know the enemy. And when you're a businessman in Russia or anywhere else in the new commonwealth, that's definitely the bank. Developing a financial relationship with a Russian bank is like playing poker with a guy named Doc. You know you're getting taken. The problem is that you can't immediately figure out how, although the way most banks operate, it soon becomes obvious.

Any foreign company, partnership, or joint venture that has ruble receipts and disbursements will need to open a basic corporate account, which means the company has to be officially accredited as a legitimate business—a process that can take as little as three months or as long as forever. Under current Russian law, for example, American companies have to gather documentation from the state in which they're incorporated, along with backup materials from the U.S. State Department and the Russian Embassy in Washington, and present the entire package for approval to the appropriate trade ministries and banking authorities. At that point, no further progress can be made until all necessary fees and honoraria have been paid in full.

More elaborate accounts allow companies to trade in foreign currencies, assuming they're doing business abroad for the overall benefit of the Russian economy—something that must be proven to a collection of bank officials and government ministers. But having a foreign account and actually using it to change money are two different things. Assuming hard currency is available, there are two ways of getting it:

- The company must produce a currency request for review by banking authorities, who will judge it on the basis of its legitimacy and reasonableness. Invoices for "services rendered" by lawyers or consultants are generally regarded as deceptions designed to steal foreign currency from the government.

- The company wishing to convert rubles to foreign currency must fill out an application for a bank auction. Auctions occur regularly, usually weekly, although the application has to be submitted one month in advance. The company indicates how much foreign money it wants to buy and what price it's willing to pay in rubles. Should the amount and price coincide with the amount available for sale and the price the bank is looking for, the transaction is consummated. If not, try again next time.

There's just one precondition. To participate in an auction, a company must have its rubles in a special bank account and get prior approval for each withdrawal to buy hard currency. Banks need so much advance warning because most have little or no money on hand. That's why there are so few Russian bank robberies. The government has always beat the crooks to the loot. Soviet banks had long been a source of funds for Communist Party activities. Stalin robbed banks to finance the Bolshevik revolution, and the practice of misappropriating bank assets has never really ended.

In the past, all foreign-currency transactions had to be handled through the Vnesheconombank in Moscow, which took its share of every dollar or Deutsch mark that moved through its accounting system before slowly passing whatever was left to the parties owed the money. Because of its virtual domestic monopoly on access to foreign money, Western intelligence agencies considered Vnesheconombank an extension of the KGB and Soviet Military Intelligence (GRU). This monopoly changed in 1991 when other banks in Russia were given permission to deal in foreign currency. But what amount of money is still being siphoned off by the authorities is unknown, though it could be considerable, since the Russian government desperately needs foreign technology and has to pay for it in hard currency.

Another Soviet bank with experience in the area of foreign currencies is the Moscow Narodny Bank, with branch offices in London and Switzerland. This famous bank's original purpose was threefold: to finance KGB and GRU espionage operations abroad, to borrow foreign currencies in order to bypass political prohibitions against loaning money directly to the Soviet Union, and to act as a kind of safe-deposit laundromat for the nomenklatura's multimillion-dollar retirement fund.

The Moscow Narodny does occasionally function as an actual "bank," but a prudent businessman should never rely on it for accurate information. Its principal function for years was to spread disinformation about the credit worthiness of the Soviet Union, and because many of its old habits persist, any advice received from the Moscow Narodny should be discounted more than the official value of the ruble.

Whether the Commonwealth of Independent States has a

strong central bank, the republics create banks of their own, or some combination of both ideas is eventually adopted, how thoroughly the entire banking system is reformed will be a good indication of how serious the Soviets are about establishing a sound economy and regaining control of their money supply.

Despite the appearance of regulation, Soviet banks have failed miserably in their money-monitoring responsibilities. In reality, they haven't been banks at all, but front organizations for behind-the-scenes thievery that's still going on. When the communists ran things, banks were supposed to regulate state enterprises; instead, bank officials, encouraged by bribes, often refinanced projects that lost money. Throwing good rubles after bad has been another Soviet banking tradition, and in the process most banks became silent partners in the same waste and mismanagement they were responsible for preventing. In the United States, that's one of the things that caused the multibillion-dollar savings-and-loan crisis. In the former Soviet Union, it's just one more reason to laugh all the way to the bank.

Chapter Eight

Undue Process

Serge is a lawyer in Moscow—a member of a private firm—but ten years ago he worked at the Institute of State and Law, at the time one of the Kremlin's leading think tanks. Whenever government officials wanted a made-to-order legal opinion, researchers went to work immediately, as Serge did in 1982, when several army generals came to the Institute with a question the military had been puzzling over. Would it be a violation of international law, the generals wanted to know, if the Soviets shot down an American spy satellite?

"International law was my field," said Serge, "so I was assigned to find the answer." But after weeks of trying, he couldn't locate any laws that applied in this case. With top military brass assembled in the Institute director's office, Serge explained that shooting down another country's spy satellites fell into a legal gray area. Nevertheless, it probably wouldn't be a good idea to pursue the project, he added, since it might lead to war with the United States.

When the generals voiced their disappointment, the director of the Institute jumped to his feet, denouncing Serge for his shoddy work. Then, turning to the generals, he assured them that their plan was on solid ground. "Anything the military wants to do," he said, "is perfectly legal."

Under communism, the practice of law was so corrupt that no one connected with it could be trusted. There still aren't many truth-seeking Soviet lawyers. The same goes for honest judges and crime-fighting DAs. Of course, there's a good reason. Despite a few brief attempts at reform, this is a country in which the ultimate legal precedent has always been the whim of the state.

The communists used rules and regulations as a form of punishment, and the legal process they left behind continues to function that way. But to understand how the current system operates, it's helpful to know how it got started. "Justice for all" has never been Russia's trademark. As little justice as possible would be more like it. For centuries, Russian rulers were the primary source of legal authority. Even after the first courts appeared in the mid-nineteenth century, the czar's word was the only law that counted. When the Bolsheviks took over, they adopted the same basic approach. Communist leaders regarded laws as antiquated bourgeois tools for the preservation of private property, and because they intended to put all real estate under their control, any legal restraints had to be eliminated.

The Party moved quickly to eliminate counter-revolutionary courts and court officials. On November 22, 1917, Lenin signed a decree abolishing Russia's entire legal system and every profession associated with it. The next year, another decree invalidated all previously existing laws. The Bolsheviks had no time to formulate policies on most legal issues, and new Soviet judges were ordered to make their decisions based on the "socialist sense of justice" (*sotisalisticheskoe pravoszanie*). So-called "people's courts" became the government's legal watchdog. "We need compulsion," Lenin declared. "The organs of the proletarian state in realizing this compulsion are to be the Soviet courts."

Just to make sure that no one escaped judicial review, an additional court system of "revolutionary tribunals" was established to deal with lapses in political correctness. Isaac Steinberg, the first Bolshevik Commissar of Justice, instructed officials to forget about the law and follow the dictates of "revolutionary conscience," the guidance for which would be provided by Lenin. As an extra precaution against any leftover sense of judicial ethics interfering with the work of the tribunals, the number-one qualification for newly appointed judges was no previous legal experience; the number-two qualification was the ability to read and write.

Yet a disturbing number of no-show cases was undermining the process, and in a get-tough move, Lenin authorized court officials to dispense with formalities, such as the requirement that plaintiffs and defendants actually appear in court. When that didn't improve attendance, Lenin had another idea. If citizens wouldn't come to court, the courts would come to the citizens. Extraordinary powers, including the license to kill, were given to Cheka, the first official state goon squad. Later, those powers were passed on to the KGB, which controlled the Soviet legal system with cold-blooded efficiency.

Given what was going on behind the scenes in most Soviet legal proceedings, it's easy to see why lawyers, particularly in criminal cases, had a hard time being advocates. If a client was accused of a crime by the state, and his attorney tried to defend him, he could find himself being charged as an accomplice. No wonder there aren't any Russian Perry Masons. That also explains why so few Soviet law students plan on careers as public defenders, a misnomer if there ever was one. Most defense attorneys were informers whose real job was to pry information from their clients and then turn it over to the KGB. Now, with the reformed spy agency cutting back its telephone bugs by a reported one-third, lawyers could become even more valuable as a source of pre-trial intelligence.

Civil laws, the type most foreign businessmen will have to contend with, are a little different. Criminal proceedings are cut-and-dried compared to figuring out which rules, proclamations, and decrees apply in a given business situation. The reason is elementary. Starting with the Bolsheviks, government policies have rarely been codified into laws. A codified law, by definition, is on the books, and the state should at least pretend to heed it. Soviet leaders solved that possible inconvenience by keeping all laws vague, indefinite, and virtually impossible to find.

Arthur Davis, a law professor from Long Island University, made his first trip to the Soviet Union in 1989 to help an American client draw up a partnership agreement with a Moscow entertainment company. Predictably, negotiations bogged down the first day over a Soviet legal requirement. When Davis asked to see the citations of the law, a dismayed Soviet lawyer, representing the entertainment company, had no idea what he was talking about.

"*Citations,*" Davis repeated. "You know, the written record of what the law is."

"Oh, that," said the Soviet attorney, who produced a six-month-old copy of *Izvestia,* the former government-run newspaper that published official announcements of all the new would-be laws.

After hearing a translation of the general provisions, Davis wanted to know more. But the Soviet attorney told him the legislature had yet to make its "clarification," a process that can take years to complete. Before a policy can be clarified, the lawyer explained, it first has to be put into practice to see if it works.

"It was crazy," said Davis. "The government doesn't want to embarrass itself by passing laws that don't make sense, so it tests them. In the meantime, people can be prosecuted for breaking a law that may never be adopted. . . . *Brilliant.* Kafka would have been proud."

Soviet lawyers may not be the most useful legal guides, but when you're doing business in a country whose legal system is this messed up, Western lawyers can be even less helpful. The prestigious Washington law firm of Arnold & Porter was among the pioneers in providing legal advice in the Soviet Union. The firm took on a group of Soviet lawyers as its joint-venture partner and devised a plan that made perfect sense on paper. The cost of its Moscow office would be paid in rubles from income generated from Soviet clients; the hard-currency profits from Western clients would go to Arnold & Porter. But once the Soviets had the business cards of a prestigious American law firm, there was no way to stop them from attracting their own clientele and pocketing the money. Since Soviet banks have yet to institute checking accounts, payment was always in cash and Arnold & Porter was none the wiser as to how much of it their partners were keeping.

Some Russian lawyers try to rationalize their rip-off schemes by pleading need. Because the law is only in an embryonic state, they can't really market legal opinions. So what's left to do but trade on their contacts? Besides, why should they be content with a mere salary while their American partners and their foreign clients stand to make sizable fortunes?

A major U.S. company got its first taste of local billing practices when it approached a legal consulting group, called INFEX, an offshoot of Arnold & Porter's Moscow operation. INFEX officials and representatives from the American company met for lunch to discuss working together on several projects. Much political discussion ensued as the Moscow consultants tried to impress their hosts with their regulatory know-how and high-level access. It was no different than a power lunch anywhere in corporate America, only here even the sales pitch had a price tag, which became clear when the meal was finished and someone from INFEX asked, "Where should we send the invoice?"

"What invoice?" the American said. The Russian responded by saying, "You owe us $500 for the time we spent at lunch." Soviets may have a lot to learn about finesse, but their urge to get paid is never in doubt.

In a society in which laws either don't exist or are in constant conflict, the notion of retaining a lawyer, in the Western sense, would be a waste of money. Smart shopping is an absolute must in finding an attorney who won't end up selling you rumors and bogus theories as $250-an-hour legal advice.

Trust your instinct. Whether you're exploring potential markets or looking for a joint-venture partner, a good Soviet lawyer should help speed up the process, not slow it down. Beware of attorneys who have nothing to offer but promises and never stop telling you about all the things that *can't* be done.

Trust your wallet. When people need a lawyer, it's usually because they're feeling economically vulnerable. Don't compound the problem by hiring a thief. Soviet lawyers, like lawyers everywhere, are in the business of selling mystery to make money. Make them earn it by producing verifiable results.

Trust the record. The American legal system is based on precedents. In the former Soviet Union, the only precedents are in the KGB archives, not exactly the best source of sound legal advice. Any lawyer selling worthwhile information should be able to supply you with references from Western companies and a list of contacts in the foreign community. If that's a problem, or things don't check out, it's *dasvidonya* time.

The most important legal questions facing Westerners involved in Soviet enterprises center around money and—if the money happens to be rubles—what to do with it. Although foreigners are allowed to *earn* rubles, there are laws that strictly limit how many they can *own* and how they can use them. Those laws are changing, but the banks and security agencies still carefully monitor what foreigners do with their revenues, both dollars and rubles.

As we've shown, transferring rubles from bank to bank or withdrawing them from a company or personal account can take months of planning. One way of speeding up the process is fictitious contracts. In fact, conducting business anywhere in the former Soviet Union would be impossible without them. Everyone, including bankers, knows about the practice, but it works so well, why stop it? Russian lawyers probably draw up more false contracts than real ones, and a transaction that occurred in late 1991 shows how the game is played.

Two Moscow entrepreneurs, Dimitri and Vlodya, wanted to buy condensed automobile paint from a company in Detroit, and then sell it to Russian paint stores. The price of the paint was

$20,000, but Dimitri and Vlodya had only rubles. That problem was solved when Vlodya found an organization in Moscow willing to lend them the money in exchange for eight million rubles from the expected profits. But neither of the two Russian partners could legally own dollars, so a fake contract was written to show that the loan was for rubles only.

That done, they carried the dollars out of the country and bought the paint in Detroit. However, to avoid import duties and possible problems on their return, they needed another fake contract to show Soviet authorities that the paint was paid for with rubles, not dollars, and another one with a second Russian firm entitled to have hard currency, showing that *it*, and not Dimitri and Vlodya, had bought the American paint for dollars. Russian law prohibits rubles from being taken out of the country.

Everybody connected with the paint deal broke the law, and everyone also profited. It's interesting to note that the $20,000 worth of condensed automobile paint, after it was liquified, had a value of more than 40 million rubles, or approximately $800,000 on the black market.

But the story doesn't end there. Once the money started coming in, Dimitri and Vlodya began to quarrel. Seeing as how Vlodya found the loan to buy the paint, he no longer wanted to share the profits with Dimitri under the fifty-fifty terms of their partnership agreement. Dimitri insisted that the contract be honored, but Vlodya refused, telling him, if he kept demanding an equal split, he wouldn't get anything.

That's when Dimitri hired members of the Azerbaijani mafia and sent them to deal with Vlodya. The plan backfired, though, after Vlodya promised to pay them more money than Dimitri had. With the mafia hit squad now working for his partner, Dimitri was forced to negotiate. Vlodya called off the rough stuff, and the two worked out a settlement. Just to prove they were serious, they drew up still another contract.

The official name for the kind of business relationship Dimitri and Vlodya had is a "cooperative." Unlike U.S. cooperatives, which are usually associations of people or private companies

joined together to buy things at discount prices, Soviet cooperatives, which became legal under Mikhail Gorbachev in 1988, are
just the opposite. They were created as a substitute for private
companies. Co-ops are essentially corporations without stock that
charge their customers the highest prices they can. A cooperative
is a little like a capitalist collective in which everyone supposedly
shares equally in the benefits and profits—yet, as the story of
Dimitri and Vlodya suggests, the division of wealth is not always
easy.

Originally set up to create a legitimate form of competition
for the illegal black market, many of the early co-ops were fi-
nanced or infiltrated by the KGB, at first to keep track of rich
Soviets, and later, when new laws allowed co-ops to deal in hard
currency, to monitor their financial contact with foreigners. This
arrangement not only enabled the spy agency to add earned
profits to the payoffs it was already collecting, but to be in a
position to skim from incoming foreign investments.

The laws governing co-ops, which have never been easy to
follow, left them at the mercy of the government if they become
too independent, and of their own partners if they become too
successful. Owing to the competitive nature of Soviet business and
the Russian impulse to seize authority, contention, not cooperation, generally characterizes co-op behavior. Co-op coups, the
Soviet answer to hostile takeovers, are widespread. Sometimes
unwanted partners are pushed out with the help of government
agencies that get an extra bribe for taking the side of the over-
thrower, and sometimes the agencies themselves stage the coups,
creating what Russians call "officially sanctioned" co-ops as a
result.

As soon as the cooperative movement was born, it ran into
trouble, and not just from the KGB and corrupt officials attracted
by the lure of easy money. At the same time cooperatives were
being held up as proof that perestroika was working, the government was doing everything it could to undermine them. Strict
rules kept co-ops out of fields like communications and medicine,
and state industry bosses did everything they could to take away

their freedom and absorb them back into the official economy. Cooperatives were on the cutting edge of a revolution few understood, but anyone could see they were encroaching on some very important and well-guarded turf.

Along with all of the other groups opposed to them, the co-ops made particular enemies of the nomenklatura, the Communist Party's ruling establishment, whose wealth and power would be threatened by an independent merchant class. Taking advantage of regulations they helped create, nomenklatura policymakers initially sought to bring co-ops under the influence of state commissions. They denied co-ops access to bank loans, imposed price limits on co-op products, and ordered "health inspections" on co-op restaurants as a pretext for closing them down. The nomenklatura was also able to alter tax laws relating to co-ops, have their licenses reviewed, and keep their legal status constantly up in the air.

But following an old communist tradition, the nomenklatura didn't content itself merely with bureaucratic methods to thwart co-ops. It encouraged a high-profile campaign of violence. Profitable businesses were firebombed and sprayed with bullets. Fortified by *Pravda*'s constant reference to co-ops as "wheeler-dealers and scoundrels," teams of police thugs killed cattle and sheep, burned down co-op farms and stores, and beat up co-op managers.

In addition to organized assaults by nomenklatura henchmen, jealous citizens began attacking co-ops in their communities. Friends turned against their co-op neighbors, calling them *capitalisti* and destroying one cooperative after another. At the height of the mayhem in 1990, sections of Moscow and St. Petersburg were turned into business war zones, as the co-ops, police gangs, and just plain folks fought it out round the clock. In Azerbaijan, state collective farms waged wars on co-ops that left hundreds dead and entire enterprises in ruins.

It was nasty business made all the more nasty by the concentrated envy of the working class, which accused co-ops of buying scarce food and reselling it at prices no semi-honest citizen could afford. New cars, new clothes, everything identified with success in the co-op business was an insult to the masses. The better cooperatives got at beating the system, the more official and unofficial resentment they caused.

In the midst of all this, another new industry was born. Seeing the need for private protection, Soviet entrepreneurs set up security co-ops. One that developed a long and impressive list of clients was a cooperative that went by the name of ALEX. Started by ex-policeman Valentin Kozakov, ALEX, by 1990, employed over a hundred men and women specially trained to protect new businesses.

On the low end of the trade were the mafia and other enterprising groups that didn't know the first thing about preparing business proposals, but saw an opportunity to profit from the rising rate of crime against co-ops. Instead of looking for customers who needed protection, they *created* them. With restaurants being bombed and co-op factories burned to the ground, the protection market was booming. Russian godfathers took the direct approach. If a co-op manager wouldn't pay protection or agree to take on mafia partners, rather than break his legs to teach him a lesson, thugs blew up his business.

In Moscow, a mafia boss explained the general thinking among his peers about their ongoing scorched-earth policy. The mafioso, in his standard black shirt and black leather sports jacket, took a thoughtful drag on a Marlboro and said, "Business is just starting in this country. And from now on, everyone will know not to fuck with us. The customers we burn out are our *investment* in the future."

As for all of those KGB agents who bugged telephones, beat up dissenters, and generally made life miserable for everybody, many of them are looking for work, and, given their talents, most would be right at home in the protection business. Even security officials admitted that ex-agents could pose a serious crime problem. While the spy agency is being reorganized into dozens of smaller KGBs, special care will need to be taken, they said, to make sure that "bad-guy" types are reemployed in the government, where their activities can be closely monitored.

"The policy of the present bosses is that these people should not be made pariahs," Russian foreign intelligence official Vyacheslav Ivanovich Artymov told *The New York Times*. "If you force them into tight corners, people with those skills could join all sorts of mafias."

But the new Russian government faces a major task in locating interesting and rewarding jobs for thousands of surplus agents, many of whom will no doubt find the financial lure of the private sector too much to resist. Then what? Soviet authorities can expect a marked increase in big-money crime directed against foreign companies, and they can expect it to be committed by some very well-trained criminals.

For most Soviet businesses, the best protection from the government and the mafia has always been a foreign partner, and once co-ops were legally allowed to trade in hard currency, many took on outside investors as an insurance policy against unwanted intervention. But until recently, any foreigners investing in Soviet business ventures were legally limited to minority-partner status. That changed in 1991, when joint-stock company laws were passed that allowed foreigners to own 100 percent of any legally licensed business—a step that almost guaranteed the disappearance of many Soviet co-ops. Another important feature of the new legislation was that it redefined the relationship between joint-venture partners by providing buy-out provisions in case the Soviet side doesn't perform as promised, which is often the case.

For obvious reasons, few Soviet businessmen thought the latest changes in the law would benefit them, and many have taken steps to protect themselves. One method has been to set up their own foreign companies. Although most are no more than a bank account and a mail drop, the address of the "home office" is usually enough to keep Soviet authorities from interfering. A number of Russian entrepreneurs have started shadow businesses in the United States for just that purpose. As the sole representatives of their own American businesses, they're protected by U.S. laws, and also eligible for privileges only available to foreigners. One of these is regular briefings by the American embassy on the latest business legislation. And with the Soviet "war of laws" in full swing, there's no such thing as being too well informed on legal developments.

In the United States, the situation might be referred to as states' rights versus the federal government, or city ordinances versus state laws. But in Russia and the other former republics, it's much more complicated than that. With each new government developing its own set of laws, often in conflict with one another, the legal environment is as unpredictable as an Aeroflot departure schedule. When former President Zvaid Gamshakhurdia of Georgia was campaigning for office in that republic's first free elections, his popularity shot up when he insisted that the legislature pass a law forbidding Georgians to marry non-Georgians. The law failed, but Gamshakhurdia was elected.

There are autonomous regions with their own laws, ethnic and religious enclaves with theirs, and cities and towns with laws of their own. This recent development is the result of shifting political power and vested interests among the various centers of authority. But for a people who have always had one source of legal authority, the experience is brand new, and contracts judged valid in one place may be invalid someplace else.

It's not hard to see why fake contracts are so popular once you find out what can happen to real ones. Unfamiliar with the concept of contract law, the attitude of an alarming number of Soviets is that all contracts are made to be broken or at least renegotiated. Recognizing their inexperience in business, most will eventually question the wisdom of any business contracts they sign. It can happen after the first major foreign investment is made, or after the first profits are made, but it almost always happens—and when it does, renegotiations will teach you why they called it the Cold War.

To put the best face on the maneuver, Soviets may suggest that certain government policies have changed and that in order to stay in compliance with the law the contract will also have to be changed. Or they might say they misunderstood the deal and were expecting more money. There may be charges of deception or accusations about the integrity of the foreign partner, both common renegotiation tactics.

In the aftermath of a 1991 lawsuit, one Soviet business tried everything it could think of to get out of a contract. When a small Moscow film company won a case in New York against Merchant Ivory Productions for nonfulfillment of a distribution contract, the Russians were awarded a judgment in rubles. But their attorneys, the blue-chip law firm of Phillips Nizer, had a contract stipulating that legal fees would be paid in dollars. Instead of converting rubles to dollars and paying the lawyers, the Russians tried to avoid paying them anything. First, company officials claimed that because the award had been in rubles, the legal fees should be paid in rubles. Next, they said they never signed a contract with Phillips Nizer. After a copy of the agreement signed by the company's president was produced, they said it needed the signature of another company official to be valid.

When the Russians' American agent advised that it would be better to negotiate a payment schedule than to waste time trying to deny any money was owed, they sent him a fax saying, "We are surprised by your attitude to the problem. However, we believe this question should be discussed in person." Months later, after several meetings between film company and agent—meetings paid for in hard currency by the agent—steps were finally taken to address the payment problem.

To develop some measure of protection from their Soviet partners, more and more joint-venture contracts are being drawn up under non-Soviet laws, and usually contain provisions for mandatory arbitration outside of the Soviet Union in the event of a dispute. Two frequently used arbitration sites are Sweden and Switzerland, partly because they are politically neutral countries with a history of fairness, and partly because Soviets can easily travel there.

But even this safeguard can end up costing the foreign partner. Every Soviet loves the opportunity to travel abroad, and a business disagreement is as good an excuse as any for a trip to Western Europe, particularly when it's at company expense. Because trips abroad cost hard currency, the foreign partner can win the arbitration and still get soaked for travel costs.

As Soviet laws change, taxes and other revised assessments will keep everyone busy trying to figure who owes what. Soviet tax policy is being changed constantly, and rates vary for businesses that deal in hard currency and soft currency. Like adjustable-rate mortgages in the United States, Soviets have adjustable-rate taxes, and no one can be sure who's doing the adjusting, or when it will occur. What's clear is that whenever the government doesn't collect enough rubles in tax revenue, it simply prints more, thereby creating hidden inflationary taxes that make the tax rates irrelevant—except for foreigners who get hit coming and going.

The base Russian business tax rate hovers between 30 and 40 percent, but additional special assessments on earnings can lead to a total tax bite of nearly 70 percent. If revenues are in hard currency, the government takes an extra helping, and foreign exchange banks also get their cut for handling any overseas transactions. Soviet lawyers are of little help when it comes to fighting off taxes. Fortunately, however, this is one area in which a shrewd Soviet partner can lead the way. Avoiding taxes has developed into an arcane Soviet business science, and the right partner can save you a bundle.

To understand the confusion inherent in the legal system, one need only notice how traffic laws are enforced. Soviets of all nationalities treasure their cars. The cost of a Russian automobile equals about ten years' salary—not a terrible inconvenience in that the waiting list is ten years long, too. Maybe the long delay is what turns Soviet drivers into kamikazes when they finally get behind the wheel. Whatever the cause, even the most suicidal among them control their impulses on streets where traffic cops might be lurking. A Soviet policeman merely waves his famous white baton and drivers come to a screeching halt.

Because the enforcement of many traffic laws is subject to the mood of each individual officer, the driver's first reaction is usually to deny any guilt. His second is to offer a bribe to the cop, who, depending on the weather and his personal supply of vodka, will frequently settle the issue on the spot.

The only vehicles that escape the police are those bearing the license plates of government officials. Traffic laws don't apply to these special motorists, and they drive wherever they like, including the sidewalk, where they scatter pedestrians and occasionally run over a few.

That's how life is for elite members of the ruling class, and it's changed very little since the communists lost power, or for that matter, since the days of the czars. They make laws, then ignore them, and when they want to get somewhere in a hurry, they just step on the gas—and drive off the road.

Chapter Nine

Dealers' School

For years, the Moscow State Institute of Foreign Relations, better known by its Russian initials MGIMO, was the Soviet Union's answer to Harvard and Yale. It was the pinnacle of communist higher education, and one of the best available tickets for trips out of the country. Founded in the mid-1940s as an academic arm of the Foreign Ministry, the school at the height of the Cold War was producing some of the top spies in the business.

In the days before perestroika, any student who got into MGIMO had to have his or her credentials in perfect order. Komsomol membership was an absolute must; so were good grades, a proven commitment to the ideals of Marxism, and the right connections: parents who were major Party figures, government leaders, or union bosses. Freshman selected to enter MGIMO were used to special treatment, and that's exactly what they got for the next five years.

The curriculum was a combination of normal academic subjects and classes in scientific communism—a series of required courses, as one graduate put it, "where you sat and listened to some old Party slave tell you how communism deter-

127

mined the outcome of everything since the beginning of time."

In Western universities, students are encouraged to argue and ask questions. Soviet universities, in the days of Khrushchev and Brezhnev, were a little different. Students were expected to memorize information and store it away for instant recall. To argue or ask questions were sure signs of an academic career—and an entire life—destined for failure.

Alexander Romanov, a Moscow trade consultant and a 1977 MGIMO graduate, remembered his first course in scientific communism. Romanov, whose father had been a member of the Soviet delegation to the United Nations, attended private schools in New York City, and nothing he'd learned there prepared him for the rigors of MGIMO.

"The first assignment was to read an essay by Lenin," he said. "So I came in the next day all ready to say what I got out of it, the same way you do in America. The teacher called on one student, and he just repeated what was in the essay. Man, I thought, this guy's in trouble. But the teacher loved it. The next student did the same thing. The teacher loved that, too.

"Then, it was my turn, and I started saying what I thought of the essay, that some parts of it were interesting and some parts didn't make sense. By the time I finished, everybody in class was looking down at the floor and the teacher was staring at me, pissed out of his mind. 'What do you call that?' he said. At first, I couldn't think of anything. Finally, I told him, 'My opinion ... I guess.' And he said, 'You don't have any opinions in *this* class, comrade.' "

It was a rude introduction to a learning process designed to produce the exact opposite of students who think for themselves. But Romanov and his well-connected classmates soon discovered that they had more power than their teachers—a lot more. One complaint to the director from an important parent and some lowly instructor could find himself out of a job.

Another MGIMO alumnus, who also graduated in the seventies, recalled having to take a compulsory course in military training that included a lot of rope climbing and push-ups. "One day, nobody wanted to do the exercises. When the teacher, this poor

Army captain, insisted, people just said, 'Fuck you, man.' That was that. We were Party brats with big-shot fathers, and he knew it."

The most successful students in Soviet colleges weren't the smartest, but the most arrogant—people with the nerve to boss around their teachers, part of whose job it was to serve as batting practice for future Party leaders. It's a Soviet tradition for parents to pamper their children—sometimes giving them an allowance well into middle age—and having more parental oversight than most colleges, MGIMO offered its students the works. In addition to enjoying the comparatively pleasant surroundings of a campus on the outskirts of Moscow, they were the recipients of free tuition, free room and board, draft deferments, and monthly stipends of 130 rubles, at one time more than half the wages of an average Soviet worker.

It wasn't a bad life when you considered how bad life in the Soviet Union could be. The state may have been an instrument of organized repression, but MGIMO students weren't the ones being repressed. Far from it. In terms of care and maintenance, it didn't get much better than this.

For graduates who were dedicated to the Party, or pretended to be, MGIMO was a gateway to the good life, highlighted by careers as diplomats, translators, and journalists—all professions of choice in the international community of Soviet espionage agents.

Many MGIMO grads were directly recruited to work for the KGB (where some, paired together to pose as husband-and-wife spy teams, met their mates); others joined the foreign service as embassy press secretaries and cultural attachés. But no matter what they ended up doing, or where they ended up doing it, their first overseas assignment was always intelligence gathering.

Then, in the mid-1980s, things at MGIMO began to change. Under the influence of the KGB's stepped-up program of spying on foreign businesses, the school offered courses to prepare students to enter the world of commerce. As Western companies expanded their Soviet operations, the authorities needed to know what they were up to. In order to make sure they did, bilingual

MGIMO graduates were planted in joint-venture offices to obtain information on everything from cash flow to long-range corporate planning. Firm believers in the theory that foreign languages are the key to knowledge, power, and industrial secrets, the KGB at one point had MGIMO teaching forty-eight of them, including several obscure African dialects, just in case there was a native tribe somewhere with information worth stealing.

The infiltration process was simple. Before any outside firm could do business in the Soviet Union, it had to submit the names of its Soviet workers to KGB headquarters for approval. Officials then merely added some of their own people to the list and started collecting data. When a 1990 presidential decree authorized KGB agents to examine the financial records of foreign companies (and of Soviet companies trading with foreigners), businessmen criticized the policy as an unwarranted intrusion by the government. Little did most of them know that the visits were often a way of double-checking figures the KGB already had. With informers in every business—and most of them still there—the giant spy network had more data at its disposal than the IRS. Of particular interest to investigators were the hard-currency profits made by Soviet partners in joint ventures. With the KGB getting payoffs as high as 20 percent, it was important to make sure that every dollar earned was accounted for.

Through most of the 1980s, MGIMO continued to produce its share of new snoops. But by the end of the decade, with Party membership on the decline and the KGB laying off employees, few students could see any future in spying. One MGIMO graduate, fed up with life in the KGB, said it took him three years to quit—not three years to work up the nerve, but three years just to get the agency to accept his resignation.

"I couldn't stand it anymore. You had to report every contact you had with foreigners, especially with foreign businessmen. Once an American asked me what time it was on the Moscow Metro, and I reported it. That was bad enough, but when my supervisor congratulated me, it made me feel like shit.

"I can't remember how many times I wrote, asking them to let me go," he said. "After a while, I assumed, somebody probably decided it made more sense to get rid of me than pay me to keep writing letters. After I left, two special agents followed me for years. . . . Nobody ever accused the KGB of being cost effective."

Brought up in a world of unearned wealth and privilege, MGIMO students were witnessing the collapse of a system they had been taught was the source of all rewards. But at the same time, theirs was the first generation of young Soviets spoiled enough to ignore the Party and look beyond small-change payoffs, bribes, and special favors to the much bigger rewards Western businesses had to offer.

Traditionalists by training, but reformers when it came to seizing economic opportunities, MGIMO students were grumbling for the type of training foreign companies looked for. After much internal debate, the administration slowly responded by deemphasizing courses in scientific communism and introducing new ones with a more practical appeal. Soon the most popular classes on campus were management, accounting, and free-market economics, a few even taught by visiting professors from the United States.

In the spring semester of 1991, the school presented a series of lectures on Mass Media and American Popular Culture that played to standing-room-only crowds. In one session, students studied magazines such as *Rolling Stone, Vanity Fair,* and *Playboy,* the latter for sale on the local black market for the equivalent of three months' salary. In the past, just bringing that kind of reading material into the building would have been enough to get arrested. But no one was there to discuss the stories. Instead, they analyzed the ads. Perfume scent strips, which none of the students had ever seen before, caused the most interest. The only aroma Soviet publications leave behind is the whiff of low-grade paper and ink.

MGIMO has been through a "cultural revolution" in the opinion of Yuri Dubinin, the deputy rector. "Not the kind American colleges had in the 1960s, but for us the effects have been just as dramatic." In the year following the coup attempt, the student body still drew heavily on the children of former government officials. But the campus and the curriculum were completely changed from what they had been in the old days. Hard-line faculty members found their positions eliminated and their courses consigned to the dustbin of the history department. Money, not Marxism, became the new school motto, and even before all the Lenin pictures were taken down, the place had been transformed into a post-communist replica of an MBA mill.

From a socialist standpoint, the failed coup turned a communist-controlled learning environment into a communist dictator's worst nightmare. One of the side effects at MGIMO, once an intellectual beacon to junior Marxists everywhere, was a mass exodus of foreign students. Cuba, Libya, North Korea, and Vietnam all wanted their young scholars returned immediately.

Disturbed by earlier signs of creeping capitalism, other leftist regimes had ordered their students home years earlier. One former MGIMO instructor told what it was like driving a group of Ethiopians to the airport after their government had issued a recall notice. "None of the Ethiopians wanted to leave," he said. "But back then, the Soviet Union wasn't in the habit of giving political asylum to refugees from other communist countries. A lot of them were crying when they got on the plane. It was a pretty sad sight. I heard later that a few were shot for exhibiting anti-Marxist behavior."

But today, no one at MGIMO wants to bring up the past. "Students have much broader horizons now than they did before," said Dubinin, whose own career at the Institute began in 1975. "The best jobs used to be with the Foreign Ministry. Now they're with foreign companies. Our graduates have always wanted to work outside the country. The difference today is that they don't have to hide what their real motives are. If I had to choose a phrase to describe how things have changed at MGIMO, I'd say that everyone now is more self-oriented."

Some observers of Soviet higher education might say that's impossible. In fact, college students in the Soviet Union, particularly those at elite institutions like MGIMO, have always been "self-oriented." So much so, they were accused as a group of sitting out the second Russian Revolution.

When the communists were deposed in Hungary, East Germany, and Czechoslovakia, students were in the thick of the action. In the Soviet Union, it was just the reverse. Although many of those manning the barricades during the three-day standoff at the Russian parliament building were young guitar-playing radicals, the real political activists were men and women in their forties, fifties, and sixties—people who got a brief taste of free expression during the Khrushchev years and then had it snatched away when Leonid Brezhnev came to power. If you want to talk reform politics in the Soviet Union, you don't, as a rule, hang out with conservative college kids.

"Most of us prefer to put our energies into economic activity," said a Moscow engineering student. "Maybe that's political because it helps the entrepreneurial system. In any case, it's more profitable for us to struggle for our own prosperity than for political miracles." There was a time when no Soviet would ever admit that his major career goal was getting rich. These days, it's hard to find anyone over the age of seventeen who doesn't.

To point students in the right direction, MGIMO recently started a mutual training project with the Price Waterhouse accounting firm. In principle, the program works like an old Soviet cultural exchange, only the objective isn't spreading propaganda, it's making a profit. The arrangement enables Price Waterhouse to learn about doing business in Russia by drawing on MGIMO's familiarity with the system, while it allows MGIMO students to spend time, with pay, out of the country, polishing their skills at company headquarters.

The Price Waterhouse London office, which first came up with the idea, saw it as a chance to train its own Moscow staff, while it positioned itself to capitalize on a growing demand for its services. Accounting is a wide-open field in the former Soviet Union, and the fact that many people still add and subtract with an abacus gives outside firms a clear advantage over local competition. Since the communists taught that all money "belonged to the people," bookkeeping was one of those professions they never tried to encourage. Embezzling funds was their specialty, not keeping track of them.

That's hardly the case anymore, with the communists out of power and the government broke. As the great patron of Marxist learning, the Kremlin had always been happy to pick up the tab for education. But with the Party dissolved and current budget planners desperate for hard currency, there's now serious talk of charging tuition—starting at the top. As a possible preview of what's in store for everyone, MGIMO, in 1991, enrolled eight Americans at $5,000 apiece. For the privileged few, the time has come to put runs on the scoreboard.

Designed to serve the needs of the Party, special Soviet colleges for decades produced welfare-dependent graduates totally unprepared to survive in a competitive setting. "Golden youth" they were called. Living the closest thing to a charmed life that anyone could in the Soviet Union, they got all the free breaks, and never faced a serious challenge from anybody—that is, until now.

On one side of the newest class struggle are the MGIMO-trained sons and daughters of the nomenklatura. On the other side is a new generation of upstarts, who have begun their own businesses from scratch, and who are determined to remake the economy by sheer hustle.

It's interesting that many of the new moguls who run Moscow's brokerage firms and consulting agencies didn't even go to college. They grew up on pirated rock music, without the benefit of Party parents and Party perks. Now they're the ones running rings around everybody. Picture the "Dead End Kids" not just controlling Wall Street, but starting it, and that's essentially what's going on in a large part of the new Russian economy.

For the first time, success in the former Soviet Union is no longer an exclusive function of who you know, but how much you know and what you can do with it. No wonder so many young Soviets are confused about their futures. How can five years in college help them take advantage of financial opportunities that may not exist five years from now?

At MGIMO the same worries are heard, accented by an even greater note of anxiety. It's easy to see why. When they enter the suddenly cutthroat job market, many of the offspring of the old upper class will be on their own. And what's worse, they'll have to compete on a level playing field with people who wouldn't have been allowed in the game a few years ago. But then, for all Soviets, these are times full of historic reversals of fortune.

The speed with which they built barricades during the coup attempt proved that Russians are good at piling up junk. Yet how fast they can dig out from under years of Party corruption and mismanagement could depend on the success of a small group of young go-getters who might have been driving cabs if the times hadn't changed so dramatically. Like their MGIMO contemporaries, most are economic conservatives. But in this case, conservatives with a street-wise dedication to making it big, such as 25-year-old Herman Sterligov, college dropout and founder of Moscow's most successful brokerage firm.

Sterligov has become a popular hero, not just because of the wealth he's managed to accumulate, but because of the way he had to fight the old system to do it. "Communists killed everyone and everything they touched," he told *The Washington Post* just before the aborted coup. "This was the richest state in the world and they destroyed it all, down to the bone! Older people don't understand us. Their psychology is all screwed up. They are so used to being equal in poverty that they assume if you have any money you're a crook."

When the junta tried to sieze power, Moscow's stockbrokers dropped everything and joined the resisters. They marched through the streets carrying a giant Russian tricolor and contributed 15 million rubles to buy food for protesters at the barricades. With the junta promising to put them out of business, these self-made capitalists had good reason to be on the front lines. As some of the richest people in the country, they had a lot to lose.

In a strange way, though, many were driven to take up the defense of free enterprise by the same utopian fantasies that inspired the original Bolsheviks to fight for communism. Granted, they were protecting their business interests, but more than a few had bigger things in mind. Besides running his brokerage business, Sterligov, an exemplary go-getter, owns the first Soviet professional hockey team and is working on plans to build an American-style town 150 miles from Moscow. Every house will have a backyard pool, a garage, and a satellite dish on the roof. There will be shopping centers, schools, modern highways, and factories. The fact that this dream town already exists in Northern New Jersey doesn't make it any less of a Tomorrow Land in Russia. The blueprints, however, are still in Sterligov's head.

Unlike a lot of financial dreamers in the Soviet Union, Sterligov has the money to make his projects come true. He earns it in what's become the meeting place for many new free-market capitalists just like him—the Moscow commodities exchange. Here, everything from bricks to computers can be bought, sold, or traded. In May of 1991, the exchange set a seven-month record by doing one billion rubles worth of business. That was over $555 million at the then-going rate.

The last time any Soviet commercial market saw this type of action was in 1988, when Sotheby's, the London auction house, held the first-of-a-kind sale of Russian art in Moscow. Paintings were snapped up at six-figure prices that had even Sotheby's people doing double takes. But Soviet art that was selling in the $300–400,-000 range only a few years ago has taken such a nose-dive that many artists are now willing to accept rubles for their work.

"The worth of Soviet art during the big boom period of the late 1980s was directly related to the times," said Moscow dealer Tanya Kolodzei. "Political repression made the paintings more interesting to buyers and, therefore, more valuable. When the repression was taken away, the demand dropped off and prices went down."

Unlike their Soviet counterparts, commodities markets in the United States and other Western countries often deal in things that don't exist when they're sold—such as pork, wheat, and soybean futures. Futures! For Soviets, the only concern is present reality. For them, nothing else exists but the here and now, and a succession of failed Five-Year Plans has destroyed most people's belief that anything else ever will.

As governments try to create a new economy, commodity exchanges have become like wholesale markets for materials and finished products of every description. What used to be done by Gosplan, the sprawling state agency in charge of allocating supplies that never showed up, is now done more profitably and efficiently by hundreds of private dealmakers.

"This is great," said U.S. Treasury Secretary Nicholas Brady as he toured the Moscow trading floor a month after the coup flopped. That the former capital of communism actually *has* something like this is amazing enough, Brady marveled. That it produces as much money as it does is an economic miracle. The action on the floor, a converted hall in Moscow's central post office, is part yard sale, part Animal House, as brokers in Hawaiian shirts and miniskirts scurry around making deals for things that aren't even supposed to be available: sports cars, airplanes, and sugar by the ton. If it's out there anywhere and has a price tag, it moves on the exchange.

Middlemen, like Sterligov, whose companies make the deals, are in the vanguard of Russia's first wave of newly made millionaires. In anticipation, Sterligov started a Young Millionaires Club two years ago. The entrance requirement is proof of one million rubles in assets. Although the current rate of inflation makes the question of who's in and who's out a matter of constant debate, members *are* sure about one thing: They got where they are on their own.

Still, no one's counting the former communist kids out. For all their rhetoric about a free market, Russian political reformers, many privileged-class products themselves, have done little to create a real one. Aside from higher prices, much of the old economic apparatus remains in place, and with it many of the old corrupt practices of communism.

"At the exchange, you can earn a lot of money quickly and honestly," said Igor Kaminsky, at age 29 the owner of his own brokerage company. "Before, the only way to earn a lot of money quickly was dishonest."

There's a commodities exchange in the predominantly Moslem republic of Azerbaijan, and another in Tyumen, one of the richest oil-producing regions of Siberia. Recently, a group of people in the city of Celenograd, in central Kazakhstan, decided to organize an exchange and phoned a new Moscow consulting company, Organization Management, for help.

Marx and Engels, the co-forefathers of the communist movement, reserved their worst criticism for go-betweens, fixers, and consultants. To Marx, they were the lowest form of human parasite, living off the labor of others and producing nothing but deals and advice. To Engels, the heir to his father's textile business, middlemen were a constant annoyance and added expense. The fact that consulting now happens to be a booming business everywhere in the former Soviet Union is a fitting tribute to the duo whose writings started it all.

"We really began from scratch," said economist Tanya Kletchko, who, along with several of her colleagues, spent a week in Celenograd teaching aspiring brokers how to do business. "On the last day," she said, "we talked about client relations, and used that to get into a subject we always like to stress. We explained to them that honesty is their real capital. Honesty, we tell them, will build trust and give people faith in your business. Everyone understands that honesty is important. But nothing in the old system allowed us to do things in the right way. In school, nobody talked about being honest. And if you brought it up at work, people thought you were crazy."

Then a man raised his hand.

"That's fine," he told the people from Moscow. "But what happens when the money starts coming in?"

"That," Kletchko said, "will be *your* problem."

Back at MGIMO, Yuri Dubinin believes it will be a long time before the legacy of the old regime is fully eliminated. The communists corrupted the moral values of the country so thoroughly, it's almost impossible to think of doing anything in business without first thinking of ways to cheat and steal.

"That tradition has been handed down for four generations, and it won't disappear overnight," Dubinin said. "But it *will* disappear. As new values take hold and new generations grow up knowing that honesty is the best policy, lots of things in this country will change."

A lot of things at MGIMO already have. There's even some discussion about introducing a course in business ethics. "Well, there has been talk about it," admitted Dubinin. At the moment, however, he's having a difficult time finding a teacher.

Chapter Ten

The Man in the Gray Flannel Overcoat

"Condoms," Nebraska businessman Charles Simmons said to a group of Moscow doctors interested in starting a medical-supply company. "Let's open a plant and make condoms."

With a growing AIDS problem and abortions virtually the only reliable means of birth control, Russia would seem like the ideal place to sell prophylactics. But when Simmons began talking about all the money they could make, the doctors suddenly broke out laughing.

"I'm serious," he said. "Seventy percent of the condoms could be sold in Russia and the rest marketed overseas for hard currency." But the laughter only got louder.

Finally, Simmons stopped talking and asked what everyone thought was so funny. "You'll never get Russian men to buy condoms," a psychologist told him. "Our penises are the only private property we have in this country, and we're not going to hide them."

The doctors weren't kidding. The lack of private ownership caused many problems in the Soviet Union. This one, however, has to be the *most* private of them all. In a country in which everything, in theory, once belonged to "the people," the average citizen has little to call his own.

Privatization is supposed to change that by breaking the cardinal rule of Marxism and transferring ownership from the state to the individual. Yet, with no tradition of private property to fall back on for guidance, and special-interest groups such as segments of the still-powerful nomenklatura doing everything they can to delay total reform until they can exploit it, the process could take years before it even gets started.

The history of private ownership in the Soviet Union could be written on the back of a matchbook cover, assuming you could find a book of matches in the current rash of shortages. For centuries, Russian serfs, a universal symbol of hard luck, were considered the property of wealthy landlords. During the empire, all real estate in Russia technically belonged to the czar, and people occupied space by his consent. After the Bolsheviks seized power in 1917, farms were collectivized, capitalism became a crime, and what little private property that did exist was appropriated by the state.

Today, most new Soviet leaders agree that, in addition to Western money, only two things can save their crumbling economy: a free market and private property. Nearly every former republic now allows some form of both. A Soviet businessman can own his own company, form a partnership or a joint venture, or become a participant in a cooperative. Most of these concepts are less than five years old, and laws that govern them, to the extent that laws govern anything, are constantly being revised.

The historic lack of private property and the slow pace of conversion in most republics have contributed to a continuing economic malaise that newcomers from the West often find hard to believe. Soviets see no point in working longer or harder if they can't improve their living standards by doing it. And as those standards gradually worsen, few have the means or the incentive to maintain their present level of existence, let alone escape the pull of downward mobility.

Traditionally, the only way to advance in the Soviet system

has been to gain political power or to accumulate easily transportable luxury items—such as jewelry, cars, or foreign currency—for sale on the black market. But for the average Soviet tied to a poverty-line paycheck and trapped in an environment of deteriorating apartment buildings, roads, and factories, the prospects of owning anything of value, much less translating that ownership into a better life, is an unaffordable dream.

Consider the living conditions of typical Soviets and how privatization would affect them. In the United States, a man's home, as the saying goes, is his castle. In Russia, a man's home is usually more like a rented prison cell, and a dilapidated prison cell at that. Trash-filled hallways, broken elevators, and an overcrowded one-room flat are what most Soviets are forced to call home.

Asked why he let garbage accumulate in the corridor outside his apartment, a man in the Kievskaya section of Moscow offered this explanation: "It's not my garbage. It's not my corridor, either. Why should I bother to clean up?" As his anger intensified, he got more to the point. "The government built this pile of shit, and they can throw me out anytime they want. Let *them* clean it up. Besides, if we make this building too clean, some big shot will tell us to leave so he can move in. Then where would I take my family?"

Unable to own her apartment, a single mother in Vladimir had another complaint. Although divorced, she still shared a small flat with her former husband and his occasional lovers. When the communists were in power, the government officially allocated eleven square meters of living space to each person. That's about the size of a walk-in closet. If a family got bigger, it was entitled to more space, although it rarely got it. If it got smaller, it might be forced to move to tinier quarters, a threat that over the years has led to many strange living arrangements.

"I want privacy, at least for my daughter," the woman in Vladimir said. "How can I raise a child with any values under these conditions? Sometimes when my ex-husband's girlfriends aren't ready to leave, I make them tea so they know when it's finished it's time to go. Is this any way to live?"

One of their first priorities, some reformers say, is the privatization of homes—not out of human concern but economic necessity. In order to make the ruble convertible and at the same time avoid massive devaluation, the government must first eliminate so-called ruble overhang, the term used to describe the hidden personal savings of millions of Soviets that account for an estimated 400 billion dormant bank notes. One method favored in the past to deplete this secret stash was an "instant recall," a surprise government swap of new bills for old ones. But with the central bank printing more paper money than ever—in August of 1991, 57.3 billion rubles rolled off the presses—the situation has reached a crisis. How can privatization help? If Soviets were allowed to purchase their apartments, much of the stored cash would be returned to the state and taken out of circulation.

But the masses are understandably suspicious of any new housing policy that might be reversed by local governments the minute they put their money down. And it doesn't help to know they'll have to buy the apartments they now live in—apartments in the same buildings they refused for decades to clean up and repair.

On top of that, there's the question of who gets to profit from the big turnover. The Communist Party, Komsomol, and other organizations were all once big property owners, and they're not about to give up their claim without a fight that could drag on for years. As plans now stand in Russia, privatized apartment buildings won't be sold to individual buyers but to co-operative groups of tenants. But there's a catch. The governing committees of these co-ops will likely be run by the same government bodies that granted tenants the license to privatize, making residents only nominal owners, while transferring the effective control of their jointly owned property from one absentee landlord to another.

Similar to everyone else, the elite nomenklatura, no matter what it's calling itself these days, has been hyperactive in the real-estate market. The once powerful Soviet ruling class is subdividing into competing feudal baronies, and each is busily grabbing up land and buildings with the determination of thousands of die-hard Donald Trumps.

The process began in the early years of perestroika, when Party officials started removing choice property from state records and transferring control to banks, joint ventures, and special committees. Like insider trading on Wall Street, all of this was done in a way that makes privatizing seem more like privateering, which, under many of the reform governments in the cities and republics, is exactly what it's become.

The Russian word for privatization is *razgosudaslenie,* literally meaning "de-state-ization," the transfer of property from the state to private hands. Private ownership is not regarded as a fundamental right, but the "personal expropriation" of government property, which may explain why local city councils, now among the nation's most important land managers, are reluctant to hand over potentially valuable real estate to ordinary citizens.

But they *are* making large pieces of property available to foreign investors willing to renovate or rebuild. Prime locations are available in the center of cities, where offices can be constructed or apartment buildings renovated. Privateering local governments are actively seeking foreign investors and construction companies to rebuild what's left of their municipalities. And to sweeten the pot, they're providing extremely favorable investment terms, provided the councils themselves are cut in as partners, which is the Soviet way of saying: You put up the money and do the work—we'll help collect the profits.

In Russia, Boris Yeltsin's government has granted incredible economic power to mayors and city councils. For example, ex-Moscow Mayor Gavril Popov, a former economist turned politician, was appointed Yeltsin's prefect for the entire Moscow region (population roughly 15 million) and given the authority to control prices, raise taxes, and close businesses, a prerogative Popov was not reluctant to exercise.

When the Raddison Corporation decided to build a hotel in Moscow, it negotiated the original agreement with the Kremlin. But just as the hotel was about to open in 1991, the Moscow city council claimed that because the building was constructed on city land, the council's jurisdiction prevailed, and it would have to be made a partner in the project before the hotel could receive an operating license. The matter was delayed until mid-1992, when it was finally resolved with a limited partnership plan.

A year earlier, the Moscow city council used a variation of the same approach on Pizza Hut. This time it informed the management that its public sanitation facilities were substandard, and closed down the restaurant. Moscow, it should be pointed out, is a city in which public bathrooms consist mainly of holes in the ground (and if you want the luxury of toilet paper, you have to bring your own). It was a classic shakedown. "You will have to satisfy our needs," local officials told the restaurant's director.

Those needs apparently included a renegotiated partnership agreement that already gave the city council 51 percent of the ownership. A quick phone call to Donald Kendall, head of Pep-siCo's executive committee, proved to be the best way to beat city hall. Kendall called Anatoly Dobrynin, former Soviet ambassador to Washington, then an adviser to Mikhail Gorbachev, and Pizza Hut was reopened for business in no time. How many Soviet business ventures, though, have a Donald Kendall to help them ward off sneak attacks by privateering city councils?

Privateering takes a slightly different form in the industrial sector of the economy, which for years has been run by the Soviet military. Although the ideology of communist world domination is now seen as a practical joke by most Soviets, decades of continuous investment and special attention by the Party has left the country's military-industrial complex in the best position to address the nation's changing economic priorities.

But any alterations in the system will first have to be approved by the managers of individual military factories, who make up one of the most powerful groups of people in the country. Still in control of a disproportionate share of budget and resources, they are the ruling class of Soviet industry, and even government leaders pay them homage.

The first steps in converting the military economy began in

1987, and since then, the process has been supervised in typical central-command fashion by various military commissions and the Ministry of Defense. The military has traditionally manufactured many Soviet consumer products, including 95 percent of all radios, video recorders, sewing machines, and televisions. It also produces household appliances such as stoves, refrigerators, and vacuum cleaners; optical lenses; tractors; toys; oil drilling equipment; and kitchen utensils. When the government predicted that by 1995 a total of 60 percent of the country's production capacity would be devoted to consumer items, the idea of developing a civilian sector to make these products wasn't even considered. The job automatically went to the military.

In the United States and other Western countries, most military items are produced by civilian industries. In the Soviet Union, the military controls industrial technology and produces everything it needs, and much more. Imagine what the American economy would be like if General Motors, Boeing, CBS, and other major companies suddenly merged into one giant conglomerate that not only made cars, airplanes, and TV shows, but took part in wars, holiday parades, and coup attempts. That's what the Soviet military did, and its power over the nation's output of goods was staggering.

Yet, despite this concentrated authority, several important roadblocks have interfered with the military's rapid conversion of Soviet industry from a defense to a consumer mode. The most notable among them is the fact that despite its preeminent position—perhaps, in some ways, because of it—the military's management of industry is acutely inefficient. The waste factor alone is mind-boggling. While exact figures are a closely guarded secret, based on the amount of scrap metal, wire, pipes, glass, defective spare parts, and other factory rejects found around most military plants, the total amount of discarded material has to be enormous.

Many of the products that don't reach the scrap heap should have. Take military-made television sets. Soviet televisions, which explode regularly and without warning, are a principal cause of fires in Soviet homes and hotels. Foreign hotel guests, unfamiliar with the threat, are always advised to unplug their TVs when leaving their rooms or going to sleep. The consequences for not doing so can be fatal. An exploding television set was the apparent cause of the deaths of a dozen people in a 1990 St. Petersburg hotel fire.

As for its principal cash product, weapons, let's just say that the military's performance record would not impress *Consumer Reports*. Forces using Soviet arms and the instructions that come with them have suffered five straight defeats between 1967 and 1991.

1. The Six-Day War (Israel and Egypt), 1967
2. The Yom Kippur War (Israel and Egypt), 1973
3. The destruction of Syria's air power in the Bekka Valley (Israel and Syria), 1982
4. The Afghan War (Soviet Union and Afghanistan), 1979–1988
5. The Gulf War (United States and allies and Iraq), 1991

It's no mystery why the Russians agreed to an arms-reduction treaty. With endorsements like these, the only clientele they have left are the Cubans and the North Koreans, and they don't have any money, either.

Even when Soviet spies managed to steal valuable defense industry secrets from the United States and other countries, the military was so lacking in basic know-how, thanks in large part to having captured an inferior batch of German scientists after World War II, that it couldn't even put them to use.

The GRU, the Soviet Army's ubiquitous espionage division, had as one of its missions setting up a garbage company in the Silicon Valley to see what useful information it could find in the trash. Another of its top priorities was analyzing American computerized toys, which were years ahead of some of the Soviets' best military equipment. The fact of the matter is that Western "throw-away" technology is more advanced than much of what the Soviets had, and the longer the arms race continued, the wider the gap would have grown.

To develop consumer products, particularly if they are to be sold on the international market, obviously requires more efficient production techniques and higher quality-control standards than typical Soviet military factories possess. Nonetheless, as badly as they may function, military industries are far superior to their resource-poor civilian counterparts. Which is why the military is in charge of converting the economy to the production of more consumer goods. But the process has actually gone in the *other* direction by transferring many civilian and consumer industries to the direct control of the military.

A detailed account appeared in *Pravda* a few years ago of an instant-potato factory becoming the responsibility of the Ministry of General Machine Building, which specializes in control systems for spacecraft, and the duties of the Ministry of Power and Industry expanding from work on nuclear weapons to include producing dairy-processing equipment.

The results have not been encouraging. There's the rocket factory that couldn't produce sausages as directed; the Ministry of Aviation that failed to meet even 20 percent of its shoemaking-machine quota; and a military plant in St. Petersburg that gave up trying to make electric tea kettles because it was too complicated.

The entire undertaking has the same Marx Brothers quality that characterizes most Soviet efforts at modernization. The Russian weekly *Ogonyok* picked up on the idea, in an article by economist Alexi Kireyev that ridiculed the decision to transfer the manufacture of food-processing equipment to military industries—offering such new names as the Ministry of Aviation and Macaroni and the Ministry of Defense and Ice Cream.

But the cause of the current industrial dilemma isn't just an identity crisis. It's the mental process behind the system itself, a system that attempts at reform have only made worse. The instinctive approach to problem solving in a command economy is to give orders, but the collapse of the old chain of command caused by the demise of the Party and an outbreak of privateering at all levels almost guarantees those orders won't be followed.

Central planning ministries are closing down and commodity

exchanges are opening up. The problem is that the old system is dying faster than the new one can take over, and, until it does, tens of thousands of factory managers have become players in a vast economic crap shoot. In Poland and Hungary, holdover bosses in some factories slated for privatization have declared bankruptcy and tried to pocket the proceeds from liquidation sales. In Russia, where that's not a viable option, managers are keeping plants open by bartering for supplies and making whatever outside profits they can.

Many military industries no longer want to cooperate with defense ministers or any other government officials, except to continue receiving their share of the annual budget. Nor do factory managers want to sell their plants to foreigners, although they *are* ready to talk about doing business.

"We represent the leading industries in the country," said the civilian director of a military plant in St. Petersburg. "We sacrificed our lives to make this nation a superpower. Now everybody's making money but us. We're the professionals, and we won't continue to carry the whole country on our backs for nothing. We want to make money, too."

Like other top officials in the military-industrial complex, the director, let's call him Boris, was once a Party leader. Now all he has is the factory that he and an army general run, for the time being a lucrative asset neither is willing to give up.

"The general and I want to get our money first," Boris said. "But we have to do it before the Americans bring in their high-tech machinery and computers and put us all out of work."

The old Soviet defense industry was funded by the government to produce goods and sell them at prices controlled by the state. Ever since the start of perestroika, though, plant managers have been making hard-currency side deals of their own.

Boris, an affable balding bureaucrat of fifty-eight, laid out a long list of products he could provide, from light bulbs to umbrellas. Despite producing some classic lemons, a few Soviet military plants make first-rate goods, and Boris claimed his factory consistently ranked near the top of the quality charts. But before gearing up for a sophisticated production process, it's much easier, he suggested, just to tap into the country's plentiful reservoir of rejected materials.

"There's tons of scrap metal from military projects to make spare parts for automobiles and other products," he said, flashing a sly smile. "Nobody wants it, and nobody in the government knows what to do with it. So we come along, melt it down, and sell it for nice money." In reality, this was no what-if scenario, but a deal in progress. The St. Petersburg factory was in the middle of privateering a junk transaction with a company from Cleveland that sells decorative brass. And here's where the story gets interesting.

The owner of the Cleveland company, having done business in Russia before, was concerned that the brass Boris and the general had promised might be coming from an illegal source. So, in order to protect himself, just in case the supply might be shut off, he approached another military factory, this one in Moscow, and placed an order for a second shipment of brass. The next day, he learned that the Moscow plant was going to the same source that the factory in St. Petersburg was using. But the Moscow director bragged that a generous bribe had persuaded the suppliers to cancel the St. Petersburg deal and sell the brass to him instead. The man from Cleveland had become the victim of his own backup scheme.

He abruptly ended his dealings with the Moscow plant and went back to St. Petersburg, only to discover that the factory there was unable to make the brass fixtures he wanted; it didn't have enough money to buy the necessary machinery. At this point there was no alternative but to lend the factory the funds it needed and go into business together, although the owner of the Cleveland company made sure to take his partnership interest as a percentage of future sales rather than stock in the new business. That way, it would be harder, he said, for Boris and the general to hide his earnings.

Soviets can be good at hiding things. So good, in fact, that locating and identifying military factories suitable for conversion into commercial enterprises is an art in itself. When William Schneider and a delegation of Ford Aerospace executives were invited to visit the Kirov tank factory in St. Petersburg to discuss buying it for conversion into an automotive assembly plant, they ran into a common problem. Military factories are often classified as "secret," and touring them is not usually permitted. So, the Ford executives, six people in all, spent their time doing everything but seeing the plant they wanted to buy.

The Soviets, who think their military factories are second to none, seem to feel that foreigners should be willing to buy them sight unseen. In part, this attitude reflects the Soviet notion that money is a minor detail. The government had always supplied whatever funds most factories needed, and large American companies should be willing to do the same thing.

Schneider and his group were assured that the site was being readied for commercial production. But whenever they asked to go inside and have a look for themselves, the answer was always *nyet*. Fed up, the Ford executives left the country after ten days without once having set foot in the factory. So much for the military side of privatization.

If you've ever wondered what the American workplace would be like without computers, advanced automation, pollution control, safety regulations, building codes, and a line of products people actually want to buy, look no further than Soviet civilian industries. Non-military factories are like mortuaries attended by demoralized zombies. Consumer items were never high on the government agenda, which may explain why the current facilities for producing them were out of date when the Nazis invaded a half century ago.

These plants *are* being privatized, and most are available for immediate purchase by foreign investors, but this is one case in which it pays to shop around. The best asset a non-military factory has is often its good location, an important factor when it comes to receiving raw materials and transporting the finished product.

Most good Soviet roads are a series of potholes intermittently connected by broken concrete and destroyed asphalt. The bad ones aren't much better than pure mud. Just the same, having a road nearby is an absolute must, in that air freight is virtually nonexistent and the use of trains to carry goods usually means paying regular bribes to entire railroad crews.

Even in a prime location access to raw materials can be problematic. Many ethnic groups will not sell their resources to rival groups, an inconvenience that military industries previously resolved by coercion. With that option no longer open, and ethnic unrest aggravated by the independent spirit of republics that boycott their neighbors, any supply chain is bound to have a few broken links. These links are easily repaired, yet the job almost always necessitates an application of hard currency.

When purchasing or joint-venturing with a non-military factory, consider the workers who come with the property a liability, especially those over thirty years of age. Only the younger generation of Soviets is untainted by socialist doctrine. A large percentage of the over-thirty crowd is either preoccupied with being provided for by the company or plagued by latent health problems related to smoking and chronic alcohol consumption.

As democracy spreads, workers—many believing they're entitled to benefits such as factory-owned vacation resorts—will undoubtedly demand rights that nonsocialist bosses don't see as their responsibility. Under the communists, the labor force was guaranteed cradle-to-grave care and protection, even though those guarantees were never fulfilled. Now, with no one to look after them, workers spend most of their time away from the job—hunting for food, gasoline, and vodka. Having no experience with corporate capitalism's need to make a profit, Soviet employees are likely to be insensitive to the limited resources of a private enterprise, and could resort to strikes to get what they want.

Remember, it was labor unrest in the form of coal miner walkouts in Siberia and Ukraine that brought on hard times for the communists just before they went up in smoke. Worker rallies have a long history in Russia, and you don't want to become the object of anger among your rank-and-file employees. But by paying them a fair wage and throwing in a few perks, as McDonald's experience has shown, you might become a local hero.

Soviet workers are used to being promised the moon, then getting next to nothing. If you follow through on your pledges, no matter how modest, you'll be helping to reverse a legacy of on-the-job deception few thought would ever end, and that can't hurt employee relations or your bottom line.

The value of real money is something most Soviets are just learning to appreciate, and finding ways to keep track of the cash flow will be a challenge for every new factory owner. Soviet managers of civilian industries are not trained in cost accounting, only in methods of manipulation and survival. It's generally assumed that once Westerners acquire a factory, most of the old management will be terminated, which might not be a bad idea. It's much easier to train your own people than to retrain Party functionaries, and departing managers will have no trouble landing jobs as fixers and middlemen in the expanding private sector.

With the increasing sale of state property, go-betweens are turning up everywhere. A population totally lacking in business skills, with nothing to sell but their time and introductions, has suddenly become the most in-demand talent pool in the former Soviet Union. The Russians euphemistically file this type of work under the heading "intangible products," a conditioned nod to Marxist terminology. But at present, the cost effectiveness may not justify the expense. Many top-dollar facilitators lost their real clout when the communists were toppled and their contacts were fired or arrested. The best advice is to choose your advisers wisely.

There's one more industry up for sale: collective farms. Prior to 1917, Russia was a net exporter of food and grain. Following the famine of the 1920s, under Lenin's New Economic Policy, Soviet farmers, some of whom were allowed to work the land as individual proprietors, were so successful that convincing them to join collectives eventually cost millions of lives. Since then, the Soviets have fallen hopelessly behind in agricultural techniques and have spent the last several decades purchasing many basic food products from the West. Today, private farms, while representing less than 5 percent of the land, yield more than 40 percent of the total agricultural output.

Some collective farms set up by Stalin are now being privatized, but interested buyers should exercise extreme caution. These collective farms are not real farms, but outdoor versions of Soviet factories, with all of the same problems, and two more: bad weather and worn-out soil. Collectives were never designed for efficient cultivation; they have no reliable means of getting what they produce to the market, no adequate irrigation, no pest control, and no proper storage facilities. What they *do* have is antiquated machinery, undependable workers, and mud, sometimes so deep and impassable that seeds have to be sown from helicopters and harvests called off when farm vehicles get stuck in the fields and have to be abandoned.

These are, however, just secondary reasons for potential farm buyers to be cautious. The main reason is that the laborers, many of whom have worked on the same farms for decades, believe they should have the first chance to acquire the land. What they need is money. What they have is plenty of anger, and a history of burning down or destroying any farm they think should be theirs. In other words, buy a collective farm and you could become the victim of a peasant's revolt right in your own south forty.

There are unlimited opportunities to buy or create businesses in Russia and the other former republics. Yet, unlike business opportunities elsewhere, they often first appear as problems, not the least of which is finding out who *really* owns what. A run-down factory or an unproductive farm are exactly that to some businessmen with no imagination or spirit of adventure. But to others, they're a chance to test their best economic survival skills, and, if their luck holds out, to walk away with a nice profit.

"Informed determination is the most worthwhile talent to have in this country," said Charles Simmons, the Nebraska businessman who's still looking for a way to make condoms in Russia.

"Succeed and you've earned it. Fail, and, believe me, there are always lots of good reasons why. The Americans say, 'Success has a thousand fathers, but failure is an orphan.' In Russia, it's just the reverse."

Chapter Eleven

Midnight Plane to Georgia

A year after the official end of communism, every Aeroflot departure still begins with the flight crew's parade to the cockpit. Once a ritual designed to reinforce respect for Soviet authority, it has become a way to let people waiting on board know that takeoff could occur any hour.

But when the crew for a recent trip to Georgia strutted down the aisle, passengers had to be wondering if this bunch came to fly the plane or steal it. In a move apparently intended to make potential hijackers think twice, the pilot and copilot were both carrying wooden clubs, and the navigator had a gun under his belt big enough to qualify as excess baggage.

Aviation itself is just a few years older than the ill-fated Bolshevik Revolution, and in this part of the world only slightly more advanced. Consistently rated one of the worst airlines, Aeroflot wasted no time living up to its reputation. Seat belts were missing, the bathrooms didn't work, and judging by the noise coming from the engines, the country's shortage of spare parts had reached crisis proportions.

Yet worries about personal safety won't get you anywhere in

Soviet air space. With no competition—which means no frequent-flyer miles, no champagne, and no free movie—the choice of domestic carriers is strictly limited to one.

In less troubled times, the two-hour flight from Moscow to Tblissi would be business as usual. But these days, what the Georgians might be up to when it landed could make getting there seem like fun. During the past few years, a little of everything has been going on in the tiny yet turbulent former republic. In Tblissi, the Mediterranean-style capital, the legislature declared independence in 1991, and ever since has been at war with itself over what to do next. To add to the uncertainty, there have been fuel shortages, power failures, ethnic feuds, and a civil war. Since Georgia severed most of its ties with Moscow, life in the region has become like an armed folk festival, with private militias bivouacked in the countryside and a general public going about its business against the background pitter-pat of sporadic gunfire.

On April 9, 1989, Soviet troops, using shovels and poison gas, killed nineteen peaceful protesters outside Tblissi's parliament building. The event sparked outbreaks of violence, and fears grew that the region could turn into another Lebanon. In some ways it already is, though it's hard to picture any true Georgian putting up with a war that might interrupt dinner for fifteen years.

Despite a future full of political question marks, the Georgians on Aeroflot Flight 923 to Tblissi all seemed glad to be returning home to the warm weather, red wine, and spicy dishes their native land was famous for until the eggplant hit the fan. But rather than being the mid-air riot several Russians making the trip had predicted, the closer the plane got to its destination the more activity inside resembled a flying picnic, at least for the Georgians, who came prepared with suitcases full of food. Between courses, a 25-year-old Georgian jewelry dealer named Mamuka, now living in Israel, talked excitedly about his first visit to Tblissi in years.

Georgians have the reputation for being the shrewdest businessmen in the ex-Soviet Union, and Mamuka, no longer a Georgian citizen, was explaining how he bought his plane ticket for rubles, even though a new law requires foreigners to pay in hard currency. "All it took was a little *shokhad*," he said, using the Hebrew word for bribe. The payoff, also in rubles, which no Soviet in his right mind thinks of as real money, saved him $180 each way.

"What can I say?" Mamuka laughed. "I'm a Georgian." And with that, he invited everyone to shop at his family's black-market store in war-torn Tblissi.

Below, the snow-covered Caucasus Mountains gave way to rolling green farmland and highways lined with palm trees. From the air, Georgia bears an uncanny likeness to Southern California, and as the plane descended into its capital, the brown smog hanging over the city made it look like a scaled-down version of Los Angeles.

After the crew emerged from the cockpit and left the aircraft first (another Soviet tradition), passengers made a mad dash for the exits. Old women suddenly became NFL fullbacks, running for daylight and plowing through anything in their way. Two beefy stewardesses tried to hold back the crowd, but its forward thrust was too great, and they were soon swept through the doorway themselves. Once outside, it was easy to understand why people were in such a hurry to leave. Following the damp and rainy weather in Moscow, the bright Georgia sunshine was immediate biotherapy.

In the spring of 1991, the political atmosphere in Tblissi had been so pro-Western, there were even American flags flapping above the main airport terminal. As it turned out, they were part of a ceremony welcoming Richard Nixon to town. After his talks with leaders in Moscow, the former president showed up on the last leg of his fact-finding mission, and Georgians, eager for any contact with the outside world, were happy he came. Through confrontation and détente, Nixon was one capitalist most Georgians had heard of, and just having him around while the communist system was finally conking out was a big inspiration.

Even before the fall of the Party, it was impossible to find a Georgian anywhere who thought the Kremlin had done a good job running the republic, although the Georgians have yet to show they can do any better. "For seventy-four years we've been ruled by monsters," said Jansung Charkviani, a well-known local poet, who thought it would take more than a revolution to eliminate the damage communism had done. But, he added proudly, "It's better to die standing up than to live on your knees."

Georgian history is full of rich cultural achievements in poetry, architecture, and music. It has also known long and bloody wars that often left Georgia in the hands of world-class tyrants: Genghis Khan, Tamerlane the Great, and, in more recent times, its own native son Iosif V. Dzhugashvili, better known as Stalin.

Older Georgians continue to hold dear the memory of Uncle Joe, and it's not unusual to see pictures of him in restaurants and private homes, particularly in rural areas, where he's remembered less as a ruthless dictator responsible for the death of millions than an old-fashioned home boy who loved to eat meat dumplings covered with hot pepper and wash them down with bottles of Georgian wine.

In his birthplace, the little town of Gori 150 miles northwest of Tblissi, Stalin's likeness, in the form of a 90-foot statue, towers above the city square. There's a Stalin museum (closed for repairs) and a park containing his boyhood home and private railroad car. In hopes of attracting some of the hard-currency tourist trade, Gori city fathers are thinking of reopening the museum and organizing tours of Stalin's old neighborhood.

The idea of a Stalin revival isn't wildly popular in other parts of Georgia, where some people go into a panic at the mere mention of Stalin's name. "Why do people want to know about him?" asked a man from the mountain city of Telavi, where nearby vineyards produce Kinsmarulya, once Stalin's favorite brand of red wine. "The guy was crazy."

When he heard that there are a lot of Americans who feel the same way about Nixon, the man immediately regained his composure. "Nixon? No kidding?" It was nice to know that Georgia and the United States had so much in common, he said.

For many Georgians, political independence has only intensified their sense of isolation from the rest of the world. Unlike other breakaway republics, Georgia has flatly refused to compromise with economic policies that conflict with its drive to be a separate nation. The result is a reputation of political inflexibility that scares away many foreign investors. Yet, when it comes to making money, Georgians may be the most flexible investment partners anywhere in the former Soviet Union.

The hot-tempered, warm-hearted Georgians have a zest for living that may interrupt work with a gun battle now and then, but it never interferes with doing business. Georgia's geographic location, in the middle of the ancient Silk Road, made it for centuries the perfect rest stop on the main trade route between Europe and Asia. In addition to all of the fabulous recipes they've created, Georgians claim to be the originators of the business lunch. Russians treat newcomers like spies. Georgians treat them to feasts that can last half the day. And if anyone wants to talk deals between meals, the Georgians are all ears.

"Georgia is a little country, and little countries survive by making friends," said art critic Paatta Iakashvili. While the communists were in power, few outside visitors dropped in, but the Georgians kept their traditions alive. Of course, it's easy to like people when they're constantly telling you how great you are. The Georgians also credit themselves with inventing the toast, and any gathering over food is always accompanied by boozy speeches that shower endless praise on each guest. Despite grocery shortages in other parts of the Soviet Union, farms in Georgia seem to be working overtime. After a typical spread of spiced chicken, fried eggplant, grilled fish, barbecued lamb, caviar, fruit, nuts, wine, vodka, and cognac, if any part of the tablecloth is visible through the array of plates and bottles, the effort is considered a complete flop.

The most important part of any Georgian meal, however, isn't what's eaten, but what's said. Officiated by an emcee known as a *tamada,* whose job it is to keep people entertained and well lubricated, the art of toasting has been refined over the years into an intricate psychological strategy capable of turning any occasion into the Academy Awards.

With customs and traditions that antedate the Christian era, the people of Georgia could be the civilized world's first shmoozers. The purpose behind their flattery isn't just dishing out free compliments, it's laying down a friendly basis for trade. The Georgians, whose ancestors did lunch with Marco Polo, are experts in the art of the deal, and once they begin applying their skills in an expanded free market, the country could become one gigantic sales banquet.

Unfortunately, politics has proven to be a serious party pooper. Factional uprisings, religious tensions, and even the population's heaven-on-earth mentality have all hindered Georgia's opportunity to cash in on its most valuable assets: a Black Sea riviera that's ripe for the development of resorts, farm land and mineral deposits ready to produce fortunes, and the majestic Caucasuses that boast some of the world's best undiscovered ski slopes.

Everyone admits that Georgia's loaded with untapped potential. The problem is getting people to stop fighting and start tapping. One encouragement might be a new east-west "air bridge" facility that the government of Taiwan wants to build outside Tblissi. Another is the arrival on the scene of Eduard Shevardnadze, who once ran the republic as Party chief and could be the only leader capable of getting down to business.

Georgia's difficulties in making the transition from dictatorship to democracy are no different from those other republics face. In Georgia, they just take on a heightened degree of drama. The times, it would appear, are perfectly suited to the Georgians' love of show business.

Since the introduction of democracy in 1990, dozens of political parties have been formed, and each one seems to have staked out its own section of battle-scarred Tblissi. There's the Helsinki Union, the Greens, the Republican Federal Party, and the St. Ilia the Righteous Society, to name only a few. The atmosphere is a little like Berkeley in the late 1960s, except for the fact that nobody's stoned, only confused.

One of the most boisterous groups consists of followers of former bank robber Djaba Ioseliani. The founder of Georgia's best-equipped private militia, Ioseliani was arrested shortly after the new government took over and charged him with possessing a gun, which hardly seems like criminal behavior in a place where firearms have become an everyday fashion accessory.

Zviad Gamsakhurdia, Georgia's first democratically elected president, had Ioseliani put in jail, he said, "to ensure public safety." But Ioseliani's army, left more or less intact, soon allied itself with Gamsakhurdia's archrivals, the National Congress Party, making both public safety and democracy relative terms. The fact that Gamsakhurdia drove around in a $460,000 bullet-proof Mercedes gives you some idea of how events progressed in the months of comparative calm that preceded his overthrow.

After four peaceful trips to Tblissi, a correspondent from a British magazine sensed the growing danger when his passport, visa, plane tickets, and two-hundred dollars in highly desirable tens and twenties were cunningly removed from his person in the central telegraph office.

But police work on the case was impressive. Bulletins alerting the public to the reporter's misfortune (with references to its possible impact on Georgia's already less than perfect image in the world) were broadcast on television, and all stolen items—minus the hard currency—were returned by the city's pickpocket squad in less than forty-eight hours. Every Georgian he met for days afterward apologized for what happened, said the reporter, who eventually felt so guilty about being robbed he started saying it was all his fault.

Despite problems getting along with one another, Georgians believe each new guest is "a gift from God," and the concern they show for visiting foreigners, particularly Western businessmen, can be extraordinary. The members of Tblissi's warring political groups, it should be noted, are unfailingly polite to outsiders. Even a man seen carrying an AK-47 in the airport snack bar had the courtesy to put the weapon under his trench coat when a group of Europeans carrying briefcases walked in.

Maybe it's all the wine that Georgians pump into your system, but daily life in Tblissi, if you can overlook the downtown bomb craters, is a pleasant relief from the supply-side nightmare it's become in Moscow and St. Petersburg. For one thing, the city, which is at the same latitude as Rome, is remarkably clean and green. Brightly colored houses with hanging flower baskets give the Georgian capital a fresh and open feeling, as if the communists had never been there. For another, Georgians seem determined to survive their present turmoil, and to do it in the midst of an ongoing political street fair.

"Communism tried to impose the Russian psychology on the republics," said Givi Gomelauri, a Georgian film executive. "But it didn't work in Georgia. We kept our language, our culture, our Christian religion. That's what helped us to survive. No one can stop us from being Georgians." Which many now think is a big part of their problem.

Exhausted by centuries of battling with its bigger neighbors, and usually losing, Georgia, in 1801, signed a treaty with Russia that incorporated it into the empire of the czar. Like the citizens in many small countries, Georgians have had to depend on the kindness of strangers, who haven't always been that kind. In 1921, after a three-year period of postrevolution democracy, the Red Army invaded Tblissi, and the Georgian Republic became part of the Soviet Union. Bitter memories of the forced collectivization and executions that came later are part of every family history. As in the case of Lithuania, Latvia, and Estonia, all free states before the communists took over, Georgian nationalism is fueled by a long history of on-again/off-again repression.

In 1991, when the deposed Gamsakhurdia (whose hobby is translating Shakespeare's plays into Georgian) was elected president, Moscow punished the republic by reducing deliveries of gasoline, electricity, meat, and milk. Georgia, whose farms produce some of the best Soviet agricultural goods, retaliated by curtailing shipments of luxury items such as wine, citrus fruit, and its prized mineral water to Russia. The food fight continues, but it's been overshadowed by other hostilities that began when Gamsakhurdia issued orders to close down newspapers, arrest his political rivals, and confiscate all Communist Party dachas for use by members of the new government and their families and friends.

Asked why he wouldn't allow his opponents access to Georgia's circa-1953 TV facilities, which they eventually took over anyway, Gamsakhurdia said, "They want . . . to spread hooliganism. . . . There is no legal right to use the television to attack and slander the president."

In many independent republics, democratic leaders are as sensitive to criticism as the communists used to be. Gorbachev, several months before the failed coup against him, issued a presidential decree that outlawed painting his face on *matrioska* dolls, those one-inside-the-other figures that some enterprising Russian artists had redesigned to show Czar Nicholas II, Lenin, Stalin, and Khrushchev all stacked up inside Gorby. Gamsakhurdia, in a similar vein, fired everybody in the government who disagreed with him, and once suggested that anyone caught defacing his picture should be put in jail. With a coalition of military leaders and intellectuals now running the country, Gamsakhurdia's quirky decrees sound like ancient history.

Political life in Georgia is surprisingly orderly and disorderly at the same time. When he was boss of the local Communist Party, latter-day reformer Shevardnadze was credited with stabilizing the economy by arresting and torturing some 25,000 people accused of corruption. In 1991, a leadership dispute in Georgia's Adzharian region was settled when the acting provincial president was shot by the acting vice president, who in turn was shot by the acting president's bodyguards. The good news is that new elections were held within weeks.

The situation in Georgia could be a preview of what will happen in other republics as leaders fight it out for power. But Georgians prove it's possible to live, and live well, in the midst of any crisis. During one period of fighting in Tblissi, opposing government and rebel factions set up barricades at either end of Rustaveli Avenue, the city's main shopping street. However, thousands of strolling Georgians turned the no-man's land in between into a pedestrian mall, and went on enjoying themselves as if nothing else mattered.

*   *   *

Although the Georgians may be learning how to be democrats, they need no instructions on how to be capitalists. Actually, the present crisis has only shown what skillful dealmakers Georgians can be. As soon as they declared independence, Georgians, famous for their entrepreneurial talents, adopted one of the most aggressive economic policies of any former republic. In one of its first official acts, the legislature passed laws guaranteeing foreign investments and extending tax breaks to new businesses. A civil war soon made these measures meaningless, but at least Georgians had the right idea.

Austrian firms were the first to take advantage, building a ski resort in the Caucasuses and Georgia's first four-star hotel, the Metechi Palace, in Tblissi. The Metechi deal is a classic example of start-up capitalism. The Tblissi city government supplied the land, building materials, and construction workers, and the ABV Corporation of Vienna arranged $77 million in outside financing. When the Austrians make back their investment, along with a profit, in an estimated fifteen years, the agreement calls for the city to take over the property and sell it to Georgian buyers.

Hotel policy is to hire only people who have never worked for Intourist, the huge state travel and accommodations bureau. According to Metechi general manager Frank Pfaller, Intourist trains its employees to be "prison guards, and that's not what we want here." In fact, the thoroughly modern and efficient Metechi could be the model for all hotels in the future—and it's still the only place in town where you can make a direct phone call to the United States.

"We look at this as an opportunity to be pioneers," said Pfaller, who once ended a dispute among Russians and Georgians on the kitchen staff by removing borscht from the menu. "The political situation doesn't bother us at all. To tell you the truth, we've been too busy to pay much attention."

But in the aftermath of communism, Georgia's jumbled economy has forced some businesses to pay a lot of attention to what they're doing. Unlike the Metechi, which accepts only foreign currency, the problem for most companies is what to do with their rubles. To overcome that obstacle, an Italian agribusiness firm set up a joint venture there that works like a multinational connect-the-dots project.

Georgians produce apple juice concentrate, which the Italians then sell to a German soft drink factory for hard currency—some of which goes to the Georgians and Italians as profit, and some of which goes to pay for farm equipment the Georgians use to raise pigs supplied by the Italians, who take a percentage of the pork for sale in Italy—and the Georgians sell the rest at home for rubles.

So far, the operation itself has proceeded without a serious hitch. The one problem the Italian firm encountered came when it invited several of its Georgian partners to a meeting in Genoa, where they ran up a $10,000 bill for room service and long-distance phone calls. The next time the Georgians came to Italy for talks, they were put on a tight budget. But they retaliated by refusing to discuss any business—and at one point even threatened to dissolve the partnership—until a $500 ceiling on long-distance calls was lifted. After a day of negotiations, the Italians finally gave in.

Georgians say they are born businessmen, and a swing through Tblissi's bustling black market suggests they're probably right. Now part of the legal economy, even though it works in the same shady fashion it always has, Georgia's black market is a testament to the strength and durability of the profit motive.

In Moscow, when the communists were in power, the black market often operated in vacant lots, parks, and other open spaces. That way, KGB agents, who demanded a 15- to 20-percent protection fee, could keep an eye on the take. "They were better accountants than I was," said one merchant. "I always knew when I was having a good month. The KGB wanted more money."

In Georgia, where the authorities were less strict—and often in business themselves—the black market has operated in slightly more permanent surroundings. The only thing democracy changed is that the bribes now go to corrupt local police officials. Everything is for sale, assuming you're willing to pay big rubles— Deutsche marks are the preferred hard currency—and aren't that particular about being an accessory to an international smuggling operation, which few Georgians seem to be.

Under the communists, the black market corrupted countless government administrators, many of whom doubled as market bosses themselves. Georgia's Vasily Mzhavanadze, a member of the Politburo during the 1960s, masterminded a network of secret factories and black-market stores in Tblissi. Mzhavanadze raked in millions of rubles in profits and millions more in bribes before the Party, in one of its periodic crackdowns, arrested dozens of his accomplices. Mzhavanadze, whose involvement was hushed up at the time, was allowed to step down quietly from the Politburo in 1972, and take millions in illegal earnings with him.

Today, the black market is so indispensable not even Boris Yeltsin and his brain trust of Russian economists can think of a way to change it. It thrived under the communists and continues to do so, because it's a better provider than the government. In Georgia, the results are obvious. The Russians, who can't seem to transport a potato from point A to point B without losing it (or having it go rotten en route), could learn a few things about distribution from the Georgians.

Tblissi's black-market stores are like international carryouts. If the customer wants something that's not in stock, he places his order, puts down a deposit, and the system does the rest. If an item isn't available locally, the store will send someone to Turkey to buy it, often in the black market there. It's a little like having your own personal shopping service. Customers get suits that fit and shoes that match—all in less time than it normally takes to buy a rationed bottle of wine. From purchase to delivery, the process is a model of economic efficiency, and nothing the Kremlin ever came up with could match it.

What makes Georgia's black market work so well is that it consists of dozens of small businesses, many of them run by Jewish families, all aggressively competing with one another. When financial squabbles break out, as they frequently do, they're usually settled by negotiations. Stores that don't pay bills on time might have their supplies cut off or a family's name cursed—as Shevardnadze's was when, as local Party secretary, he ordered winegrowers to dilute their product to meet higher production quotas—but nobody in the Georgia black market has ever been killed over money. At any rate, that's what black marketeers claim. But then, there's never been so much money floating around in Georgia's black market before, and the tradition could soon be in for a test.

That's little consolation for Mamuka, the Israeli jewelry dealer who came to Tblissi to visit his relatives. Mamuka had fallen in love with his 18-year-old cousin, Rita, a turn of events that didn't go down too well with his family or hers, both pillars of the black-market community.

But Mamuka had a plan. In New York, where he lived before moving to Israel, he was in the retail diamond business, and doing well, he said, before a Georgian gem dealer stole over $1 million from him. He had reason to believe the man was in Tblissi, hiding with another black-market family, and Mamuka was determined to find the guy and get all or part of his money back so he could marry Rita. His financial needs were made more urgent by the fact that Rita's brothers had let him know that if he ever came near their sister again, he was a dead man.

"I know it looks bad," Mamuka sighed, admitting this was no ordinary affair of the heart, even by Georgian standards. "But I can't help it. I'm in love."

His original idea was to kidnap Rita and take her to Israel, but on second thought, they both have so many relatives there, they could never live incognito. Then he thought of running off with her to Italy or maybe the United States. Before he could do anything, though, he needed to find the man who stole his money. As an added incentive to hurry up, Rita's father, who was in jail for manslaughter, was about to be released, and had vowed to kill Mamuka with his bare hands if he was still in Tblissi by the time he got out.

Family feuds, especially black-market family feuds, can be messy business in Georgia. Some have been known to last for centuries, and this one looked like it was destined for the record books.

As the release date for Rita's father got closer, Mamuka's romantic resolve showed signs of weakening. The pressure was getting to him. With no luck tracking down the man in possession of his million dollars, maybe the best thing to do was go back to Israel for a while. Love and money were taking on lethal implications.

"There are two things about Georgians you have to remember," said Mamuka. "They never forget their family or their enemies. And when you happen to be both, you're in real trouble."

Chapter Twelve

Location Is Everything

When Armenians decide to have a revolution, they like to do it in a businesslike fashion, even when it comes to dismantling one of the last reminders of communism. In this case, the object in question was a thirty-foot statue of Lenin that for years had dominated the center of Yerevan, Armenia's capital. Other former Soviet republics have had to wrestle with versions of the same ideological eyesore, but none went about it as deliberately as Armenia.

"There were two choices," said Yerevan's newly elected mayor Hampbartsum Galstian. "We could blow it up, or we could take it down in a way that made a good impression on the rest of the world." So, the city council met to debate the options. A committee was formed, and in the spring of 1991, the statue was unceremoniously hoisted from its pedestal by a crane and hauled across the street to its current resting place behind the Museum of Culture and History.

"It was the only responsible thing to do," said Galstian, who headed the removal committee. "But as a historian, I have to admit, I don't like the idea of destroying the past, even when it's a statue of Lenin."

Given the way Armenians feel about communism, getting rid of the giant bronze memorial was an absolute must. What's amazing is that the operation was carried out with such orderly efficiency.

"That's how Armenians are," Galstian added, with a distinct note of pride in a job well done. The only visible indication that emotions came into play was a single bullet hole right where Lenin's heart would be. But one question was still unanswered; namely, the whereabouts of the Great One's missing head.

"It's being kept in a special place," hinted a local official, concerned that communists might try to rescue the 1,000-pound cranium. The special place, it turned out, was the museum's basement, where the head, sporting a few recent dents, was leaning against a panel of electrical switches, the perfect spot for a guy whose ideas all seemed to blow a fuse at the same time.

"Maybe we should sell tickets," said a security guard, as he and some of his friends obligingly rolled Lenin's bald noggin under an overhead light for closer inspection. Everyone agreed the idea deserved looking into.

In an era of dramatic and unexpected changes, Armenians these days are keeping one eye on politics and the other on the bottom line. And who can blame them? After centuries of invasions, wars, and persecutions, they've learned what it takes to survive. And as they launch out on their own, survival is likely to become a major concern.

Even though communism has ended, its creepy presence continues to be felt all over Armenia. Red and white propaganda signs can still be seen along roads in the countryside, and, at the Hotel Yerevan, Intourist brochures in the lobby advertise the Party and its mission as if nothing has changed.

"Present-day Armenia is an example of the implementation of the CPSU's Leninist national policy," one pamphlet proudly declared. "It is convincing evidence of how within a short period a backward province of czarist Russia has made spectacular progress in advancing its economy, culture, science and the people's well-being, and has turned into a highly developed socialist country. It has achieved this in conditions of the new social system born of the Great October Socialist Revolution and under the guidance of the Communist Party of the Soviet Union."

Communist touches are also noticeable in Yerevan's urban architecture. The city looks like it was designed by cubists improvising on Stalin's master plan. Buildings appear to be made of solid stone blocks piled one on top of the other, with windows and doors cut into them with drills. There are avenues wide enough for tanks to make U-turns and spacious squares for Party rallies.

Yet, as shoppers and vendors take the place of policemen, reminders of the old regime and its strict control on the pursuit of free enterprise are fading fast. Suddenly, everyone in Yerevan seems to be in the retail business. There's an amazing assortment of Western products for sale on every corner: Old Milwaukee beer, Madonna albums, Bic pens, Air Jordan basketball shoes. Take away the language barrier, add a few neon signs, and you could be walking down any main street in Middle America.

Everywhere in Yerevan, whose skyline is set against the twin peaks of Mt. Ararat, now inconveniently part of Turkey, Armenians are letting their economic impulses express themselves in ways that are primitive but impressive. One cigarette salesman on the outskirts of town advertised his product by constructing the full-size figure of a man entirely out of Marlboro cartons and hanging it from a tree. Throughout the country, people appear confident in their ability to make ends meet, especially now that they don't have the Kremlin cutting into their profit margin.

Constituting less than a thousandth of the Soviet landmass, Armenia, whose power as a nation may have peaked in biblical times, has a formidable task on its hands. With few natural resources, a dilapidated infrastructure, and a population of only 3.3 million, the new democratic government is trying to start a country and an economy at the same time. Throw in a guerilla war, a growing refugee problem, and the constant threat of earthquakes, and you begin to realize why Armenians talk so much about suffering. "Sorrow," said one old man in a Yerevan park, "is the one thing all of us share."

But Armenians have other connections. They are, without a doubt, the best networkers of any Soviets. Most families have relatives, often wealthy and influential ones, living everywhere, from Paris and London to Fresno, California—and they haven't lost contact. That not only makes Armenians feel like part of the outside world, it gives them access to outside know-how and money that's already starting to pay off. AT&T recently installed a satellite telephone system that gives Armenia 184 new international phone lines. That's more than Russia and all of the other former republics combined. Calling across the street can take days, but thanks to advanced American technology, calling New York is almost like being there.

"We'll be okay. We're a nation of businessmen," boasted David Rostorian, manager of Yerevan's new Benetton store. "It's the one thing we take with us wherever we go." And Armenians *do* go places. More Armenians now live in the so-called diaspora—the United States, France, Syria, and elsewhere—than in their own homeland. Only 34 percent of the world's Armenians actually reside in Armenia.

Lately, however, it's difficult to find a native Armenian who doesn't think it's time that more exported business skills were put to use at home. It's also difficult to find a native Armenian who has the faintest idea of where to begin, which may explain the government's initial cautious approach toward autonomy.

Whereas most of the fourteen other former Soviet republics declared some form of independence after the failed coup, only Armenia carefully followed the guidelines for secession spelled out in the Soviet constitution, including holding a referendum and giving the Kremlin six months' notice. Armenians, led by their President Levon ter Petrosian, a scholar of ancient history, like doing things by the book.

"Many asked what was the meaning of leaving the Soviet Union when the Soviet Union, in fact, no longer existed," said Feliks O. Mamikonian, Armenia's onetime representative to the

State Council of Republics in Moscow. "But the political situation may again change, and we would like to lay the legal foundation for our independence so it cannot be challenged."

Two days after 1991 elections in which Armenians voted overwhelmingly to leave the union, Armenian officials and their counterparts from neighboring Azerbaijan agreed to a cease-fire to end the fighting over Nagorno-Karabakh, an ethnic Armenian enclave inside Azerbaijan. The previous year, rioting Azerbaijanis killed hundreds of Armenians living in Baku, Azerbaijan's capital. Ever since, the two republics have been involved in repeated clashes, caused in part by religious hatred between the Christian Armenians and the Moslem Azerbaijanis, and in part by political antagonisms stirred up by Moscow when the communists were in power.

The peace agreement, negotiated by Russian President Boris Yeltsin, called for an end to the shooting, the disarming of local militias, and the beginning of talks to settle the question of which side will control the Karabakh region. Shortly after the treaty was signed, new fighting broke out, and it's still going on.

The situation could be a preview of things to come, not just in Armenia but in other former republics. With the removal of political and military forces that once kept local tensions under control, hopes for the peaceful conversion of what used to be the Soviet Union into a working commonwealth could be replaced by scattered ethnic shootouts just like this one.

The communist strategy had been to defuse unrest by the systematic relocation of ethnic groups. As a result, some republics, such as Kazakhstan, with a population only 40 percent Kazakh, have become potential combustion chambers of opposing national factions. In Armenia and Azerbaijan, both with largely homogeneous populations, old disputes over land and religion are what set off the most recent hostilities, which include livestock slaughters, deportations, and an Azerbaijani oil embargo that's crippled Armenia's economy.

It doesn't take long in Yerevan to discover that many Armenians won't be satisfied until every Azerbaijani is driven out of the contested area. Terms such as "butchers" and "animals" are often used to describe their next-door foes—the same words, incidentally, that Armenians use to describe their traditional archenemies, the Turks, who massacred 1.5 million Armenians during World War I. So, this conflict could be a long way from over. Feuds here are ancient, and after a century or two take on a life of their own. If revenge is sweet, no one knows it better than people who have been at one another's throats almost from the beginning of recorded history.

One Armenian politician, who suggested a compromise with Azerbaijan to settle their differences, was gunned down in the streets of Yerevan. As a cab driver said, in a brief lecture on Armenian psychology, "Our problems are not the kind that disappear overnight."

Armenia's dilemma has all the ingredients of a mini Arab-Israeli conflict: a small country surrounded by enemies, a growing number of angry refugees, and old-time animosities amplified by horror stories that won't quit. One man in a refugee camp near the Armenian resort city Tskhazor told how his town near the border had been fired on point blank by dozens of Soviet tanks. Others recalled being awakened in the middle of the night by the Azerbaijani militia, beaten and tortured, and then loaded on buses and deported to Armenia. All of their possessions, they said, were stolen and their homes turned over to Azerbaijani families.

"Even if we go back, what will be left?" said a 35-year-old woman who hadn't seen her husband since he joined the army. Many young Armenian men have gone off to fight in the hills along the border with Azerbaijan. A month before the peace treaty reduced direct Russian involvement, the military action took many forms. In one strange encounter, Soviet forces in Azerbaijan crossed the border and stole 2,500 sheep, killing three Armenian shepherds in the process. (Being a shepherd in Armenia or Azerbaijan nowadays is a high-risk profession.) The following night, Armenian soldiers invaded Azerbaijan, drove the Soviet troops away, and recaptured the herd, minus a few dozen the Soviets had eaten for dinner.

The same week, a soccer match in Yerevan between the Red Army team and the Armenians became a small-scale version of the war when fans attacked Soviet players with rocks and bottles. The melee went on until the fire department arrived and hosed everyone down, which had about as much lasting effect on cooling off tempers as Yeltsin's peace treaty did.

But even in the midst of combat, the opposing sides always seem to find plenty of time to do business. Reporting on the commercial side of the war, *Commersant,* a Moscow weekly, printed complaints from Armenian villagers that Soviet Army personnel were overcharging them for ammunition. Soviet soldiers are notorious for selling their equipment, but this time, the paper charged, they were clearly guilty of discrimination by making Armenians pay a higher price for bullets than Azerbaijanis. To settle the argument, *Commersant* suggested that a uniform price of five rubles per machine-gun round be charged to all buyers. Now that Soviet troops have withdrawn and the Azerbaijani government has nationalized all military hardware, there's no telling how high the prices will go.

Continued battlefield business shows how dependent on one another adversaries can be in a place where trade has as much importance as religion. In many ways the center of life in this part of the world isn't the church or mosque. It's the bazaar, the stock market of the Middle East. As politicians in Moscow and other capitals argue over the best way to manage a free market, the Armenians and Azerbaijanis already have theirs running just fine—classic open-air shopping centers, teeming with buyers and sellers, where anything and everything has a price.

"People here don't particularly think in terms of producing goods," said a Yerevan street vendor. "We have a middleman's mentality. We're merchants. We make deals. It's genetic." How quickly that changes, and area residents become producers as well as traders, will determine how quickly both Armenians and Azerbaijanis advance to the next stage of economic development.

With former communists still holding onto power in Azerbaijan, most economic development there exists outside the law in the black market. Azerbaijanis are Moslems, moderate in their religious practices but relentless in their pursuit of behind-the-scenes deals. Traders by tradition, they can be tough bargainers and demanding business partners.

Azerbaijan's black market functions like a minor-league American Mafia. Lonya Leshbeck, one of the most powerful black-market bosses in Baku, even has a car that plays the theme from *The Godfather* when his driver honks the horn. Leshbeck, whose Jewish ancestors came to Azerbaijan from Poland at the turn of the century, runs a construction supply business that would make money anywhere. But the fact that he's a Jew and everyone who works for him is Moslem makes the operation something of a managerial miracle.

One reason for his success is that Leshbeck spares no expense when it comes to impressing investors. A group of Americans, visiting Baku to talk about a project to collect money abroad for fixing up neglected Jewish cemeteries in Russia, were treated to a succession of feasts between business meetings that left their heads spinning.

There were dinners on yachts, lunches in the country, and a ten-course meal on the shores of the Caspian Sea, with tables and chairs set up in the sand, that lasted an entire day. But Leshbeck, who never goes anywhere without bringing his cook and private food supply, is no soft-around-the-middle chairman of the board. When one of his lieutenants pulled ahead of his car on the trip to the beach, the offending driver was motioned over to the side of the road and told the next time he passed the boss without permission he'd be walking.

If you want to do business in Baku or anywhere in Azerbaijan—and sizeable oil reserves almost guarantee an influx of foreign energy companies—get ready to deal with people who conduct their affairs in the time-honored style of an eye for an eye and a tooth for a tooth. In other words, renege on a promise or back out of a deal and be prepared to leave town in a hurry, or be very well protected. Azerbaijani goon squads are known for an uncompromising dedication to their work.

Baku is a mixture of East and West. Divided in half by the border between Europe and Asia, it's the sort of town Chicago must have been in the 1920s, or Las Vegas was when Bugsy Siegel invented it. There are nightclubs with big-spending black marketeers and leggy Russian show girls dancing the lambada. The Moslem prohibition against drinking and X-rated entertainment has not turned Baku into a city of dour ascetics. Azerbaijanis are the original fire worshipers, and still live their lives that way. Incidentally, the fires they worshipped were flaming natural gas deposits, the same ones people are interested in now as potential sources of hard currency.

Azerbaijanis say they don't like Armenians because they make too much money, which isn't that apparent in Armenia, although the Armenians could surprise everyone with their get-up-and-go. One group trying to hasten the process is the Armenian Assembly of America. From offices in Washington and Yerevan, it funnels technical assistance into Armenia and coordinates a potent pro-Armenian lobbying effort in the United States. Armenians have more support groups than any other Soviet nationality. There are Armenian-American associations that raise money; others send volunteers to help restore villages and churches; and one in California publishes a slick monthly magazine that looks exactly like *Time,* only it's full of political news from Armenia and upbeat success stories about Armenians in America.

"People in Armenia see the example of Israel and it gives them hope they can make it in a hostile environment," says Linda Bedeian, director of the Armenian Assembly's Yerevan office. A big part of the organization's goal is to get Armenians living in the United States to contribute time and money to the cause. "Relative to other ethnic groups, Armenians are very generous," says Bedeian.

In 1991, the Assembly opened a $2 million plant in earthquake-ravaged Gamauri (formerly Leninakan) for producing home-building materials, and soon expects to be constructing 10,000 homes a year. It also sponsors programs to teach Armenians how to set up joint business ventures with foreign partners.

"Right now, the focus is on electronics components, textiles, and computer technology," says Michael Kouchakdjian, an Armenian-American with a Wharton School MBA, who volunteered to assist the government in attracting outside investors. One of the more interesting projects is a two-year-old American-Armenian venture called Armen Toy that assembles a mechanical "monster" truck called The Animal. The company sells the toy trucks in Western Europe and the Arab countries for hard currency and anticipates profits of $4 million dollars by 1993.

But it's not only Armenians from abroad who are helping to generate revenue. Another recent arrival is Benetton, the Italian clothing manufacturer. After a three-year search for a factory site around Moscow, the company gave up and decided to locate in Armenia instead. The reasons why sound like a capsule summary of everything that's wrong with the Russian approach to doing business. They didn't have the right equipment; the workers had the wrong attitude; the material wasn't any good. Russians mix all of their fabrics with synthetics. The Benetton people are purists. An American consultant involved in the factory search reported that the final straw came when a former director of light industry in Moscow told Benetton executives: "We don't need you. What we need are better quotas."

"There was too much bureaucratic red tape to contend with in Russia," says Lucino Colusso, technical supervisor of Benetton's new plant outside Yerevan. "The government here is much more flexible. Besides, Armenians are more business oriented than Russians. We have very high standards and the workers here meet all of them."

Benetton, which now has a total of four stores in the ex-Soviet Union (three in Moscow and one in Yerevan), hopes its Armenian plant will be supplying all of them with clothes in two to three years. "To assure the high quality Benetton is famous for, we had to totally retrain the people we hired," explained Colusso. "We started with a small group and added more and more as we went along until we finally had a whole factory."

Benetton's initial investment in its Armenian joint venture

came to about $700,000. But as new shops are opened, it expects to spend more money expanding its production facilities in Yerevan. In addition to the plant in Armenia, the company has 6,000 stores and eight other factories in countries around the world.

"I'm absolutely sure, with our emphasis on bright colors and international goodwill, we can change the psychology of Soviet life," said Colusso. "Benetton's product is for young people, and Soviet kids have been waiting for the day when they can live like kids do in other countries. I think the fact that we're here is one more step toward that goal." The political situation in Armenia will take care of itself, he added. "To me, politics is always a little crazy. I'm from Italy, so I'm used to it."

Government officials are hoping Benetton will be the first of many international companies to locate in Armenia, and they're prepared to offer attractive inducements to get them interested, including reduced labor costs, a reliable work force, investment guarantees, and tax breaks. If foreign businesses do come, it would be a pleasant change from the past, when most outsiders saw Armenia as something to exploit or destroy rather than invest in.

"Other countries have tried for centuries to wipe Armenia off the map," said Kouchakdjian. "There's a feeling here now that the worst is in the past. What will happen in the future is up to us." But Armenia's immediate future, like that of other former Soviet republics, is anything but certain. For one thing, Armenians are on hostility-alert status with three-fourths of their neighbors: the Turks to the West, the Iranians to the South, and the Azerbaijanis to the East. The only people in the region they seem to have relatively friendly relations with are the Georgians, currently considering a deal that would give landlocked Armenia access to ports on the Black Sea. Even as talks were progressing, though, there were telltale signs of trouble ahead. A spokesman for the new Georgian government in Tblissi confirmed that a seaport deal might be possible. "But frankly," he said, "we're afraid if a lot more Armenians move there, pretty soon they'll start claiming they own it."

Problems come with the territory for Armenia. "Being everybody's victim has become a way of life for us," said an Armenian journalist in Moscow. "We're born defensive. There's an old Armenian saying that goes: Always protect the Jews because we're next." Historians trace the problem back thousands of years to a time when the Romans and Persians used Armenia as a place to fight their wars. During the intervening centuries, it's been partitioned and subdivided so many times the country is now only a fraction of the size it once was. "Armenians have seen their homeland chopped apart for years," said historian Levon Avdoyan. "There are many old wounds that people find very hard to forget."

A union with czarist Russia in the nineteenth century probably saved the nation from complete destruction. But after the communists took over in 1920, Armenians found themselves at the mercy of a dictatorship that outlawed their business skills and put their economy in storage for the next seventy years.

When the Party was toppled from power, there were signals that Armenians might be willing to give up at least some of their long-standing grudges. In a major surprise, the new government under ter Petrosian has said it might even be ready to explore the idea of peaceful coexistence with Turkey. On a scale of difficulty, settling the Turkish problem ranks right up there with bringing peace to Northern Ireland. But these days anything can happen.

Obviously some hard political choices lie ahead. Then again, hardship seems to be Armenia's natural environment. Even nature is out to make life difficult for the Armenians. Yerevan in the summer can be as hot as a bread oven, and buildings sometimes shimmer in the haze like a dusty mirage. The shimmering isn't always an illusion. This is earthquake country, and Armenia has its share of tremors. The most recent in 1988 nearly destroyed the northern cities of Spetak and Gamauri and countless small villages in between.

In the mountain village of Gogoran, near the epicenter of the 1988 quake, inhabitants are still digging out from under the rubble. Life in Gogoran has never been easy, and the most recent catastrophe pushed conditions back a century or two. Helping with the reconstruction work is an Armenian relief group called the Land and Culture Organization. Every year, the New York–based group brings Armenian students from countries around the world to remote sections of Armenia to help restore churches and other historical sites.

In Gogoran, during the summer of 1991, students from England, France, and the United States were restoring a fifth-century church that was leveled by the earthquake. All of them were from Armenian families, and for most, this was their first visit to the land of their ancestors. In addition to other damage, the quake had destroyed the church graveyard, and part of the job of getting things back in shape involved gathering up skulls, ribs, and other bones and stacking them in neat piles for reburial later.

"This kind of close contact helps you learn where you come from," said a pretty American co-ed, placing another skull on the stack as a dozen or so young men from the village looked on, smoking cigarettes and trying to make eye contact. "I've learned I'd never marry one of these guys, that's for sure," said Armineh Cartland-Stuart, an 18-year-old girl from London. "All they want to do is get laid. They treat women like slaves around here." The young men, while not exactly denying the charge, said foreign women wouldn't make good wives anyway. "They talk too much," said one. "They have a whole different mentality from our women. The perfect wife, as I see it, has to keep the house clean, feed the guests, and take good care of your cows."

If people in Gogoran find foreigners unusual, they've learned to take earthquakes in perfect stride. But their occurrence, both in Georgia and Armenia, so close to areas of political unrest, does have a few conspiracy buffs working on theories that the KGB was responsible, planting underground nuclear weapons to trigger instant disasters as a way of diverting attention from local independence movements.

If that's true, the plan failed, and in the area around Spetak, a half-dozen new communities have been built with foreign aid from dozens of countries. The effect is surreal. There's a Swiss village that looks like a pre-fab ski resort, an Italian village that only needs a pizza restaurant to be more authentic, and a Russian village that's already falling apart.

Armenians seem to be building and digging everywhere. Armenia was the first of the former republics to privatize farmland, and the result has been an explosion in food production. While other governments play around with the idea of dismantling collective farms, one of communism's most counterproductive concepts, Armenia did it. In rural villages, residents signed up for the type of crops they wanted to grow, and then land was given out by lottery. The size of a family's plot depended on the size of the family.

For the first time in years, fields were well tended and bountiful. The fall 1991 harvest was 50 percent larger than the previous year's. Yet the impact of a quick agricultural turnaround has been minimized by a state-run distribution system that's still a nightmare of inefficiency. Land reforms won't be a complete success until the entire economy is privatized, and Armenians claim that because they never lost their entrepreneurial spirit or their willingness to work, complete privatization will occur faster there than it will anywhere eles. "The truth is that Armenians are good workers," said Dr. Avdoyan. "Communism never afforded them a chance to show it. Give an Armenian some land or a business and he'll work at it night and day to make it a success."

That point was illustrated along the road to Lake Sevan, where an enterprising Armenian chef had opened a restaurant in a converted Aeroflot passenger jet he had bought for a million rubles and trucked all the way from Yerevan. Business was so good, he was thinking of buying another plane. That's another indication of confidence in Armenia's future as a prosperous and peaceful nation, despite constant reminders of its far-from-peaceful past.

A few miles from the airplane restaurant, there's a bust in the middle of a cow pasture dedicated to the nineteenth-century Armenian patriot Sassom Soloman ter Petrosian. What was his claim to fame? "Oh, he was a very great man indeed," said the chef. "Every time he saw a Turk, he killed him."

Chapter Thirteen

Hong Kong on the Baltic

Stasys Lozoratis may not have been the loneliest guy in town. But he came pretty close. In Washington, where the diplomatic pecking order is almost a religion, Lozoratis for years was a voice crying in the wilderness. Officially known as an ambassador without portfolio, for all practical purposes he was missing a lot more than that—starting with his country, Lithuania, which was annexed to the Soviet Union in 1940 as part of a deal between Hitler and Stalin. Lozoratis managed to escape with his family before the Russians moved in, but the imposition of communism sentenced him and thousands of other Lithuanian expatriates to more than a half century of political exile.

"It wasn't like representing an abstraction. We always had plenty of work to do," he said of his job in the old days before Lithuania regained its independence and he achieved full ambassadorial status. "We were sure the Soviet regime would collapse some day. The question was when. Now that it has, the real work begins."

A top priority, say officials in the Lithuanian capital of Vilnius, is giving "some polish" to their threadbare foreign service corps,

185

whose new mission will be to impress Western investors with their noncommunist style and efficiency. Scandinavian governments are helping out with a training program, and the British have pledged financial aid from a special "know-how fund."

The embassy in Washington, staffed by Lozoratis, two full-time assistants and a dozen volunteers, is a good example of Lithuania's determination to succeed on a shoestring. A prime piece of real estate when the tiny Baltic country bought it in 1924, the embassy now sits in the middle of an inner city neighborhood where most of the signs are in Spanish and the drug dealers outnumber the cops. That's on the outside. Inside the four-story building little has changed in sixty years. The desks and chairs, tables and couches are all 1920s originals. The lights are kept low to save electricity, and in the dimly lit hallway a mural depicts a parade of precommunist government officials, all dressed in black and looking more like pallbearers than politicians.

"For a long time, it was an appropriate scene to depict the mood of our country," said Lozoratis, who's quick to point out that recent events in his nation's history clearly call for redecorating. He only wishes he had the cash to afford it.

Lithuania, like its Baltic neighbors Latvia and Estonia, is severely strapped for hard currency. Unlike most of the other former republics, though, the Baltics have a plan that could—if it works—make them the Hong Kong of Eastern Europe, a conveniently located corporate headquarters for companies doing business in the ex-Soviet Union and a reliable outlet for hundreds of value-added finished products.

On the financial front, Baltic banks over the last few years have become high-volume clearinghouses for buying and selling rubles. Entailing far less red tape than the ruble auctions in Moscow, transactions have become so large that Baltic exchange rates (considered the closest approximation to the real market value of the ruble) are now published daily in the Russian and European press.

Banks in the Baltics, particularly in Riga, are not only involved in arbitrage for companies and business associations, they also convert millions of rubles for local and national governments.

There are rumors that prior to the 1991 coup attempt Baltic bankers helped Party bigwigs in Moscow funnel money into Europe in return for the Kremlin softening its hard-line stand on independence.

In what could be the most significant development of all, the Baltic exchange market has begun to replace the black market as the preferred mechanism for currency conversion. Scores of people from Europe and the former republics arrive every week with suitcases full of money for sale. And much to the consternation of black marketeers (who literally stand outside bank doors with their own bags of loot waiting to make deals), Baltic bankers give better rates and also have more cash on hand.

With reorganization hampering operations at the Vnesheconombank (in the old days the Soviet Union's only financial institution authorized to make hard-currency transactions), Baltic bankers are scurrying to fill the vacuum. "Westerners trust us more than Russians," said one bank officer visiting Moscow. Then, pointing to himself in his new double-breasted French suit, he asked, "Wouldn't you?"

Having once satisfied Russia's historic ambitions for ice-free harbors, the Baltic states are perfectly positioned to serve as commercial loading docks for trade in and out of the newly created Commonwealth of Independent States. Estonia and Latvia both have two major ports, and while Lithuania lacks comparable facilities, it is a key depot for food and dairy products. But location isn't the only selling point.

Although their size and population constituted only a small fraction of the U.S.S.R., the Baltics contributed heavily to the most advanced sector of Soviet industry. Under the old centralized system, Baltic factories produced computers and military equipment, as well as precision medical and electronic instruments. That same brainpower can easily be put to work providing goods and services for Western customers.

"The Baltic people aren't just Western-oriented; they *are* Western," said Gailius Draugelis, a Canadian-American businessman working as a full-time commercial adviser to the Lithuanian mission in Washington. "They still have a memory of what capitalism was like. They also have one of the highest concentrations of educated workers anywhere in the world. In Lithuania, for instance, out of a population of 3.8 million people, over 1.2 million have university or technical degrees."

Even with such an impressive talent pool, the problems involved in redirecting former Soviet enterprises toward foreign trade are formidable.

"The tragedy of many of our old industries was that such capable workers were wasted by a system designed to produce trash," explained Lozoratis. "No matter how poor the quality of goods happened to be, there were always Soviet buyers. That's not the case anymore. We have to adapt our production to Western standards."

Now that the Soviet economy has collapsed, depriving heavily subsidized industries of a market that would take even the worst-made products, more and more state enterprises are being forced to compete or go out of business. After 50 years of communist mismanagement, many factory managers are learning they can neither sell their shoddy goods to impoverished Russians nor find the flexibility to adapt to Western markets. The result on the consumer level is the same as it is throughout the old Soviet Union: a growing frustration with capitalism and in some cases an open nostalgia for the old communist system it replaced.

"It was better during Brezhnev's times," said a well-educated Russian woman, summing up the feelings of those who have soured on the hope for instant improvement that the free market was supposed to bring with it. A common complaint heard among Soviets everywhere is that life has become too unpredictable. Add unemployment, recession, and inflation to the latest list of woes, and it's easy to see why the biggest threat to the success of economic reforms could be an impatient population that's simply unwilling to give them enough time to work.

But that's where the Lithuanians, Latvians, and Estonians say they have a distinct advantage over those in the other parts of the once unified Soviet Union. Besides Georgia, the Baltics were the only breakaway republics not to join the commonwealth. There is the sense in all three new nations that what's needed is not a redefined dependency on Moscow or Minsk but a fresh start. If the Russian tendency is to make things bigger, the Baltic approach— influenced partly by ethnic temperament, partly by geography—is to operate on a smaller scale. Their limited population is one reason why all three Baltic states are completely self-sufficient in food production.

Culturally, the industrious Balts, who tilt toward Western Europe, have more in common with Finns, Poles, and Germans than they do with the Russians and Ukrainians. Little Estonia (population 1.6 million) has a legitimate claim to being the most westernized of all the former republics, at least in terms of its video habits. While the rest of the Soviet Union had to watch Party propaganda on state-controlled TV channels, Estonians had the luxury of being able to tune in Helsinki, a mere 50 miles away, and catch episodes of "Dallas," "Falcon Crest," or whatever else Finnish television happened to be showing—including the latest in European and American consumer products.

Estonians were preconditioned to capitalism, and now theirs is the only republic, according to *Fortune* magazine, whose joint ventures have been consistent net exporters (meaning that revenue from Estonian goods sold abroad for hard currency surpasses the amount of foreign investments coming into the country).

Despite a dependence on Russia for such necessities as oil, transportation, and phone service, political sentiment in the Baltics is for separatism rather than confederation. It's no coincidence that Lithuanians were the first Soviets to defy the Kremlin with open elections in 1990, or that their continued defiance led to a bloody confrontation with Soviet troops a year later, marking the beginning of the end for Party leaders.

Throughout the Baltic states, in fact, opposing communism had been an underground activity for years. Generations of armed partisans kept up a resistance movement inside Lithuania that lasted as long as Soviet occupation. Next door, Latvians gave their own special twist to the anti-Moscow campaign by sticking swords through their hats during ceremonial drinking bouts and ridiculing their Russian oppressors with curses and colorful insults.

Part of their anger undoubedly stems from a sense of betrayal after helping Lenin come to power. Fearing that he couldn't trust Russians to kill other Russians en masse, Lenin relied on the Latvian Riflemen and the Lithuanian Reserve Regiment to squelch his Russian opposition. Without this assistance the fragile Bolshevik coup d'état might never have succeeded.

The days of Soviet domination may be over; just the same bitter memories of life under Kremlin rule will take a long time to erase.

After annexation, Stalin set out to subdue the Balts with waves of deportations to Siberia. Some 60,000 Lithuanians made the trip in 1945, followed by an estimated 40,000 the next year. Few survived the ordeal. One of the earliest milestones of Gorbachev's glasnost was the public disclosure of secret documents detailing the extent of Stalin's ruthless treatment—the memory of which inflamed passions and further fueled the drive for Baltic independence.

Estonians, Lithuanians, and Latvians were the first Soviets to tear down the symbols of Party authority, the first to banish the KGB, and now, while other former republics waste valuable time in ethnic and religious feuds, they could also be the first to capitalize on the free market.

Estonia began lifting price controls long before the other ex-republics and, in stark contrast to tax-gouging Russia, has kept its business tax rate at a livable 35 percent. Lithuania, with over 225 working joint ventures, has passed laws allowing foreign companies to own businesses and lease land for up to 99 years. Latvia has been slower than its neighbors at implementing economic incentives, but 310 miles of sandy beaches directly opposite Sweden may be all it needs to attract resort developers and a hard-currency European tourist trade.

A Baltic Riviera, with beautiful people, chic hotels, and film festivals, may take a while to materialize, yet dreams of being a business gateway to Russia aren't that farfetched. What the Baltics have to offer, aside from economic and political stability, is an "ethnic density" that, officials say, assures smooth and rapid progress through the most difficult stages of reform.

Lithuania is 80.1 percent Lithuanian; Estonia is 61.1 percent Estonian. But even in Latvia, where Russians, Byelorussians, and Ukrainians account for nearly 50 percent of the population, plentiful food supplies and a relatively high standard of living among the hardworking Balts make minorities happy to stay.

As the experience of strife-torn Georgia has shown, a large native population isn't always the best guarantee against trouble. But at a time when other republics are beset by factional discord, Balts seem to be more interested in repairing their economy than fighting.

"Baltic people have never been aggressive," said Ojars Kalnins, Latvia's minister counselor in Washington. "Throughout our history we've been occupied by foreigners. In order to survive, we had to learn how to get along with everybody."

During a time in the Middle Ages, the Baltic rulers dominated the Northern European plain. Today the Baltic way of life, along with inherited characteristics like patience and cooperation, provides an ideal environment for nurturing a fledgling market system. All three Baltic countries have essentially agricultural economies. Still, slowly but surely a new generation of entrepreneurs—most of the domestic variety—is beginning to emerge. Some, like the Lithuanian-American joint-venture Grigishkes, which makes wood and paper products, also do business abroad. Grigishkes has a brisk trade going in Sweden, Denmark, and Germany, where it sells low-cost building materials. It's had less success, however, marketing its toilet paper to overseas buyers, though the distinctive brown rolls that show little pieces of wood shavings in the sheets continue to be big sellers in Russia, particularly since a paper shortage there has forced *Pravda* to stop regular publication.

What early success Baltic businessmen have had is due largely to the thoroughness of the region's postcommunist house-cleaning. In Russia, Ukraine, and elsewhere, most Party officials merely changed their name tags after the failed coup and started calling themselves capitalists. They still control the important ministries and the banks, and they still keep a tight hold on most of the new business opportunities. In the Baltics, all the communists who opposed reform were given early retirement. The rest, as one Lithuanian diplomat said, "have been pushed into third- and fourth-level government jobs where they can't do any damage."

It's no longer communism that poses the biggest threat to the survival of democratic reforms in the Baltics and other parts of the former union, it's nationalism. "Communism, as it developed in the Soviet Union under Stalin ... was effective in sedating nationalism," wrote Connor Cruise O'Brien in *The New York Review of Books.* "As communism wore off, nationalism woke up again and the disintegration of multinational polities set in."

The initial signs of nationalism in Georgia, Moldova, Russia, and the Baltics seemed to be democratic, but later manifestations, namely in Georgia, where the first democratically elected president was overthrown in a mini civil war, were not.

"Democracy," O'Brien continued, "is more vulnerable than nationalism, in that, among people who have not grown accustomed to it, democracy is more likely to be judged by its immediate results. Thus economic hardship tends to discredit a new democracy. . . . In Eastern Europe, many of those who are now attracted to democracy, because of its associations with success and economic well-being in the West, may well recoil from it when they find that democracy does not immediately deliver those good things. Also, the discovery of things like corruption in elected governments may be followed by a tendency to repudiate not just the particular people concerned, but the system they are felt to represent."

In such cases conditions would be right for national saviors with military or paramilitary backing to take over.

The mild-mannered Balts say that could never happen where they live. Citing Riga, Latvia's capital, as an example of international togetherness, Kalnins explained that Baltic people, especially Latvians, have no trouble getting along with anyone. "Riga was developed by the Germans seven centuries ago, and since then, we've always had a lot of foreigners. Because of our history, we're used to being caught between the East and West. We get along well with the Russians in Latvia. We also know how the Russian system works. We can be very good go-betweens."

Those comments were echoed by Ilya Schneider, a Latvian businessman living in Boston. "History has made us very practical people," he said. Schneider acts as a broker between Russians and Westerners, putting together deals of his own and picking up the loose ends of others that have unraveled. One day, he's selling containers of Russian textiles sitting in Rotterdam and a Russian patent for air filters that the Russians are unable to produce themselves. The next, it's thousands of board feet of timber and a Russian water purification process.

The reason Russians trust the Balts, Schneider said, is because, "We're half Russian, or at least we've been Russianized." They're also able to help Russians keep their hard-currency profits out of Russia, and thus out of the hands of the tax-hungry government, a critical component of any foreign trade deal in these uncertain times.

Under the communists, the Baltic states built mini-vans, locomotives, radios, and televisions. They produced 80 percent of the pharmaceutical drugs used in Soviet hospitals. But when the flow of Soviet raw materials to make these goods stopped, so did production. (Moscow apparently felt that destroying their principal source of pain-relief medication was a small price to pay for keeping the Baltics in their place.) Kremlin economics was a form of mercantilism that kept goods and supplies moving in a more or less steady flow from Soviet manufacturers to Soviet consumers. But with that network permanently closed down, the Baltic nations are eagerly looking for replacement partners.

Estonia has found a substitute for the Soviet Union in Finland, its longtime Western role model. Lithuania and Latvia are looking to Germany and the United States, with the Latvians so far scoring the biggest deals. The Germans are refurbishing three shipping facilities in Latvia, and the American cereal maker Kellogg's is negotiating to set up a huge corn flakes factory.

"The only problem," said Kalnins, "is that we don't grow any corn."

Everywhere in the Baltics you hear politicians talking of creating "trade bridges" and "commercial corridors" between Russia, with its rich abundance of natural resources, and the West, with its rich abundance of wealthy investors. One plan being seriously considered by the Japanese calls for making Latvia a "transshipment depot" for products made in Japan and sent across Russia by rail to Riga, where they would be distributed to Western markets. Relying on thousands of miles of Russian railroads to deliver the goods may not insure profitability for the Japanese or the Balts, but it will certainly enrich scores of enterprising thieves all along the way.

All three Baltic countries want to become service and assembly centers, and with worker productivity 10 percent higher than that in next-door Russia and salaries considerably lower than cheap-labor outposts like Poland and Hungary, they're in a position to make a serious bid for business.

For foreign companies, the Baltics offer a low-cost manufacturing base right on Western Europe's doorstep. Here's a unique opportunity to invest in the emerging post-Soviet markets without taking on some of the built-in risks that come with doing business in other former republics. That's not to say that Baltic business ventures will be hassle-free. Even simple things like finding a hotel room, ordering a meal, and placing a phone call can be a full-time occupation. Also, any effort to start a new business in the Baltics will involve reeducating workers about what it means to *do* business.

"It will require a special kind of investor," said Lithuanian ambassador Stasys Lozoratis. "What we need right now are people with the resources and the patience to teach us. I think what they'll discover is that we're very good at learning."

Chapter Fourteen

Buried Treasure

For a wheeler-dealer Texas lawyer with no diplomatic training, who couldn't speak a word of Russian and, by his own admission, knew next to nothing about U.S.-Soviet relations, Robert Strauss seemed like an odd choice to be named American ambassador to the Soviet Union. Strauss was someone used to shmoozing oil company executives and industrial tycoons, not new-age revolutionaries. But he wasn't picked to go to Moscow for his skills as a diplomat. He was going there to take care of business, and for that, Washington decisionmakers believed, it would be difficult to find a better man for the job.

Here's the former Soviet Union, a place of vast natural resources, resources that might as well not exist for all the good they're doing anybody. And here's 73-year-old Robert Strauss (roughly the same age as the Soviet state itself), whose reputation for causing money to appear out of nowhere has become part of corporate American mythology. Strauss' assignment, according to President George Bush, who appointed him to the post, is to help U.S. companies turn all of those raw resources into hard currency, and do it before the Germans, Italians, French, and everyone else in the world beats them to it.

The idea of choosing a person such as Robert Strauss to be our man in Moscow wasn't that unique. Take away his official political status, and Strauss is merely the latest in a long line of big-business types that stretches back to the early days of Bolshevism, including Armand Hammer of Occidental Petroleum, Donald Kendall of PepsiCo, and Dwayne Andreas of the Archer-Daniels-Midland Company. In the wake of the failed coup, what American businesses in Russia and the other runaway republics needed wasn't another thumb-twiddling foreign service officer, but a man of action, or someone who acted like he was a man of action—and that's what Strauss was.

In a letter attached to his financial disclosure statement, Strauss promised to sell his stock in PepsiCo, where he was a member of the board, and in ADM, whose chairman he had accompanied to the Soviet Union on his only previous trip there.

TOP FOREIGN BUSINESS INVESTORS IN THE SOVIET UNION

JOINT-VENTURE PARTNER	NUMBER OF WORKING JOINT VENTURES	DOLLARS INVESTED (MILLIONS)
Germany	244	284
Finland	175	194
United States	172	288
Austria	99	113
Great Britain	96	118
Italy	95	279
Switzerland	69	60
Sweden	56	102
France	54	244
Canada	37	75
Japan	27	49
Spain	21	30
Australia	21	117
Netherlands	20	38
Others	70	173
	Total 1,256	Total $2,164 billion

Source: PlanEcon Research Associates, June 1990.

However, he didn't promise to mothball his time-honored Mr. Fixit act.

One of his first official excursions outside the Russian Republic was a get-acquainted visit to Kazakhstan for talks with President Nursultan Nazarbayev. Kazakhstan is the focus of the largest Western investment proposal in Central Asia, a plan by Chevron to develop the Tengiz oil field, estimated to hold 25 billion barrels.

"I've been helping people negotiate and get together all my life. . . . I've made a success of that, professionally and personally," Strauss told *The Washington Post.* "And I hope to do that here. I guess that's what I'm here for, to make these transactions work."

But Kazakhstan is the East, not East *Texas,* and, as others before Strauss have discovered, the rules for doing business are a little different. You drink tea, and you have long conversations about deals that may take months, even years, to work out. If you haven't got the time or patience to build relationships—and many Western firms don't—you can't expect to win any contracts.

Are Americans too interested in a fast buck to make any serious money in Soviet ventures? Strauss' attitude so far hasn't been reassuring. Looking forward to parleying his latest political appointment into new business for his Washington law firm, he showed up in Moscow saying that he planned to stay on the job only for a year or two. That's fine for taking home the coveted, and highly marketable, title of "Ambassador," but by Soviet standards it's hardly long enough to say hello.

As with any high-profile middleman, Strauss thrives on hype, much of it so moldy by now it's taken on a life of its own. Like an old golf pro at a country club who spends most of his time kibitzing in the lounge, he's a living legend, and his natural element is a power lunch. But in a country like Russia, notoriously short on food and established leaders, it's not clear where to have lunch or who to have it with.

"Virtually everyone in Washington recognizes that Bob Strauss is 99 percent hot air," columnist Michael Kinsley wrote a few years ago, "yet they all maintain this 'elder statesman' . . .

routine like some sort of elaborate prank on the rest of the world."

If that's true, Strauss' mission to Moscow could put him in the same league as another great pretender, the late Armand Hammer. Regarded as America's unofficial emissary to every Kremlin leader since the revolution, Hammer traded for more than half a century on one twenty-minute meeting with Lenin. No one was better at playing the role of an expert on Soviet business and politics, and whenever his credentials were questioned, he merely pulled out his trump card. Once, while General Secretary Konstantin Chernenko was giving a speech in Moscow, Hammer fell asleep in the audience, and by the time he woke up, he'd missed almost the entire address. "Did he see me sleeping?" Hammer asked one of his assistants. The answer was yes. "Well, watch his mouth drop," Hammer said. When Chernenko asked him what he thought of his talk, Hammer paused for a moment. "I was surprised about some of your remarks," he told the Soviet leader, giving the impression that he'd spotted some grave ideological error. "When I was talking to Lenin, he said just the opposite."

Hammer, whose father founded the American Communist Party, started his career by opening the famous Sacco and Vanzetti pencil factory in Moscow. Later, as chairman of Occidental Petroleum, he embarked on a number of ambitious Soviet enterprises. He made his early fortune, though, not by shrewd investments or carefully laid plans for developing oil projects, but by purloining Russian artworks and selling them in the West. Faberge eggs, paintings by Old Masters, and other art objects that might otherwise have been destroyed by the Bolsheviks were all part of Hammer's vast inventory, and essential props in his campaign to portray himself as the savior of Russian culture.

Hammer consistently lost money on Occidental's activities in the Soviet Union, and soon after his death in 1990, his successors at Oxy bid a hasty retreat from his projects there. Clearly, they didn't share their predecessor's costly obsession with Russia. The company's biggest profits came from oil deals with Libya. But that hardly mattered to Hammer. He never really thought of the Soviet Union as a profit center, anyway. Instead, his Russian adventures were designed to promote his image as an international genius, and later his candidacy for the Nobel Peace Prize, an honor he was still trying to buy on his deathbed at the age of 92.

What Armand Hammer knew, and Robert Strauss soon found out, is that it's a lot harder to do business with the Soviets than it is to act like you're doing business with them. Recent reforms have made dealmaking even more complicated than it was in Hammer's time, when dictators ruled and democracy was suppressed. It was always much easier dealing with people whose word was law. Now nobody has any idea what the law is.

Then there's the costly and time-consuming matter of cleaning up after the Party. Each new industrial operation is also a salvage and rebuilding project. The reason for the extra work is the previous regime. The communists had a reverse Midas touch. Everything they got their hands on is either broken, missing, or lethal.

"They could turn gold into lead," said an engineer working for a German joint venture. "Just look at the mess they made. Every industry in this country needs a complete overhaul, and that includes the gold industry, too."

One of the reasons the former Soviet Union qualifies for last-frontier status is the undeniable richness of its natural resources. But developing those resources will require cleaning up decades' worth of pollution and decay created by the old system. To some companies, that's all part of the challenge. To others, it's just too much trouble. An Italian firm considering building a resort complex along the Caspian coast of Azerbaijan backed out when it learned that the water in the picturesque location was so toxic it could send vacationers to the hospital.

Industrial development will also mean creating an infrastructure to transport products, since—once again, thanks to the communists—no workable system presently exists. To maximize political control and make it more difficult for European nations to stage invasions, Party leaders purposely kept Soviet communications and transportation facilities primitive. The plan succeeded, only now it presents a major obstacle to outside businesses that will either have to work around the problems or find some way to correct them.

The Soviets have never been very successful at applying their technologies or management theories to their own industries, or anyone else's, as their forty-year experience in Eastern Europe shows. The fault lies in a litany of contradictions that kept their production tied in knots that no amount of twisting and turning could undo:

- Enterprises that were supposed to depend on one another were in competition, but those that could have benefited from competition were purposely isolated.

- Exporting technology, except in the form of military weapons to client governments, was considered tantamount to cooperating with the enemy, but importing technology that could have helped Soviet researchers improve their own was seen as an admission of defeat.

- Decentralizing the production of vital goods would have made the system less dependent on single sources of supply, but because that would have weakened central control, delays or shutdowns in one plant could throw the entire network out of whack, as the following table suggests:

SOVIET MONOPOLY*

PRODUCT	SOURCE	PRODUCTION PERCENTAGE
Cigarette filters	Armenia	100
Oil-well pumps	Azerbaijan	100
Electric irons	Kalingrad	93
Die-casting machines	Moldova	99
Tramway rails	Russia	100
Sewing machines	Russia	100
Forklifts	Ukraine	86
Corn harvesters	Ukraine	100
Cotton harvesters	Uzbekistan	100

*Figures for 1989.

The Soviets need construction and road-building equipment, telecommunications technology, and food-processing machinery, none of which their own factories can produce. If they had to invent a plan for crippling their industrial capability, it would have been difficult to come up with a better one.

The energy industry shows how much needs to be done to put things in good working order. When it still had fifteen republics, the Soviet Union produced a quarter of the world's coal and natural gas and a fifth of its oil. This provided the central government with slightly less than half of its hard-currency income, revenue it desperately needed to purchase goods from the West. With that level of dependency, any other nation might have refined the management of its energy industry into a science—but not the Soviets.

Soviet oil and gas exports fell from a high of 12.5 million barrels a day in 1987 to 11.4 million barrels in 1990. In January of 1991, production dropped 9 percent below 1990 levels, and later that same year Aeroflot temporarily closed ninety-two of its domestic airports for lack of fuel. If the trend continues, the Soviets could soon become energy importers. But without the money from oil sales abroad, how can they pay for foreign energy, let alone imported food and consumer goods, both of which are tied to earnings from oil exports?

"If . . . there is major cooperation from international agencies and substantially increased direct investment of energy multinationals, a turnaround is possible," concluded a 1991 report by the Congressional Research Service. If not, there will be more of the same "falling levels of efficiency, inadequate technology, and poor environmental safeguards that are characteristic of Soviet energy production."

The blame for this incredible state of affairs goes to industrial managers in every oil-producing republic who control production and steal profits. Yet, even if there weren't massive amounts of administrative corruption, outmoded Soviet technology would still be unable to produce oil efficiently or safely. As things stand now, it will be impossible to tap proven reserves without material assistance from the West. Unfortunately, when assistance in the form of advanced technology is provided, a new set of problems comes into play. The Soviets, Western oil officials claim, ignore the instructions, destroy the machinery, and end up creating more pollution.

In the late 1970s, the Soviets wanted to expand oil drilling in Azerbaijan but didn't want foreigners involved because they might mingle with the locals and give them dangerous democratic ideas. So, they decided to buy Western oil equipment for hard currency and operate it themselves. What happened next was a typical Soviet how-*not*-to scenario. Since the equipment was extremely expensive, Soviet bosses didn't want to waste parts that would be too costly to replace—so they simply didn't use them.

One such part was a filter crucial to preventing the release of poisonous sulfur. As the wells were drilled, sulfur was freed from the ground, and with no filters in place, it polluted a large section of the Caspian Sea, defoliated the region's vegetation, and killed or injured hundreds of people. When the extent of the disaster became known, the Soviets blamed the European suppliers for not selling them better technology. The Europeans responded by saying the Soviets should have read the operator's manual more carefully.

Just as it was in the days of the California gold rush, when more people got rich selling mining tools to the prospectors than discovering gold, there's probably more money to be made in Soviet oil fields selling anti-pollution technology than there is drilling for oil, assuming the Soviets have the mineral barter to pay the bill.

Since 90 percent of all Soviet oil is located in Russia, which now has sole authority over it, oil concessions and development contracts should be easier to negotiate than they were when the commissars were in charge. That doesn't mean they *will* be, or that, once wells are drilled, operations will run smoothly. Usually, Russians insist that modern oil drilling equipment be brought in, arguing, correctly, that without it production will suffer. At the same time, the new Russian government has the habit of insisting that the supplier pay all import duties in dollars. That's not the only extra cost. Normal wear and tear on the machinery—normal, that is, by the Russian definition—can also be a big expense.

The damage issue is an acute problem, particularly in Siberia, where winters are so harsh that equipment often freezes solid. Fires are used to counteract the cold, and it's not unusual in some areas to see blazes burning under trucks, oil rigs, and other valuable hardware. Orange growers in Florida and California do the same thing to protect their crops from the frost. In Russia, though, the same technique has sent entire drilling operations up in flames.

If that's how they treat their oil wells, many concerned observers wonder how they're taking care of their large and potentially harmful supply of nuclear materials. The question involves what nervous types might call the survival of mankind, and the answer isn't likely to lower anyone's anxiety level. Stored in Russia and Ukraine, site of the Chernobyl meltdown in 1986, Soviet atomic weapons and other assorted byproducts of the Cold War present two distinct problems: They could fall into the hands of an evil dictator (take your pick), or they could remain in Russian hands. Either possibility is not encouraging.

Over the years, the Soviets have displayed a unique talent for destruction, and channeling it in useful pursuits won't be easy. Look at the timber industry. Soviet forests constitute over a third of the world's total timber area, some 747 million hectares. That represents an estimated yield of more than 79,000 million cubic meters of lumber. So why is the country constantly running out of wood and paper? Again, it's a matter of planning. It's easier to cut down the closest trees and forget about the rest, and that's exactly what the communists did for decades, clear-cutting the entire landscape in some places and leaving others untouched. What's left, more than 70 percent of the country's timber, is either inaccessible or over age.

There is a market for Soviet wood products in the West, even for old-growth wood. Moldings, door parts, and window frames could all be produced and sold, and companies such as Russian Wood Express, an American-Soviet joint venture, are taking advantage. But, as always, the first step is to supply Soviets with the right tools and training to do their part.

"It's our intent . . . to sell equipment from the U.S. to the Soviet Union and, in return, get a product that's manufactured correctly—to U.S. and Canadian standards," said Robert Prezzano, vice chairman of Russian Wood Express. "We're not talking about super technology. Heck, we could even sell them used equipment. . . . Many of [the Russian] saw mills look like mills we had fifty to eighty years ago."

The woods have always been a place of great mystery to Russians, and not even the animal inhabitants have been safe from attempts at managing what goes on there. In 1982, a bureaucrat in the leather industry got the idea that obtaining deerskins would greatly simplify meeting the leather quota for his factory's Five Year Plan. After convincing his superiors that the plan was workable, the next order of business was to preserve the deer. So, hunters were loaded into helicopters and flown into the woods to shoot wolves that preyed on the deer.

All went well for the first year. Then, the deer, undisturbed by predators, began propagating so profusely the factory couldn't keep up. Deer hunting teams killed the animals in such great numbers they no longer had the time to carry away all the carcasses, which had been supplying the villages near the factory with meat. Whereas the factory met its quota, local villagers, who depended on the deer, went hungry as tons of meat rotted in the distant woods.

But the story goes on to illustrate a uniquely Russian domino theory. Villagers were involved in the timber business and had their production quotas to meet, too. Without ample food, they had to plant gardens, taking away from the time they could spend harvesting trees. When their timber quotas weren't met, it created a ripple effect, which hurt the furniture and construction industries and reduced fuel supplies to wood-burning factories, one of which was the local leather plant.

Some people think of cultivating their gardens. Russians have always thought in terms of expanding theirs, taking whatever they wanted in one place, then moving on to the next like nomadic gatherers, whose wealth of natural resources made them complacent about planning ahead. The Russian historian V. O. Klyuchevsky (1841–1911) proposed that "Russia's history is the history of a country colonizing itself." But it was never colonization in the constructive sense, merely wasteful exploitation. Nor did their colonial excursions stop at the border. In the early 1800s, while Napoleon was entering Moscow, Russians were establishing settlements in northern California, apparently looking for more easy pickins. The search continued well into the next century.

As wasteful as the Russians have been with their resources, at least they didn't systematically destroy them. Enter the Bolsheviks and their descendants. Over the years, hare-brained communist industrial priorities have poisoned Soviet soil and polluted rivers and lakes, turning many portions of the country into "dead zones." One such disaster area is the Aral Sea, between Kazakhstan and Uzbekistan.

The problem began sixty years ago, when blacks from the American South, fleeing white repression, came to the Soviet Union, where they helped establish its first cotton fields. Hoping to maximize productivity, the government channeled entire rivers into the fields. But after decades, the once-abundant water supply has declined, the cotton industry has fallen on hard times, and the Aral Sea, where the rivers would have flowed if they hadn't been diverted, is disappearing.

Poor land management is as old as Russia itself. The Bolsheviks merely improved on the tradition, especially when it came to food production, where leaders saw the political benefit of controlled shortages. Meager diets kept people tired and lethargic and, therefore, deterred their counterrevolutionary impulses. The only agricultural conservation in Soviet history has been in the area of calories, which Lenin decreed should be held to minimum levels, sufficient enough to keep people alive but not enough to supply them with energy that might be directed against the state.

Another reason for the low output of food was the backward conditions of Soviet agricultural research, which, for almost a

generation, was based on the scientific application of Marxist-
Leninist political theories to the growth of farm products. In the
1930s, a Russian peasant agronomist named T. D. Lysenko declared that biology and genetics work according to the same laws
that Marx ascribed to society; namely, that plants and animals
would change characteristics with proper training, just as people
do when they're educated in the wisdom of socialism. To any
committed bureaucrat, this was merely a logical extension of
Marxist thinking, and as such made perfect sense.

In 1948, the Central Committee officially adopted Lysenko's
conclusions as dogma, and Soviet farmers were told to "teach"
their plants to grow differently. That same year, the Kremlin
announced to the world the invention of a new science called
agrobiology, destined to revolutionize agriculture. The revolution
lasted until the late 1950s, when Khrushchev was forced to admit
the idea had been a failure. But by then it was too late to save
Soviet agriculture, which was already being supplemented by
food purchases from the West that today account for the biggest
part of the nation's multibillion-dollar foreign debt.

In one attempt to improve domestic food production, Soviets
in the 1980s bought a huge shipment of fertilizer and superphos-
phoric acid from their old friend Armand Hammer at Occidental
Petroleum. The chemicals were spread over vast stretches of
farmland, but when they failed to produce the desired results,
officials threatened to sue Oxy for misrepresenting its product.
Dismayed by the charges, company representatives rushed to the
scene. It didn't take them long to discover what the problem was.
The Russians hadn't diluted the powerful fertilizers. In an attempt
to make their crops grow faster, they poured them directly onto
the ground and burned out the soil.

Into this environment comes the Western businessman with
his high technology and new ideas for increasing production,
reducing waste, and generally keeping things neat and clean. But
to do all this first means reforming the world's ultimate throw-
away society. Controlling the waste of raw materials would make
a good place to start. Tons of virtually every type of discarded

scrap material document the Soviet attitude that manufacturing mistakes are unimportant because new resources will always be available to try again.

There are big profits to be made from Soviet junk. In one example of turning waste into wealth, a foreign newspaper correspondent heard about a Russian factory manufacturing thermostats that contained platinum wires. Aware of the high reject rate in any Soviet enterprise, he managed to get into the waste area of the factory, where he saw piles of broken thermostats, most still containing the platinum. Patiently taking apart as many as he could, he filled his suitcase with platinum wiring, transported it out of the country, and made a killing.

In the process of improving their economy, the Soviets, either with or without outside help, will have to dismantle many existing industries and rebuild them again from scratch. This will add to an already staggering amount of debris, but it will also increase the amount of enriched junk available to any prospector with the time to look for it. An American businessman, Arthur Skidell, worked out a way to salvage used copper from broken city street lights and sell it in the West. The problem was determining who owned the stuff. Even though it was clearly tossed out, because it was installed by the Kremlin, it technically belonged to the government. But which one? Russia and the city of Moscow also had their claims to ownership. Fighting over Soviet garbage has become a major occupation in itself, and when Skidell was last heard from, the copper controversy was still going on.

In the field of processed metals, the Soviets seem to have found their niche, although some might argue they're still essentially peddling junk. Unable to meet the purity levels for Western aluminum, they sell their own low-grade product cheaply to manufacturers of construction materials or castings for automobile parts. Here's a case in which offering inferior goods has actually helped the Soviets to take over nearly 10 percent of the Western market, a share that experts predict will increase now that the military is cutting back on its purchases.

But until more manufactured goods are marketable in the

West, the best investment return is in natural, not man-made, resources. For years, many successful foreign companies have profited by obtaining payment for their goods and services in coal, wood, and other commodities. Besides Pepsi and McDonald's, corporations such as General Electric and Xerox have traded turbines and photocopiers for such items as whale bones and building materials. Coca-Cola traded coke syrup for Lada cars, which it later sold in Asia. In a recent turbine deal, General Electric agreed to be paid in timber, which it planned to turn into plywood and sell to the Japanese. "The only real issue now," said a spokesman for GE, "was deciding how many trees equal a turbine."

Barter, or countertrade, as it's sometimes called, remains one of the few profitable ways of doing business in Russia and the other former republics. Just don't get stuck with a trade product you can't sell, or what's worse, can't take out of the country. It's usually more difficult to obtain export licenses for raw materials than for semi-manufactured products. And keep in mind, dealing in raw materials requires dealing with government officials, whose requests for bribes can drive up the price of any bargain.

Many resource items, such as coal, oil, and precious metals, are sold directly by government officials, and reformers are just as active in the business as the people they replaced. According to Central Committee records, now in the hands of the Russian government, three years before the 1991 coup attempt, the Politburo started transferring gems and hard currency to banks in Western Europe. During the same period, more than a few directors of state enterprises, anticipating the collapse of central planning, played follow the leader and began exporting vast quantities of strategic metals, such as titanium, nickel, uranium, and rhodium, and keeping the hard-currency profits.

Confusion over ruble convertibility and the scarcity of dollars have made resources an even more important medium of exchange than they were under the communists. Everyone in the barter game is competing for resources. Yet there are pitfalls to watch out for. Many a Western businessman has shipped his merchandise to the Soviets only to learn that the return shipment of a promised barter item had been delayed or canceled.

With the republics now in control of their own resources, transactions could move more efficiently. Some places, such as Ukraine, even have food to trade. Still, it's often hard to be sure who has the authority to sanction deals, and until you find out, it's just as hard to be sure what deals to make.

The new commonwealth structure, dominated by the Slavic countries of Russia, Byelorussia, and Ukraine, might be the beginning of a better system than the one the communists developed, provided it substitutes incentives for quotas, decentralizes the production of vital goods, encourages competition, and promotes smarter land and resource management. However, in a part of the world in which ethnic conflict is par for the course, religious and nationalistic differences can always turn ugly and ruin everything.

Meanwhile, General Electric is wondering what do with the several tons of Russian nails it picked up as part of a trade for its turbines. GE officials, though, know how to look on the bright side. After all, these are people who believe that progress is their most important product. In a country that needs wood, hammers, and saws, cornering the market on that many nails has to pay off someday.

Chapter Fifteen

Lights, Comrades, Action

On Saturday night, April 6, 1991, Soviet state-run television preempted its usual weekend schedule of lectures and talent contests to air a rebroadcast of the Academy Awards Show from Hollywood. The program was watched by millions of viewers, and what they saw was difficult for many to believe. There was Madonna, Kevin Costner, and hundreds of other glamorous celebrities, all looking well dressed, well fed, and visibly pleased to be where they were—which was the exact opposite of the way most Soviets seeing the show felt about being where *they* were.

Russians love American movies because everything in them is an escape from reality, and given all the reality there is to escape *from* in the former Soviet Union, U.S. films are more popular than ever. The titles of the year's biggest hits may have been unfamiliar to most Soviets as they watched the Oscars handed out, but within a matter of months pirated copies of *Dick Tracy, Dances with Wolves,* and all the rest would be on sale in the black market and playing on VCRs all over the country.

There was a time when the Kremlin used movies to drill socialism into the minds of the masses. Yet, during the final years of the Party, theaters and video parlors throughout the Soviet Union were showing hundreds of American films that not only made audiences want more of everything they saw on the screen—including freedom—but demand it. Rather than reinforcing the Party's hold on power, motion pictures were one of the influences that helped to destroy it.

Going to the movies at the height of communist oppression was a far different experience than it became during perestroika. Since the days of the first Bolsheviks, Soviet films had served several functions, none of them having much to do with entertainment. For audiences, what played on the screen was immaterial. A movie theater was a better place to be than a cold, overcrowded apartment. It could also be a useful hideout when you skipped work or just wanted to be alone with your girlfriend.

For the government, though, movies were serious business. They were political tools for educating the public, or at least keeping people's minds off how miserable they were. On another level, films gave officials a way to monitor intellectuals by forcing writers and directors to express their ideas in a tightly controlled environment that reduced everything they said to propaganda.

Historically, the psychological tendency of Russians is to be pessimistic and depressed. "Go to Russia," wrote the French dramatist and travel writer the Marquis de Custine after a trip there in 1839. "It is a useful journey for every foreigner. Whoever has examined that country will be content to live anywhere else. It is always well to know that a society exists where no happiness is possible, because by a law of nature, man cannot be happy unless he is free."

After the revolution, the formal policy of the government was that all citizens should be optimistic and happy with their lot in life. Movies reflected this official change from sad to glad, and to be certain that Russian artistic talent followed the program, an organization known as Glavlitt was established to supervise the content of all creative activity, including making movies. (One reason the Soviet Union never signed an international copyright treaty is because Glavlitt wanted to edit foreign movies any way it wanted.) Get an X rating from Glavlitt, and you might as well start packing for Siberia. Deviation from the Party's view of life and human nature was regarded as a serious crime against the state, and countless screenwriters, directors, and actors were put in prison, some even put to death, for straying into areas Glavlitt considered taboo.

The Party controlled the Soviet movie industry with iron-fisted ruthlessness. But politics wasn't the only problem Soviet directors had to deal with. In the silent era, shortages in raw stock were gotten around by shooting scenes without film until the actors were thoroughly rehearsed, then cameras were loaded for the one-and-only take. Noted director Sergie Eisenstein overcame the film shortage by an imaginative editing process that eventually led to the creation of the montage, a technique that made him famous worldwide. Once the movie industry became a full-time vehicle for propaganda, film supplies increased because it was often necessary for directors to shoot scenes over and over until they pleased the censors from Glavlitt.

With the arrival of glasnost, many moviemakers challenged Glavlitt's ideological guidelines. Among the earliest pioneers in the movement was a small Moscow-based film company called Paritet. The enterprise began in 1988 as an experiment by the Soviet Film Fund, a kind of government bank for state movie studios. The Fund's president, Nikholai Ivanov, was a strong-willed Party member, who also believed in the right of free expression. Leonid Golovnia, a Soviet director and Paritet's founder, persuaded Ivanov to lend the new company 20,000 rubles, and, using that as start-up capital, Golovnia obtained licenses from Goskino, the state film organization, to produce and distribute movies.

Within six months, most of the money was used up, but Paritet had an ace in the hole. Golovnia had friends in the United States, who persuaded a group of Americans to form a partner company that would bring foreign films to the Soviet Union for distribution and find Western investors for co-productions. Although inexperienced in the movie business, the American company, Washington Film Associates, succeeded in persuading New World International to sell Paritet the distribution rights to a 1985 release titled *Black Moon Rising*. The transaction marked the first time an American movie company had ever agreed to license a film for rubles.

To convince Hollywood movie executives to accept Russian money was bad enough, but because foreign companies, under old Soviet regulations, weren't allowed to own rubles, New World was also breaking the law by just being paid. On top of that, currency rules prohibited the American company from even having a bank account, although that problem was solved when Paritet opened a "sub-account" in a Moscow bank to which New World would have access.

At a dinner in Moscow shortly after the contract signing, the president of Paritet, Boris Komarov, proposed a toast to his American partners: "Let's drink to our future," he said. "What we have just done may not be legal, and in six months we could all be in prison."

While it bombed in the United States, *Black Moon Rising*, a sexy technothriller starring Tommy Lee Jones, Robert Vaughn, and Linda Hamilton, was an enormous success in Soviet theaters, where it broke box office records from Moscow to Tashkent. And why not? What Soviets liked about the picture is the same thing they like about every American film—escape—as long as it's fast-paced and exciting, with a lot of high-tech thrills, which, from the Soviet point of view, means cars that don't need a push to get started.

When all of the tickets were added up, Paritet had made 16 million rubles, a profit that sent shock waves through the state film industry, which was getting its first taste of what competition is like. The success of the movie caused a typical Russian reaction—anger and fear. A senior official of Sovexportfilm, the government organization responsible for importing all foreign movies, invited the Americans to his Moscow office to discuss the implications of their new sucess.

"You can imagine my surprise," he said. "Here, I thought I had a monopoly on all foreign film distribution, and then I see your name in all *my* theaters." But didn't the theaters belong to "the people" asked one of Paritet's American partners. Whereupon, the Soviet official informed him that if he didn't cancel its contract with Paritet and deal exclusively with him, there would be "serious problems." "If you want to know what serious problems are," replied the American, "you'll find out when we put a full-page ad in *Variety* and tell everybody how you threatened us. No one in Hollywood will do business with you for the next twenty years."

The Soviet, who had been speaking in English, reverted to an arrogant pre-perestroika posture and dropped into Russian, forcing the Americans to use an official interpreter. The meeting abruptly ended when the Soviet official explained that the government was putting Sovexportfilm on "quasi-independent" status and all subsidies would soon end. This meant that the organization would have to be self-supporting, a state of existence that goes against every socialist instinct there is.

Sovexportfilm's World War II executive bathroom, with its broken toilet seats and exposed plumbing, was evidence enough that the organization was strapped for cash. The Americans offered to make a deal. "You need rubles, and we have millions of them," they told the Soviet. "Maybe we can work something out." Six months later, the offer was made again when Sovexportfilm needed funds for a project, and a relationship was established. Paritet had broken the official monopoly.

Sovexportfilm is no longer the force it once was. Now, each of the former republics makes its own movie deals, a turn of events that requires foreign companies to be extra careful, in that films "on loan" for distribution are often pirated for making into videocassettes. In 1991, this resulted in the Motion Picture Industry of America's initiating a boycott against distributing U.S. films in the Soviet Union. But so far, the action has had little effect.

Almost immediately, the influx of foreign films began putting poorly equipped Soviet filmmakers out of work. The Soviets offered a classic socialist solution to correct the problem, suggesting that Western filmmakers help out by giving them state-of-the-art equipment. The "exchange," they argued, would help create joint productions from which everyone would eventually profit. The reaction in Hollywood was not positive; still, some companies agreed.

Coproduction deals between Soviets and Westerners came to be structured so that the Western party would bring cameras and equipment as part of their investment, and leave them behind when the production was completed. The Western partners were also asked to bring raw stock and equipment for processing "rushes," and hard currency for paying bribes, a critical component in any Russian film deal.

Paritet continued to distribute foreign movies, earning millions of rubles. It also produced its own films. One was a murder mystery called *Fools Die on Fridays*, which sounds better in English than it does as *Jerks Die on Fridays* in Russian.

Paritet coproduced films, too. Since it's relatively inexpensive to shoot movies in Russia, foreign companies approached them with all types of projects. Once, a film producer from Greece wanted to make a children's movie about a little deaf girl who befriends an escaped convict. The producer, who grew up in Detroit, claimed to already have the Barbie doll people interested in a product tie-in. "What's a tie-in?" Paritet's president Boris Komarov wanted to know. The Greek explained that companies pay to have their products shown in movies, and in this case, he said, "If the little deaf girl carries around a Barbie doll, we could get $25,000." "Tie-in good," said Komarov, who'd been studying English for just such occasions as this. And what about splitting the profits when the picture was shown in Soviet theaters, he asked. "Greeks have no problem accepting rubles as real money," the producer said. "Don't forget, we have drachmas."

Children's films are big in Russia, where the government has always promoted family togetherness, even during Stalin's time, when kids were encouraged to spy on their parents. One of Paritet's first big coproductions was another children's movie, a 1.5-million-ruble joint venture with a Florida company to make a Soviet version of the Grizzly Adams story, this time focusing on

Misha, the Russian son Grizzly never knew he had. Original plans called for the film to be shot in Soviet Georgia, using an American and Russian cast with English dialogue. But a combination of money delays, political turmoil, and a shortage of trained bears caused constant problems. The veteran movie bear Paritet wanted to use as Misha's faithful companion in the picture was also unavailable. In its last film, the final scene called for the animal to be killed, and an overzealous special-effects person shot him.

Despite setbacks, Paritet was riding high. Yet certain managerial shortcomings were already showing themselves. Never having earned more than three or four hundred rubles a month in their previous jobs, company officials, many of them former state film industry bureaucrats, suddenly found themselves in control of millions.

First, they invested money in their friends' movie projects, most of which were unfinished fiascos. In the past, when all films were produced by the government, there was no accounting or accountability for how funds were spent. If a director ran over budget, he simply asked the state for more money, and nine times out of ten he got it.

Since films were never thought of as commercial products in the first place, no attention was ever paid to how much money they cost, or whether they made a profit. A year, two years, three years, the making of a Soviet movie, like the making of anything in the Soviet Union, could go on forever. Before long, various filmmakers working at Paritet began to insist that the company finance their personal projects. Paritet often had to agree, or face prolonged office squabbles until they did.

Paritet's management splurged on cars (including two Mercedes), clothes, and group vacations for the entire staff, a staff whose size seemed to increase weekly as new people were hired to sit around and do nothing. The company was turning into a private-enterprise copy of every state bureaucracy. Of its forty-five employees, only the accounting department and a few dedicated production people put in a full day's work. The rest appeared when they felt like it, and did as little as possible.

Similar to most Soviet organizations, Paritet was run like a collective. The slightest decision required the approval of a majority of the staff. To Soviets, "majority" means "unanimity." Everyone has to agree. But unlike simpler times, when the workers always agreed with the boss, in the collectives that sprang up during glasnost, a lone dissenter could stifle any proposal in the name of "democracy." Komarov, a bureaucrat from the Ministry of Culture before he became Paritet's president, often labored for days, even weeks, over how to get everyone to agree with a policy.

Imbued with the collective mentality himself, Komarov failed to notice the problem. He only saw how many people were employed by his company (in the Soviet Union, size has always been important) and assumed that the organization would run itself.

Meanwhile, Paritet's American partners were growing frustrated. *Black Moon Rising* had proven there was money to be made distributing U.S. films. But Paritet seemed to feel it had made enough money for the time being. Its board of directors in Moscow abruptly decided that the company didn't need any more American movies for distribution. A "unanimous" decision was made to produce Soviet films, even though Soviet movies are rarely exportable and invariably lose money at the box office.

The Americans disagreed with the new direction the company was taking, particularly after they were informed that some of their millions of rubles in past profits would be used to cover production costs of the new movies Paritet wanted to make. The money was in Paritet's bank account because the Americans, by Soviet law, couldn't open one of their own. Until 1991, when banking regulations were changed, every outside investor with money in a "sub-account" was at the mercy of his Soviet partner.

During this period, Paritet's financial director visited the United States to help resolve the growing conflict. It was her first trip to America, and she was awed by what she saw. While on a tour of New York with a Soviet émigré interpreter hired by Paritet's U.S. partners, she confided that her objective was to use the Americans to obtain financing and learn about business, after which they would no longer be needed. The Americans were so naive, she said. They didn't realize they would never control the rubles they earned, let alone have any say in joint productions. When that news came back to them, the Americans' worst fears were confirmed. Paritet wasn't just going down the tubes, it was taking their money along.

Under socialism, everyone milked the cow, but no one thought about feeding it. When the cow stopped producing milk, somebody was blamed and a new cow had to be found. Noticing it was losing money on films, Paritet concluded that the film business itself was at fault and decided to diversify. So, with some of its remaining rubles it leased a bee farm.

If this weren't happening in real life, it would have made an unbelievable movie. In desperation, the people at Washington Film decided to try dealing with Paritet one last time. The Soviets wanted to make movies. Very well, they said, let's make a movie.

The vehicle chosen for the attempted reconciliation was the Grizzly Adams picture, which had been on the back burner for months, waiting for money to arrive from an American investor in Florida. The movie, assuming it was made at all, could do well in the Soviet Union, and possibly the United States. But at this point, there was no guarantee there would even be film in the cameras.

The script had a little of everything—sex, adventure, and male bonding. According to the plot, Grizzly, as a young man, has an affair with a beautiful Russian girl who lives with her family in Northern California. The girl's father finds out that his daughter is pregnant and sends her back to the Urals, where Misha, Grizzly's son, is born. When he grows up, Misha learns who his real father is and journeys with his pet bear all the way to America to find him.

Since perestroika, a number of Western films have been made in the Soviet Union, including *Russia House,* with Sean Connery and Michelle Pfeiffer, and *The Clearing,* a sort of Russianized *Quest for Fire,* starring George Segal. A Russian film typically takes two to three times longer to shoot than an American movie. But even American movies made in Russia can seem to take forever. Frank *(The Doors)* Whaley signed to do a picture titled *Back in the USSR,*

a joint Soviet-American production shot in Moscow in 1990. Mid-
way through the filming, Whaley, showing signs of fatigue,
moaned to one reporter, "Three months and two weeks. That's
how long I've been here, and it seems like seven-and-a-half years."

To a Russian crew, though, time is money—good money.
From the director to the gaffers, the aim of any Russian production staff is to draw out the moviemaking process as long as they
can. When the government was paying all of the bills, this allowed
everyone to earn an income that could carry them for years.
Scouting locations, building sets, and bribing local officials were,
and still are, used as excuses to stall the shooting schedule and
increase the costs of production. Also, the longer a film takes to
shoot, the more opportunities there are for the crew to steal
furniture from the sets and clothes from the costume department.

The Misha project started out as an opportunity for international cooperation. There was an American director, an Israeli
producer, a British supervisor of photography, Italian animal experts, and actors from the United States and Russia. But problems
started on Day One.

After several weeks of sitting around Moscow waiting for the
Soviets to set up a production office, the Americans quietly obtained a copy of the contract with the hotel where they were
supposed to be staying and discovered that Paritet had not only
lied about renting adequate office space, but hadn't arranged for
business equipment. By the time additional room was found and
computers shipped from the United States, the production was
several weeks behind schedule.

Despite constantly changing regulations, hotel bills can often
be paid in rubles, but Soviets seldom tell that to visitors. Doing so
would ruin a perfect opportunity to bilk them for hard currency,
something the American crew found out when they got a block of
rooms for rubles by doing the same thing Russians do. They
bribed the hotel manager.

Angry when they heard that the foreigners were fending for
themselves, the Soviets retaliated with their secret weapon—inac-
tion. Paritet's drivers refused to drive, the translators refused to

translate, and the company treasurer refused to provide the American contingent with its daily allotment of rubles for living expenses. Paritet also demanded artistic control of the film and final authority over the entire production. This time, it was the Americans who refused, and the war continued.

Company transportation was at a standstill, except on one occasion, when a driver deliberately tried to run over one of the American crew members. Having lost control of the film, the Soviets were so mad that one of the foreign coproducers remarked, "I don't care about making the movie anymore. I just want to get out of this country alive."

Finally, the hotel, acting on a counterbribe by Paritet officials, began demanding dollars instead of rubles. When the crew balked, the director was removed from his room one night as he was taking a bath. The producer returned to his room to find his bags packed and his girlfriend guarding the door against three menacing Russian chambermaids.

This only intensified the Americans' push for independence. They hired their own interpreters and drivers, got new hotel rooms for rubles, made their own arrangements for telephones and fax machines, struck a deal with the Moscow McDonald's for food, and opened a supply line to the black market.

After nearly a month of delays, the production was actually beginning to move forward. But whatever residue of goodwill remained in the U.S.-Soviet partnership was completely gone. Expecting capitulation, not progress, from the Americans, this upsurge of resourcefulness put Paritet in a temporary state of shock. In retaliation for Western ingenuity, one company administrator was a no-show for a Saturday morning screen test, and no one, including many top Russian actors and actresses, could get into the locked studio facilities to use the cameras. After several hours of waiting, the Israeli producer asked what they should do.

"How many rubles does it cost to repair a door?" asked one of the American partners. A Soviet on the production crew said about a hundred. "Wait five more minutes," said the American, "then break it in and leave the money in an envelope on the desk."

The missing Paritet official arrived an hour later with the keys and found the door in splinters.

With its influence over daily production activity almost nil, Paritet turned its attention to money. When the Americans wouldn't disclose the name of the person they bribed for hotel rooms, the Russians informed them that when the principal photography began in Soviet Georgia and weeks of hotel space would be needed, the money would have to be paid through Paritet in advance—in hard currency totalling $165,000.

Knowing that Georgians are not favorably disposed toward Russians, the Americans decided to investigate and went to Georgia to negotiate their own hotel arrangements. The price they got was 20,000 rubles, plus a $2,000 bribe to a Soviet official in Moscow.

But the people at Paritet had another ploy. They told the Americans it would cost $85,000 to rent the studios in Georgia and that part of the money had to be paid immediately in order to ensure that the production would fit into the studio's schedule. "Just bring us the money in cash," said Paritet's president. "The arrangements are sensitive and I'll have to handle them myself."

The Americans responded by organizing another excursion to Georgia for direct negotiations with the studio officials there. Paritet made an attempt to prevent them from getting visas, which are required for visits to Soviet cities, but that roadblock was overcome with another bribe, and studio space was negotiated for rubles.

The Soviets were now in full retreat. Once it had been established that the American group was going to make the film with or without Russian help, Paritet reluctantly consented to cooperate. At least they could share in the profits. But by then, after many weeks of delay, word of all of the problems had reached financial backers in the United States and the money fell through. What should have been an easy film to produce had turned into a Soviet soap opera that left everything, including the partnership, in ruins.

Accustomed to relying on the government's financial commitments, Soviet moviemakers, like other Soviet businessmen, expect the same commitment from the West. The idea that time is money is a shocking discovery. It will also take the Soviets awhile before they develop a feel for what is and isn't a viable commercial product. In the past, creativity was usually expended in getting around state censors. Openly expressing ideas on film will require some psychological adjustment to the tastes of foreign audiences.

Most Soviet movie writers have dozens of screenplays they've been sitting on for years. Now that censorship is no longer an issue, they can let their impulses take flight. The result is very often something with all of the commercial appeal of a car wreck.

When one Russian screenwriter selling his services saw that a group of Americans wasn't interested in doing a dramatic exposé on Lenin, he reached into his sausage-stained briefcase and pulled out a bundle of greasy papers as thick as a phonebook. "Wait a minute," he said with great enthusiasm. "I just happen to have a six-part series on the life of Solzhenitsyn."

Chapter Sixteen

Working Girls

Muscovites love to talk about how miserable they are. Actually, it's an old Russian pastime given new meaning by present economic conditions. But of all the things there are to grumble about, few seem to give men and women in the Russian capital more personal satisfaction than complaining about one another.

"Women should be ladies in public, slaves in the kitchen, and whores in the bedroom," said a 35-year-old Moscow bank manager, describing his ideal mate. "Women are nothing but problems," warned a twice-married Soviet Air Force major. "If you don't let them know who's boss right away, you'll regret it."

Both men are in the market for new wives, and from the sound of it, they're *not* looking for feminists, although the middle-aged Air Force officer, a hardcore Leninist, said he might be willing to settle for "someone with democratic tendencies," if no one better comes along. Other Soviet men voiced surprisingly similar feelings toward the opposite sex. In the post-communist Soviet Union, many old attitudes still prevail, among them the idea that "men are in charge," as a government official in Tblissi said. And

225

if women don't like it, he added, "That's their problem." Which, by all indications, is exactly what it is.

How does the other side feel? A secretary at a Moscow film studio summed up her thoughts in the form of a joke. "What works four hours a day, watches television eight hours a night, and lasts ten seconds in bed?" The answer, she laughed, a Russian man. In a society in which people spend much of their time waiting in line, there seems to be a lot of agreement that Soviet males hold the speed record in at least one major category.

"Women are an afterthought in Russia," said a female professor at Moscow's Institute for Economic Research. "This is a man's country, and you can see what they've done to it. Nothing here functions the way it should . . . including my husband." She went on to point out that Russian men "are the worst lovers on earth." Although her experience with foreigners has been limited to one brief fling with a visiting Austrian professor, she's hoping the influx of Western companies, and with them Western business-men, will change that. Soviet women are looking to Europe and America for relief as eagerly as Soviet politicians are. Yet, if the present mood is any indication of things to come, stabilizing economic conditions in Russia and the other former republics will be easy compared to ending the ongoing strife between the sexes.

In her book *Soviet Women*, author Francine du Plessix Gray blamed the problem on communist machismo. When the Party had a monopoly on political power, its propaganda organs used to proclaim that the Soviet Union was the first nation on earth to establish full equality between the sexes. But now, as then, male predominance in every major field of activity is an established fact of life.

"In this society, women aren't ready to run things," said a former Party stalwart, echoing a common refrain among Soviet men from all walks of life, many of whom regard females with a sense of paternal impatience and often describe them as immature and childlike. That also happens to be the way most women describe men.

Everything in Soviet life, from food shortages to alcoholism, reflects the condition of male-female relations. The chronic consumption of vodka has left the Soviet male population mired in a day-after depression that's gone on so long it's become part of the national psychology. Men exist in a state of perpetual indifference, and women in a state of perpetual drudgery. A woman wrote in *Izvestia* a few months after the coup that members of her sex "have again become the victims of the political and economic troubles experienced by this country. This has happened in our history more than once. When the country needed labor power, women were invited to work at plants and on railroads, and when they were no longer needed . . . they were reminded about their duty as mothers and wives."

Under the new demands of capitalism, what was already a hard life for women has only gotten harder. Soviet women are expected to work, take care of their families, keep house, and shop (a full-time job all by itself). No wonder a St. Petersburg sex therapist reported that 70 percent of her female patients have never had an orgasm. But that could have more to do with a chronic housing crisis than exhaustion.

"A big reason Russian women don't have orgasms is because there's no privacy," said a recent divorcee. "How can you have good sex with your mother-in-law and kids sleeping five feet away? It doesn't exactly make you feel like pounding on the walls."

Couples in the ex-Soviet Union, Gray concluded, make better adversaries than lovers. Still, relations between them are far more complicated than their constant carping about each other might suggest.

"Soviet men and women feed on each other's need to suffer," said Anna Lawton, an American film expert who's been studying the culture for years. "You notice it in real life and in the movies. Wives invariably see themselves as their husbands' keepers; husbands see themselves as their wives' responsibility. In some ways, I suppose, it's an ideal situation." And it's completely compatible with the division of labor in a country in which abortion is a substitute for birth control and grandmothers clean the streets. As a married mother of two bitterly remarked, "In Russia we have no men, only a male species."

Lawton cited a 1926 Soviet film called *Bed and Sofa* to make her point about male dependence on women. In the movie, two World War I buddies meet in Moscow. One is married and the other is single and looking for a room. The married man offers to let his friend sleep on the couch in his apartment, but before long the houseguest has begun sleeping with the wife, who soon becomes pregnant. The men decide she should have an abortion, but the woman refuses and leaves both of them to fend for themselves. The picture ends with the two men lounging around the apartment drinking tea, playing checkers, and arguing about which one will clean the place up.

While they agreed that having men around only increases their workload, most single Soviet women say they want to be married and have children. In Russia, where serial marriages are common, couples wed for different reasons at different ages. First marriages tend to be purely practical. Deprived of the opportunity to be together when they're single, young Soviet couples frequently get married just so that they can spend time alone—indoors.

"Finding a place to get laid is impossible," said a divorced professor of literature, looking back on his student days in Moscow during the early 1960s. "I can remember when I was a teenager doing it in the snow. Don't laugh. It was better there than the one-room apartment we shared with my wife's parents."

If first marriages usually don't last long for most Russians—it's estimated that more than half of them end in divorce—a lack of living space can make second marriages just as difficult. A driver for a Moscow joint venture related his situation.

"I got a divorce from my first wife, but neither one of us could afford to move out. So we stayed in the same apartment. When I got married again, she was still there. After three months, she still hadn't left. Finally, my second wife moved out."

Married life in other former republics is every bit as crowded and twice as primitive, even by Russian standards. In Uzbekistan, brides are paid for with money, livestock, and oriental rugs. In Kazakhstan, some officials are talking about reinstituting "the national tradition" of polygamy. And in Georgia, when a man wants to get married, it's perfectly acceptable if he kidnaps his intended.

Manana Khechikashvili is a television reporter in Tblissi and a dedicated career woman in a part of the world where female ambition is frowned on. "Marriage to a Georgian man is a form of imprisonment," she said. "Women here are considered to be their husband's property, and if you get divorced, it's as if you've been condemned."

For young Soviet women, marriage is often the only alternative to spending the rest of their lives with their parents. The housing shortage makes living alone an unheard-of luxury. Women get married for economic protection and stay in bad marriages for the same reason. In Soviet society, single women in their late twenties or early thirties are considered semi-spinsters, and single mothers of any age romantically obsolete.

"No Russian man wants to take care of another man's children," explained Tanya Pushkilova, a 37-year-old mother of three and the wife of a policeman she no longer loves. "I have a boyfriend who's ten years younger than I am. But my parents keep telling me it will never work out. When I'm 47, he'll be my age now, and then he'll be interested in someone younger."

Pushkilova, a former high school physics teacher who earns the equivalent of six dollars a month working as a floor supervisor in a former Party hotel in Moscow, said she feels trapped in a marriage she can't stand, but afraid she'll have no place to live if she gets divorced and then her boyfriend decides she's too old. Meanwhile, she's taking tennis lessons to stay in shape. "Maybe I'll meet a rich American my age, and I'll marry him," she said.

It's possible. Business opportunities are bringing more Westerners to Russia, and many Russian women for the first time are able to do a live comparison of foreign men and their own. Not long ago, it was against the law even to give street directions to foreigners. Now women say they can't wait to meet European and American men. During the summer the coup attempt took place, there was a popular Russian song in which American men were described as the answer to every woman's romantic and financial fantasies. It's still a big hit.

Soviet men may be just as eager to find foreign girlfriends, but they may have a problem. A woman from New York, who represents a U.S. bank in Moscow, has dated several Russian men and noticed a common pattern. "At first, they bring you flowers and pretend to be really polite, but it doesn't take long for that to wear off. There are two types of Russian males. They're either extremely aggressive or extremely weak. The aggressive ones treat you like a servant, and the weak ones want you to treat them like servants. But the minute there's the slightest problem, both kinds disappear."

Once, she was having a difficult time registering for a Moscow hotel room, she said. An argument ensued with the woman at the front desk, but instead of helping to resolve the problem, the Russian man she was with turned around and left the building.

"Can you imagine an American guy acting like that? Fear is the most common emotion in Russia. The communists are gone, but Russians are still afraid of authority figures. You see it constantly. Russian women don't have any worries when it comes to foreigners stealing their men. Who would want them?"

The one trait in Russian men that Russian women complain about most is their selfishness, particularly in bed.

Another woman offered this analysis: "Russian men could never show how important they are by what they owned, so their way of being manly is by acting like little dictators. Women have their children. Men only have their egos and their penises. The one is usually big, the other usually small, and each is very fragile."

With all the criticism they get, you would think Soviet men might be concerned about losing their women to outside competition. Not so. While some admit Westerners will probably walk off with a certain percentage of their females, others are secure in the knowledge that Russian women can't live without them, believing, as one man put it, that Soviet men and women are "spiritually joined."

But when Russians say "spiritual," according to Lawton, "it's a code word for 'miserable.' They don't have much in their lives to feel superior about, and the pretense of enjoying hardship is something they like to challenge Westerners with. It comes from reading too much Dostoevski. Most Russians I know would be very happy to trade in some of their spiritual qualities for a little less hardship."

Capitalism and the free market are giving many women the opportunity to do just that. When the communists were in power, the country's best jobs automatically went to men. Women were expected to work, but not in the prestige professions unofficially closed to them. They were funneled into service careers, teaching, health care, and transportation, and despite the lip service government leaders paid to equality, their chances for advancement were limited.

One year before the Party was disbanded, 60 percent of all Soviets with higher and special technical educations were women, yet only 7 percent of all managerial positions were held by women. Among men with the same educational training, one out of every two held a managerial post.

"It isn't because women aren't worthy, but because they're constantly being pushed aside," said Galina Semyonova, the first and last woman to be a full member of the Politburo. "Double burdens of work and family are pulling them in two different directions.... Socioeconomic conditions have slowed the development of women." But what was true for women living under communism isn't necessarily true anymore.

"During the first years of the revolution," noted Semyonova, "the idea of socialism was very attractive because of its moral ethics. Our country was the first to include equal rights for men and women in the constitution. We irradicated illiteracy. We respected women who worked. . . . Now we have a disfigured image of women because society dictated to us only one specific female role, that of the hardworking drudge. We forget about the real woman—her beauty, her individuality, her tenderness."

When she was still in politics, one of Semyonova's goals was to help women make the transition to a free-market system. "Women are a harmonizing force," she said, "and for that reason it's important that they have a chance to influence politics and the economy."

With talk of the emergence of a new angry proletarian movement, fueled by demands for more consumer goods and higher salaries, harmony is something Soviet society could use. But a growing number of educated women see little reward or personal satisfaction in adopting the same support role their mothers and grandmothers played.

"It's fine to be a calming influence, if that's all you want out of life," said a twenty-year-old co-ed at Moscow's Institute for Foreign Languages. "In the past, women were supposed to raise children and help their husbands by making sure everything went smoothly at home. Handling the big, important jobs was a man's work. . . . My priorities are education, money, and a good career, preferably with a Western company, so I can travel abroad. Marriage would be nice, but not an old-style marriage where the husband gives all the orders and expects the woman to obey, that's not marriage. That's a dictatorship."

Among many educated women in their twenties and thirties there's a feeling that the time has come to make decisions about their futures, decisions they could never have made a few years ago. For some, that means changing their lives, and for others it means starting completely new ones.

Nadya, who worked for years as an English interpreter, got a small taste of the West in East Germany, where she met her husband, Slava, a career officer in the Soviet Army. When they returned to Moscow, she soon forgot about life outside the Soviet Union. For the next six years, she was a perfect wife and mother, working a full-time job, taking care of her two children, and indulging Slava every time his friends showed up to drink vodka and sing military songs.

In many ways, they had a typical Russian marriage. Nadya, with help from her mother, raised the children, cleaned house, and cooked dinner. Slava went to work, came home, and watched videotapes, or didn't come home and watched videotapes at a friend's apartment. Like most Russian husbands, he wouldn't let his wife drive his car, which meant she had to spend her weekends doing the family shopping by subway, while he spent his time taking it easy at another friend's country dacha.

But all that changed when she got a job as a translator with a Soviet-British joint venture. Not only did she earn more money than she'd ever made before, she began to like going to work. The people she met there were different, even the Russians. Everyone was more confident, more energetic, more of everything Nadya had always wanted to be, including happy. Suddenly, what she thought was the good life of an Army officer's wife didn't look that good anymore.

As often happens in such cases, she met a man, an Englishman, and fell in love. When she told her husband she was taking the children and moving to London, he blew his top. But it wasn't nearly as bad as Nadya had expected, and after a while he gave her the divorce she wanted. Slava's friends consoled him, blaming his bad luck with Nadya on capitalism, and they may have been right. At any rate, the next time he got married, Slava said, it would be to someone who didn't speak English.

Nadya's friends, on the other hand, all said she did the right thing for herself and her children. She was still dependent on a man, but at least the man wasn't a Russian and she was living in England. And in the minds of a lot of Soviet women, that put her two good moves ahead of them.

What's surprising these days is how determined many Soviet women are to take advantage of new economic possibilities, whether they involve changing jobs or changing countries. Leaving Russia, once an act that ranked just below treason in the Soviet hierarchy of crimes against the state, is now something everyone discusses, especially career-conscious women who have an advantage over their male counterparts when it comes to attracting invitations. The more they come into contact with foreign men, the better their chances of being invited abroad.

Feminism was never popular in the Soviet Union. Its anti-domestic side is not appealing to most women. Yet clearly, under the influence of democracy and capitalism, a new type of female assertiveness is showing itself, and if it becomes a trend, as it appears to be, Soviet men may be in for some surprises.

At the Moscow Labor Exchange, a place where people go to look for jobs, it was reported that nearly 80 percent of work applicants were women. But those are women looking for traditional employment in the Russian job market, which is really a state-sponsored day-care program for adults. "We pretend to work," goes the joke, "and the government pretends to pay us."

Official labor statistics don't reflect the increasing employment opportunities for females in the joint-venture job market, where women's work habits as well as their ability to learn new skills are highly valued by foreign employers. "Women have a much better chance than men to land good jobs with Western companies," said Igor Rounov, vice president of the Trade & Economic Council in Moscow, which keeps track of trends in Soviet business. The reason? "They work harder. Women are used to putting in long hours and getting things done," said Rounov. "It doesn't take companies long to see what reliable and resourceful employees Russian women can be. The irony is that women can get better jobs with foreign companies than they can with Soviet businesses. Russian bosses think women can't handle responsibilities, but Western companies don't seem to give it a second thought, and you can see the results."

One of them is that the brightest and most capable Soviet women, who once were confined to jobs that wasted their talents and paid them slave wages, are now working for businesses that pay them what they're worth. Some companies, such as McDonald's, have started programs to train women as managers. Western law offices and accounting firms in Moscow go out of their way to recruit and promote women. And in a marked departure from the old way of doing business, some of the new Russian brokerage companies have even begun to hire more women. Every day at the Moscow Commodities and Raw Materials Exchange, female brokers prove they're just as profit-minded as men.

It's women—not men—who will be the most immediate beneficiaries of free-market jobs. While Russian politicians warn one another about possible coups and countercoups, another revolution has already begun.

"I can see a day when men and women will be equal, instead of the way it is now," said Tanya Pushkilova, who gave up a low-paying teaching job to work in a swank Moscow hotel. "That will be for my daughters to experience, though. Not me. Things may happen fast in America. Here they happen very slowly.

"At this point, I can only hope to meet a rich foreigner," she laughed. "My friends say I'm dreaming, but as long as I work in a hotel, there's always a chance."

Chapter Seventeen

Ex-Soviet Man

Vitali Kriukov is on special assignment. Six months before the Kremlin coup backfired and toppled the communists from power, Kriukov departed Moscow for Switzerland to become a business-man. As fluent in English and German as he is in Russian, he has a mind for money. But what makes him, and his job, so unusual is the amount of money he's thinking about, not to mention where most of it comes from.

At a time when there was much debate over sending billions of dollars in aid to the beleaguered Soviet Union, it wasn't widely known that some Soviets had enough cash on hand to be investing in foreign business ventures. Yet, they not only had it, like smart investors everywhere, they were eager to see it increase.

And that's where the 44-year-old Kriukov came in. When he's in Moscow, he drives a Mercedes Benz. In Zurich, he's behind the wheel of a BMW, equipped with a car phone that keeps him in touch with his own financial enterprises and those he runs for associates back home, who, despite the popular image, are by no means poor.

Kriukov, once employed in the Kremlin's Council of Minis-

237

ters, used to be an apparatchik, though he was never so committed
to the cause that he couldn't see that its future, if it had one, was
in commerce, not government. *His* politics is money, and thanks
to his nomenklatura training, he knows how to handle it—which
is why he now resides in the land of the secret bank accounts.

In Zurich's famous Moevinpik restaurant, the walls along the
stairway to the exclusive upper dining room are covered with
photos and portraits of famous past patrons, among them Karl
Marx, who probably charged his meals to *The New York Herald
Tribune,* his sometime employer. Over a century later, communists
and ex-communists were still eating at the same place, only this
time they weren't plotting to overthrow capitalism, they were
planning ways to participate in it.

"Marx should have remained a journalist," Kriukov joked to
an Austrian millionaire. "We would all have been better off. Intellectuals are dangerous when you let them loose." And with that,
he picked up the bill and paid for lunch.

Indoctrinated in the virtues of sharing, Russians can be annoy-
ingly stingy. Not Kriukov, who has mastered the art of expense-
account spending as well as anybody. A few years ago, an
American business executive waiting to meet him in the Oyster
Bar at the Plaza Hotel in New York had his pocket picked. The
theft left the man with no cash to settle his bar bill or to take a cab
to the airport. When Kriukov arrived and heard the story, he
pulled out an envelope full of crisp new hundred-dollar bills.
"Take as many as you need," he said. "We Russians are always
willing to loan Americans money."

The nonchalance of the nomenklatura, when it was fully subsidized by the state, had no equivalent in the West, except perhaps
in 1930s movies in which playboy aristocrats always seemed to
treat spending their inheritance as a sport. That's how Kriukov is.
So much so, you have to keep reminding yourself that he learned
the habit not by watching old Cary Grant films but from growing
up among the privileged elite in Moscow.

Kriukov, whose actress wife Alona is the daughter of famed
Soviet film czar Sergie Bondarchuk, began his career as a journal-

ist, which, under the communists, had less to do with delivering the news than laundering it. But Kriukov took the job seriously, and after becoming the editor of a Central Committee newspaper, his pursuit of actual information turned what had been a flimsy Kremlin house organ into a muckraking Western-style scandal sheet.

Needless to say, this did not go over too well with the powers that were, and Kriukov was fired. In a less enlightened era, he might also have been shot. Considering that he came from a good family, though, the promise to get out of journalism and stay out was sufficient. Kriukov didn't get mad or get even, he got a promotion. In the late 1980s, the Kremlin was beginning to explore new ways to earn hard currency, and one of those ways was going into business. By then working for the Council of Ministers, Kriukov, a skilled negotiator and comfortable dealing with Westerners, was given the task of starting various enterprises abroad that would function as semi-private corporations, earning money for the state and for state officials.

The nomenklatura, to which Kriukov belonged by birth, was the only group in Soviet society that knew what business was. These were the privileged few who ran parts of the government like private family concessions, and when perestroika came along, they were poised to expand into "enemy territory." Behind the facade of socialism, most high-level communists were always capitalists at heart. Lucky for them. After the world they were used to was gone with the wind, anybody who didn't have outside investments was history.

"Perestroika itself showed that the Party was on the defensive," said Kriukov. How long it could defend itself, however, nobody knew. As early as 1988, smart communists were already looking ahead to second careers in the private sector. Start-up funds were no problem, thanks to exclusive access to the state treasury. But time was.

Within a year, Kriukov had several trading companies off and running in Switzerland and England. Yet none of them was producing the big money officials needed. For that, only America would do, and in 1989 he came to the United States as part of an advance team, preparing the way for a visit by Mikhail Gorbachev. His objective was to launch a special project with so much earning potential it had the Kremlin tremblin'. He was scheduled to get input from Armand Hammer, but Hammer, preoccupied with plans for his art gallery in Los Angeles, had little interest in making deals, so his staff introduced Kriukov to other American businessmen who did.

The Americans who met him in Washington were immediately impressed with Kriukov's perception of the changing nature of the Soviet Union, and with his ingenuity. He had brought a personal computer with him from Russia, but it wasn't compatible with American electrical outlets. Not letting that stop him, while everyone else was sipping tea, he pulled off the plug, stuck the exposed wires into two live sockets, and proceeded to keyboard the finishing touches on a business proposal. It was the centerpiece project of a scheme to save the Soviet economy.

The basic idea was to hold a dual national lottery in the United States and the Soviet Union, the purpose of which would be to raise money for the Soviet government in both countries. A large part of the millions of dollars collected on the American end would go to the Kremlin, and the rest would be used to buy U.S. products—television sets, VCRs, automobiles, tractors, and clothing—that would then be distributed as prizes to winners in the Soviet lottery.

Kriukov anticipated there would be more than 20 billion rubles spent on tickets. Soviets, he explained, love to gamble. They have such a passion for it, not even communism could stand in their way. Even though the Party was successful in stamping out other vices, it would have been overthrown long before it was if it had ever tried to eradicate gambling.

But there was more involved here than just making bets. Soviets who bought tickets in the lottery would be doing their part to stabilize the monetary system. Some of their rubles would be funneled into a Moscow environmental fund, one of the many organizations Kriukov works for, and the rest of them, billions and billions of rubles, would be burned.

The Americans, most of whom had never seen a ruble in their lives, politely listened to his proposal with a mixture of curiosity and amazement. *Burned?* Step One in making rubles convertible, Kriukov explained, requires removing them from circulation as fast as the government prints them. And what more painless way to do that than to let people spend them trying to win nice prizes?

The Soviet economy in 1989 had yet to become the public fiasco it is today. It was still being administered behind closed doors—doors Kriukov was now opening to reveal a recovery plan so bizarre it almost sounded like fun. It would be, he assured, and for anyone who wanted to lend him a hand in making the arrangements, it might be very profitable, too.

Here was a representative of the Soviet government putting out feelers for the type of business opportunity you don't even hear about on late-night TV. It definitely got several people thinking, and a few signed on. The principal American participant was the Ford Motor Company, which was scheduled to provide automobiles as part of the grand prize. In exchange, Ford was promised a manufacturing plant in the Soviet Union. The first setback came when negotiations for the plant fell through, and Ford backed out of the deal. Undeterred, Kriukov lined up prizes from other corporations all over the United States, but putting together a nationwide lottery was harder than he imagined. Given all the different state laws that come into play, it would take years to organize the event. With more rubles rolling off the presses every day, he didn't have years. So, plans for a lottery in America had to be canceled.

The decision was a particularly difficult one for Kriukov, who was just getting to like the United States. All the same, business is business, and he needed to act fast. On the advice of Scientific Games, an Atlanta-based consulting firm, he decided to shift the hard-currency end of the lottery to what was then East Germany. Tickets could be sold to Soviet troops for Deutsche marks, since part of the force withdrawal agreement called for the West German government to pay the soldiers in hard currency. The contracts were signed by the Soviet commander and Kriukov's lottery was finally about to begin.

But days before the drawing there were more problems. First, a group of Soviet Army officers defected to the West, taking with them some very important military secrets. Then, several Soviet generals were arrested for accepting bribes from European businessmen who supplied the shops on Soviet military bases with Western products. This matter became so sensitive that West German Chancellor Helmut Kohl telephoned Gorbachev and asked him to send a plane to pick up the generals before the incident became a national scandal. The officers were discreetly hustled back to Moscow and put in jail. A day later, Kriukov was informed that until a thorough investigation was completed, the Kremlin was reluctantly calling off the lottery.

A lesser man might have folded on the spot. It would have been right in character for most Russians to have given up a long time before, but Kriukov kept the project going. This time, he turned his attention to the Soviet Union. Half of his plan was still on track, and if winning rubles as prizes wouldn't be as exciting as winning a Ford Bronco station wagon, at least when the drawing was over, the government would have a stupendous pile of money to burn.

Had Kriukov been an American, he might be just another nose-to-the-grindstone entrepreneur. The fact that he's a Russian makes him a phenomenon, a type the West will be seeing more of in years to come—polished, plugged in, and showing up out of nowhere to broker deals that once would have been impossible to imagine.

The coup and the dissolution of the union only intensified many forms of business. With former communists in important new government positions, the transfer of money out of the now defunct Soviet Union continued, and so did industrial spying by the reformed KGB. Even if the Soviet Union didn't exist, the central spy agency always would, insisted Yevgeny Primakov, its director of foreign intelligence gathering. "Of course, our emphasis will shift to the commercial sphere. That's quite natural," he told a group of foreign visitors to security headquarters in late 1991, just before the Russian government assumed control of operations. Traditional espionage of the Cold War variety had dropped off, but spy work in other areas, such as monitoring the development of critical technologies, had sharply increased, both on the government and private levels. In addition to handing information over to the new authorities, top-flight Moscow spies also sell it to competing Western companies for personal profit.

To outsiders, it must seem incredible, Kriukov conceded, that a nation unable to control its own money supply or provide enough food for its people is talking about keeping up with the latest breakthroughs in advanced technology. But Soviet life, he pointed out, has always been full of contradictions. Likewise, despite headlines about empty shelves and idle workers, it's business as usual in parts of an economy that very few foreigners even know about. Keeping things out of sight is something that Russians are good at. Kriukov has always believed that the biggest bargains are sometimes the easiest to miss, and the present situation proves it.

"No one will say so publicly, but what used to be called the Soviet Union is for sale," he said in his Moscow office, as a fax machine hummed in the corner and half a dozen people worked the phones like volunteers at a telethon. "We want Westerners to buy it, or at least rent it with an option to buy, and I'm trying to help them do it for everybody's benefit."

Exactly what forms that benefit will take, he didn't say. But one of them could be the cheapest shave in the world. With extensive connections in the Soviet military-industrial complex, Kriukov's trading companies stock a full line of products nobody in the West has seen before, such as sapphire razor blades. He pulled one out of its plastic case to allow a closer inspection. It looked like any ordinary razor, but inside was a blade that *never* wears out.

Similar to so much else the Soviets have to sell these days, the sapphire blades were originally developed by the military. They were intended to be used by soldiers in the field, who need to shave but can't be bothered changing blades all the time. For those who think the Soviets have nothing to offer in the way of consumer goods, here's something millions of men could use. Kriukov is negotiating with the Wilkinson Company in England and Gillette in the United States.

"Our military industries have developed some unique products," Kriukov said. "The problem right now is getting them onto the market. We have to commercialize them to make money. When that happens, our military economy will change into a consumer economy."

Using engineering laboratories in Finland to authenticate some of the products he represents, Kriukov has convinced a number of Western buyers that Soviet goods are for real. There's a new-age, fuel-efficient automotive engine, revolutionary hinges for doors and windows, technology for putting out oil well fires, diamond scalpels for eye surgery, and a lot more.

After the first Russian Revolution, the Bolsheviks sent teams of "missionaries" all over the world to convert the masses to socialism. Now the reform government of Russia is doing its version of the same thing, with one big difference. The missionary brigade this time is a sales force, many of whose members were taught by the communists to serve the Party, but who are now fully committed, and often surprisingly well-prepared, capitalists.

Kriukov's nomenklatura upbringing has served him well, but there still is room for improvement. When the communists were in power, business ethics were unheard of. The only rule everyone believed in was deception. Learning Western corporate niceties, Kriukov confessed, is sometimes difficult for Soviets, whose basic training in Party policy only made sure they paid lip service to honesty. Fear and force were the two motivating factors in communist commerce. If you wanted something, you took it. If you wanted to keep something, you made sure it was well hidden. Doing business in the Western sense requires an openness few Soviets have ever known and even fewer have practiced.

"We can produce products, but we have no idea how to market them," said Kriukov. That requires proof the product works, something the communists never needed to bother with. They didn't have to. After all, they ran a monopoly. Kriukov remembered trying to convince a new publishing company in Moscow that came to him for advice on raising capital in the West that they would first need to put together a business plan.

"The guy asked me, 'What's a business plan?' And when I told him, he looked at me like I was crazy. 'That's secret information,' he said. The company wanted to get the money first, then tell the investor how they would spend it. The whole idea that someone might want to see evidence that his investment wouldn't be wasted never occurred to them."

But it's not just new Soviet businesses that are having a problem meeting the demands of Western money culture; so are new governments that want the West to give them billions of dollars in unconditional aid. In Soviet society, a direct unadorned "gimme" is the accepted approach for getting what you want. Having to explain yourself has always been seen as a sign of weakness.

In the old economy, everything was based on demand, orders, and decrees. The same city council that gave someone permission to open a private shop could order it closed. Presidential decrees could make something legal one day and illegal the next. A source of supply that was "guaranteed" by a bribe to one official could be cut off the minute another one demanded his payoff. Soviet entrepreneurs have been conditioned to see business ventures as windows of opportunity that can be closed any minute. Take the money and run is usually their philosophy, and, if they demand a little more money before they take off, that's what they've learned from experience. But there are degrees of taking. The same goes for taking advantage. And the ease with which some communists have become capitalists is evidence enough for many ordinary citizens that both systems are corrupt.

Free enterprise, as it's practiced in Russia today, bears no resemblance to free enterprise in America, where capitalism went through its robber-baron period on a much larger scale in the late nineteenth century. Yet all Soviet entrepreneurs aren't the strong-arm artists and fly-by-night crooks they're supposed to be. Some, like Kriukov, conduct their affairs with an amazing degree of civility, which is even more amazing when you consider what they're up against.

If fate played a part in Kriukov's being where he is, so has a very non-communist sense of drive and ambition. He offered no apologies for getting into capitalism when the chance presented itself, or for using the state resources put at his disposal to get started. Not many Russians in his position would feel differently. In name, if nothing else, the state was, and to a large degree still is, the basic provider of all things.

Kriukov calls himself an economic patriot, trying to do the best he can for himself, his family, and what's left of his country. It hasn't been easy. Being a Soviet businessmen in the 1990s is like being a Soviet cosmonaut was in the 1960s. "People may envy or admire you," Kriukov said. "But they only see the good side, the money, the cars. They don't see the danger." And they definitely don't see the body parts scattered all over the place when something goes wrong.

Because of their success, Kriukov and his associates have encountered many problems. A few years ago, one of his closest friends was murdered in Moscow by a so-called trade mafia gang trying to take over his business. Kriukov himself was once beaten up by a mafia goon squad that broke into his Moscow offices and demanded that he pay them protection money. In both cases, the perpetrators were eventually arrested, but similar crimes are on the rise almost everywhere Soviet businesses operate.

The transition from communism to capitalism is a revolution, and revolutions by their nature tend to be unpredictable affairs full of challenges, mistakes, and long periods of readjustment. "It will take a generation before our country really changes," Kriukov predicted. And, like a lot of other ex-Soviets who can afford it, that's a generation he'd rather be spending someplace else, which makes him very glad he just moved his family to Switzerland.

Who Do You Trust?

It was a cold winter afternoon in Moscow, and an American computer executive was having lunch with his Russian partner at a restaurant not far from Red Square. The two men had been working together for over a year. The American knew the computer business. Igor, his partner, knew the Russians. Together they made an ideal team, and their profits proved it.

The two toasted each other's success, after which Igor drank to his friend's safe journey home. "You know," he said, "if you fly back to the States via Frankfurt, there's a way we can both make a lot of money." Naturally, the American was interested.

Igor told him about a German computer expert he knew in Moscow. The man, once employed by a firm in Frankfurt, had stolen design plans worth a small fortune when he left. He had been close to making a deal with the Kremlin, but the aborted coup had killed it. Now he wanted to sell the plans back to the company, and was looking for someone to act as a messenger.

"When you get to Frankfurt, just give them a call and say we'll hand over everything for $10 million," said Igor. The American was stunned. This had to be some kind of joke. But his partner wasn't kidding. He even had the name and phone number of the person to call in Germany.

"That's extortion," the American said. "What do you mean?" Igor replied. "We could make some big money." Soon, the American realized his partner had no idea why the scheme was illegal or what the consequences might be. "Interesting," said Igor when he heard that the two of them could go to jail for twenty years. "That would never happen here."

Business concepts most Westerners take for granted never applied in the Soviet Union. For the communists, the end always justified the means. And when the Party departed the scene, what it left behind, besides an economic catastrophe, was a culture of dishonesty in which making a deal means taking whatever you can.

Lenin popularized the idea of hoodwinking capitalists with this parable, once required reading for every Soviet schoolchild: If you meet a robber coming down the street and he asks how much money you have, are you required to tell him the truth? Of course not, said Lenin, who taught that a profiteer in any form was exactly the same as a thief.

Following that advice, communist logic sanctioned deception as an accepted practice in every type of commerce. Today, as a result, most ex-Soviets are not only lacking in basic business skills, but are missing virtually any sense of business ethics. From deadlines to contracts, all promises are subject to change without notice, and all rules and regulations can be altered by instant decree, or, what's more likely, overlooked for a generous bribe. Marx developed a theory that only the laws of economics matter, but in the Soviet Union, economic laws as well as every other type were made to be broken.

"The Soviets' real problem isn't money or politics, it's morality," said Richard Dean, an attorney with Coudert Brothers, who served in the law firm's Moscow office from 1988 to 1990. "Most of the time, in order to get anything done commercially, Soviet entrepreneurs have had to bend, if not break, the law," Dean said. "That attitude is pretty ingrained in the people. It's going to take a long time to reeducate them, not just in the practical requirements of a free economy, but in the moral obligations that go along with them."

In this book, we've tried to give you a picture of what to expect when you do business with Russians. What we haven't told you is what *not* to expect. There are historic changes taking place in every former republic, changes that could create profitable business opportunities for natives and new arrivals alike. But it would be a serious mistake to believe that the entire commonwealth was suddenly transformed by democracy and the free market. Banners urging people to support the Party, with slogans such as "You Are Walking the True Path, Comrades" or "The Central Committee Is Your Helmsman," may be gone, yet the thinking they encouraged—and maybe what's more important, the thinking they *discouraged*—is still very much in evidence.

Present-day Soviet society exists between two worlds: one not quite dead and the other unable to function on its own. Former Party barons, factory directors, and military brass, who continue to run a huge part of the economy, haven't left the scene. Nor has a fully independent business class emerged from the wreckage of the communist system to take their place.

"There's a funny tension that exists right now between the old way of doing things, which everyone knows wasn't working, and a new way, which nobody understands," said Dean. "In other countries caught in that kind of bind, there are often ethical or intellectual traditions to fall back on for guidance. But those traditions were all destroyed by the communists."

What Soviets do have to fall back on is their deep-rooted instinct for survival, which shows itself in different ways at every level of the economic scale. To Americans, as Scarlett O'Hara said, tomorrow is another day. To Soviets, tomorrow—any tomorrow—is going to be the worst day in the history of the world, but an excellent reason to stock up on everything in sight, from beets to bank notes. An unreliable economy has made Soviets hoarders of money and anything else of value. That may be a good way of beating the system, but it can wreak havoc on a business deal.

The only way for outside investors to succeed is to commit for the long term. But a history of having the rug pulled out from under them has conditioned Soviets to be more interested in a quick return, to get whatever they can as fast as they can out of every business relationship. It's not uncommon, say, for a Russian to insist on a ten-year contract, stop honoring his end of the bargain after the first profits come in, and then disappear altogether when he thinks he's learned enough to operate on his own.

"You have to start out with the clear understanding you could get royally screwed if you're not careful," said one seasoned American entrepreneur. "Otherwise, you might as well just wire them money and save yourself the plane fare." That's not to say no one can succeed in business. McDonald's, PepsiCo, and other companies large and small prove it's possible to build impressive sales figures and considerable goodwill, even under the most difficult of conditions. But the people behind every successful incoming business all have two things in common: They did their homework before arriving, and took nothing for granted once they got there. As McDonald's' long history of negotiations and planning suggests, if something works in Russia, it's only because the arrangements were made well in advance.

But in a country in which the idea of success itself is an alien concept, preparing the way for things to work can be a lot more than half the battle. Americans expect to succeed. Few businesses started in the United States would ever get off the ground if the people who began them didn't think they were better than their competitors—had an improved product, faster service, or if nothing else, a bigger sign. Most Soviets automatically assume that being successful means paying off the right official or neutralizing the competition by force. That had always been the communist approach, and now it's the way the new free market works.

"Soviet business is totally wild, and no one keeps his word," a member of a Moscow mafia gang told *The Los Angeles Times.* "So you have to base everything on fear. Nothing is decided by the law."

Lacking any of the regulatory controls that keep most American businessmen honest, Soviets have gone on a spree of price gouging, bribing, and bullying that makes Wall Street in the 1980s look like a Young Pioneers' picnic. A Boston commodities trader recalled hiring a Russian consultant to help him negotiate a deal to buy military scrap metal from a government salvage operation in Siberia. The man who helped arrange the deal, it later turned out, was not only working for the Russian government, but got a fat kickback from the army officers who had originally supplied the metal.

Another American became the unwitting accomplice in a Moscow ring of rip-off artists when the government office that registers new businesses regularly sold all the best ideas to his partner, who, in addition to drawing a salary and commission from the American, was still on the payroll of the business registration office where he'd been working a no-show job for years.

Then there was the case of the California juice distributor and his Georgian partner, who had a joint bank account in Moscow. Getting the Georgian to make deposits, withdrawals, or even tell him how much money they had was complicated enough. But when it came time for the two to settle their debts, the American couldn't help thinking he was getting the shaft. Finally, translating dollars into rubles and vice versa made it impossible to determine who owed what to whom. "I've got an idea," suggested the Georgian. "Why don't we just sign a piece of paper that says neither one of us owes each other anything." "Now I know why people over here define conflict of interest as an opportunity not to be missed," said the distributor.

It will be a long time before all the former Soviet republics have laws that encourage free enterprise, protect property rights, and reward investors with tax incentives. And until they do, every business day will be an adventure, each with its own rewards and punishments.

There's an interesting theory, though it's never gained much acceptance, that perestroika and the economic reforms that came with it were part of a KGB plot to undermine the West by pretending to become more like it. Accordingly, glasnost was an elaborate form of disinformation aimed at making Americans and Europeans think the Soviet Union had changed into a more open society, when, in fact, it was the same place it always was, with a few slight modifications added to suit the times.

If that was the plan, it may have worked too well. Whether intended or not, the changes took hold and became real, and while the final results aren't in yet, it doesn't look like a big win for the KGB. The spy agency has been reorganized, but, presumably, is still cooking up plots, although stopping reform probably isn't one of them, even if controlling reform is.

Without completely understanding it, many Soviets now see the free market as both their financial and spiritual salvation. Some even believe a market economy will restore the civilized society that communism supposedly destroyed. But in the current any-thing-goes environment, a civilized society seems like it will be one of the last by-products of capitalism. Yet even capitalism Soviet-style has valuable lessons to teach.

"Outside of Las Vegas and Atlantic City, nothing like this exists in the United States," said Ted Lehman, an investment broker with Project Development International of New York. "This place today is like one big Caesar's Palace, where every-body has a secret plan for getting rich. Some work, some don't. But the action can be addictive . . . and if your plan pays off, you *can* get very rich, very fast."

Nevertheless, a country famous for its failed Five Year Plans can make mincemeat out of any project that isn't conceived and executed with the greatest of care. As U.S. Ambassador Robert Strauss said, "If I were a young man with only $100,000, I'd invest it in Russia. If I were an old man with $10,000,000, I'd still invest only $100,000 in Russia."

"Russia requires everybody to start from square one," said Lehman, who's been doing business there for more than twenty-five years. "Believe me, if you can make money here—and lots of people do—you deserve to be called a self-made man. If you don't . . . well, it's your own fault for not asking the right questions."

Foremost among them is *Who do you trust?* And the answer can often determine the success or failure of any business venture. But trusting anyone in a place where so much can go wrong usually boils down to trusting your own survival instincts. Keep one eye on the bottom line and one eye on your Soviet partner, and chances are good your enterprise will survive and prosper. Lose sight of those two things, and you'll soon be wondering where all of your money went, as a joke currently making the rounds in Moscow illustrates perfectly:

An American and a Russian own a joint-venture store in a ritzy hotel near the Kremlin. One day, while the American is out to lunch, a man comes in and buys a tie, which he pays for with a brand-new hundred-dollar bill. As the Russian is putting the money into the cash register, he notices there's another hundred-dollar bill stuck to the back of the one the man just gave him.

Suddenly, he's faced with a serious moral dilemma: Should he tell the customer? The thought never crosses his mind. The question is—should he tell his *partner?*

Index